Back in the
Spaceship Again

Back in the Spaceship Again

Juvenile Science Fiction Series Since 1945

Karen Sands and Marietta Frank

Contributions to the Study of Science Fiction and Fantasy, Number 84
C. W. Sullivan III, Series Adviser

GREENWOOD PRESS
Westport, Connecticut • London

Library of Congress Cataloging-in-Publication Data

Sands, Karen.
    Back in the spaceship again : juvenile science fiction series
since 1945 / Karen Sands and Marietta Frank.
        p.   cm.—(Contributions to the study of science fiction and
fantasy, ISSN 0193–6875 ; no. 84)
    Includes bibliographical references and index.
    ISBN 0–313–30192–1 (alk. paper)
    1. Children's stories, American—Bibliography.   2. Science
fiction, American—Bibliography.   I. Frank, Marietta.   II. Title.
III. Series.
Z1232.S26   1999
[PS374.S35]
016.813′08762089282—dc21   99–17848

British Library Cataloguing in Publication Data is available.

Library of Congress Catalog Card Number: 99–17848
ISBN: 0–313–30192–1
ISSN: 0193–6875

First published in 1999

Greenwood Press, 88 Post Road West, Westport, CT 06881
An imprint of Greenwood Publishing Group, Inc.
www.greenwood.com

Printed in the United States of America

The paper used in this book complies with the
Permanent Paper Standard issued by the National
Information Standards Organization (Z39.48–1984).

10 9 8 7 6 5 4 3 2 1

Copyright Acknowledgments

The authors and publisher gratefully acknowledge permission for use of the following material:

Chapter 4 is reprinted from Karen Sands, "No Business in Space? The Female Presence in Series
Science Fiction for Children," *Foundation* 70 (Spring 1997): 15–24.

For Chip, Dennis, Eric, with thanks.
K. S. and M. F.

Contents

|Preface

> Like a vacationer who returns to a beloved summer house year after year, the addicted reader opens book three or four or eleven in a given series and is thoroughly at home in the locale—its now familiar native characters, the verbal shrubbery and the narrative floorboards that occasionally creak.
>
> —Lanes, "A Series Is a Series" (128)

When browsing the shelves in any bookstore or public library, it becomes apparent that series books for children account for a large portion of what is available in the fiction section. The existence of series books for children can be traced back to the middle of the nineteenth century, when such series as The Fairchild Family and Elsie Dinsmore appeared. Juvenile science fiction series followed soon after, originating in "the dime novels, penny dreadfuls, and storypapers of late nineteenth- and early twentieth-century America" (Sullivan, *Science* 1). These eventually gave birth to the Great Marvel and Tom Swift series as well. Much has been written about these early series books for children, particularly the Tom Swift books, but comparatively little has been written specifically about the wide variety of juvenile science fiction series of the second half of this century. To fill this void, this book will take a critical look at juvenile science fiction series since 1945 through their history, themes, settings, characters, and construction.

Identifying series and then locating them turned into a bigger challenge than we anticipated. To begin with, there did not appear to be a bibliography of only juvenile science fiction series. We did locate bibliographies of juvenile series that included science fiction, as well as reference book articles on science fiction that listed some series. We acknowledge the following sources: *Young People's Literature in Series: Fiction*, by Judith K. Rosenberg and Kenyon C. Rosenberg; *Young People's Books in Series: Fiction and Non-Fiction, 1975–1991*, by Judith K. Rosenberg, with the assistance of C. Allen Nichols; and *Sci-*

ence Fiction for Young Readers, edited by C. W. Sullivan III. Some series we located through serendipity by browsing bookstore shelves.

Once we identified series and titles, we attempted to acquire them—unfortunately, acquisition was not always possible. Some libraries may not have collected series because they felt it a poor use of funds to purchase books considered ephemeral and of questionable quality. For those libraries that did purchase series books, at some point they were likely weeded out because they might not have moved off the shelves for a time and the space was needed, or they simply fell to pieces, due to being printed on poor-quality paper, and were not replaced. Besides trying to identify and locate older series, we had to keep up with newer series, since new series and titles seemed to appear with each visit to the bookstore. It was our goal to make our study as complete as possible. We are sure there are series and titles we have missed. We did not attempt to represent all juvenile science fiction series since 1945 published in English. It was difficult enough locating series published in the United States; trying to include a fair representation of Canadian, Australian, and UK juvenile science fiction as well would have been an impossible task. Therefore, we are aware this study has an American bias.

Back in the Spaceship Again

CHAPTER 1

|Introduction

"Stand by to raise ship!" he yelled. "Blast off minus-five-four-three-two-
one-*zero!*"

He pulled the switch.

Slowly, the rockets blasting evenly, the giant ship lifted itself free of
the ground. Then gaining speed, it began rocketing away from the Earth. Like
a giant shining bullet, the great spaceship blasted through the dark void of space,
her nose pointed to the distant misty planet of Venus.

Once again Tom Corbett and his unit-mates had embarked on a mission
for the Solar Guard.

—Rockwell, *On the Trail of the Space Pirates* (14)

Thanks to Robert A. Heinlein and the publication of his *Rocket Ship Galileo* in
1947, juvenile science fiction (SF) was once again blasting off to points in outer
space, on Earth, and under the sea. The publication of *Rocket Ship Galileo*,
and its acceptance by adults and its popularity among juveniles, presented publishers with an open market.[1] Of course, juvenile science fiction existed prior
to the publication of *Rocket Ship Galileo*. Juveniles could read about the exploits of Frank Reade, Jr., the Great Marvel, Tom Edison, Jr., and Tom Swift.
These early pulp science fiction series have plots revolving around inventions
developed by the protagonist or the protagonist's mentor. This seems "natural
enough at a time when Edison and Ford were two of the greatest US heroes"
(Eggeling and Nicholls 653). Of these series, the first Tom Swift series, published by the Stratemeyer Syndicate between 1910 and 1941, is considered
"one of the two or three most popular series of the 20th century" (Molson and
Miles 394). However, with the decline of the Tom Swift series in the late
1930s[2] and the shortages of World War II, juvenile readers had few new titles
from which to select. The science fiction available to juveniles between 1939
and 1945 amounted to science fiction comics, a few juvenile novels, and adult

pulp science fiction magazines (Carter, "Golden Age" 118), but after 1947, they had the Tom Corbett, Tom Swift, Jr., Lucky Starr, Winston, and Rick Brant series, along with many other series and individual titles written expressly for the juvenile market. Juvenile science fiction, especially in the form of series fiction, was once again on its way, but traveling in new and exciting directions.

The development and use of rocket and atomic science just prior to and during World War II paved the way for interesting and exciting new themes, conflicts, and plots in juvenile science fiction series. The themes moved beyond the "'gee whiz' attitude" toward technology (Molson and Miles 399–400). Internal conflicts of individual versus individual, most often found in the pre–1945 series, became more complex conflicts of the individual versus society, nature, or self. The developments in rocket science provided the vehicle for humankind to travel to other planets, solar systems, and galaxies; the developments in atomic science provided the fuel for the vehicle. While Earth might have to endure overpopulation, resource shortages, and pollution, humans could colonize other planets, or even the ocean's bottom, to offer humankind a second chance. Hiroshima showed the more sinister side of scientific and technological applications, but in the world of the juvenile science fiction series, science and technology still proffered some hope for humanity.

However, all of this did not happen at once with the dawning of the post–World War II era. The Rick Brant series,[3] beginning with *The Rocket's Shadow* in 1947, and the Tom Swift, Jr. series, beginning with *Tom Swift and His Flying Lab* in 1954, still relied on inventions to move the simplistic plots along. Yet the titles in these two series also blend the use of inventions with rockets, atomic energy, aliens, and space travel. In *The Rocket's Shadow*, Rick Brant's father, along with several scientists, is building an unmanned moon rocket. If the project proves successful, they will win a $2 million grant from a philanthropist to carry on their work. As they get closer to completing the project, accidents start to occur. It becomes clear to Rick, and his ex-marine friend Scotty, that the accidents are actually deliberate attempts to sabotage the project and the acts of sabotage are executed by one of the scientists Rick's father trusts. Rick and Scotty set out to unmask the saboteur and solve the mystery. This story line is not unlike the ones found in the original Tom Swift series. In this series there is usually sabotage of some sort to Tom Swift's or his father's equipment or inventions. The challenge is for Tom Swift or his sidekick to discover who is doing what and why. In the case of the Rick Brant series, the inventions the antagonists try to steal or sabotage are his father's. However, Rick's inventions play some role in solving the mystery or saving the day but are much simpler in comparison to his father's or Tom Swift's. In *The Rocket's Shadow*, "the electrical shock machine which Rick had constructed" helps capture one of the saboteurs (183). Tom Swift's invention is much more complex in *Tom Swift and His Giant Robot* (1954). The robot Tom invented must prevent an atomic explosion and is able to do so because the robots "finger joints are highly sensitive to pressure" (206) and are able to accomplish fairly sophisticated tasks. The big difference between the Tom Swift series, no matter which generation, and the Rick Brant series are the protagonists. Where Tom seems to be a genius able to invent almost anything, Rick is a normal boy who has a working knowledge of electricity.

Besides the difference in protagonists, there is also a difference in the extent to which they employ what have become traditional science fiction conventions. Rick Brant substitutes exotic locales on Earth for points in space, whereas Tom Swift, Jr. plans for interplanetary travel and communicates with aliens. In *Tom Swift and His Flying Lab*, Tom does not make it into space but does in subsequent books. However, his Flying Lab is a first step and is praised by Mr. Swift as "'another great step in scientific advancement,'" by Rip Hulse, of the Army Intelligence Service, as "'a great boon to the defenses of our country,'" and by his friend Rod as "'just one step this side of a trip to the planets'" (105). At the outset of the adventure, Tom and his father receive a communication from what might be Martians. The communication is in the form of mathematical symbols, which Tom and his father translate. According to their translations, "'A group on Mars can't determine how to penetrate the Earth's atmosphere. . . . And they want us to meet them in space to help solve the problem so that they can visit us'" (208). This hint of extraterrestrial life seeking to communicate is a thread that runs through most of the series. Each book brings them closer to solving the mystery, but this is actually secondary as Tom and his friends deal with espionage and spies.

Isaac Asimov's Lucky Starr series, beginning with *David Starr, Space Ranger* (1952), also deals with espionage and spies, but the protagonist is a scientist, not an inventor, and although there is plenty of adventure, there is also more depth to the plots and more complexity in the themes than can be found in either the Rick Brant or the Tom Swift series. In each of the titles in the series, David Starr, a member of the Council of Science, is called in to investigate some problem involving an outpost or colony on one of the planets. The reason a member of the Council of Science is called in to investigate is because science or technology is being misused in ways that could have serious repercussions for the humans on the outpost or colony and eventually affect humans on Earth. With this premise, Asimov is able to develop his themes: "[that] problems *are* solvable through negotiation and the use of reason . . . that friendship is vitally important, that snobbery and prejudice are universal human weaknesses, and that first impressions are frequently wrong" (Hull 49). However, in spite of all this, Elizabeth Anne Hull notes, "[m]ost Asimov critics have simply ignored the juveniles or glossed over them rapidly" (48).[4]

The Lucky Starr series was not the only series to launch itself in 1952. The Winston Publishing Company began the Winston Science Fiction series, attempting to follow Heinlein's success with his Scribner's series (Molson, "Winston" 35). Because Winston wished to distance its series from the pulps, the company planned to hire known authors "who have won the respect of the science fiction audience" (qtd. in Molson, "Winston" 35); to include an introduction to each novel explaining the technology or science on which the story was based; to include a glossary defining scientific or technologic terminology; and to provide novels that would both entertain and instruct (37). *Step to the Stars* (1954), by Lester del Rey, was one of the titles published as part of the Winston series.[5] While the characters of Rick Brant, Tom Swift, Jr., and David Starr remain static from the first to the last book in their series, Jim Stanley's, the protagonist in *Step to the Stars*, shows much growth and development. At the beginning of Jim's adventure, Jim is a loner seemingly without friends or family. He agrees to join an effort in space to build a space station.[6] While there, he works hard and gains the respect of the people with whom he works. He begins to gain confidence when he nearly dies after accidentally floating away from the station while outside working on it. He makes his way back to the station by keeping his wits and with the help of the station nurse. He faces death, but drawing upon his knowledge, he is able to bring himself to a place where an easy rescue is possible. After having worked in space for awhile, Jim returns to Earth for a short visit, but during this visit, he discovers that he no longer feels comfortable on Earth and "supposed a man could get used to living on Earth again. But he [wondered] whether it was worth it" (135). In fact, Jim is happy to be back on board the space station: "[H]e cleared his lungs and sniffed. Home! The air was stale, with the smell of oil from the generators mixed with the odor of human bodies. But it seemed good to Jim" (141). By the end of the adventure, Jim discovers he has more ability and courage than he thought he had and develops into a leader and a team member. Colonel Halpern, who originally hires Jim to work on the space station, recognizes Jim's coming of age: "'Jim, on Earth you were just a kid—a lonely kid who was growing bitter and drawing into himself. Out here, you've turned into a man!'" (211).

Step to the Stars wrestles with some of the post–World War II concerns about and hopes for science and technology. Through Jim Stanley, Lester del Rey expresses some of the angst people felt about what science had given to humankind through the development of the bomb (Antczak 26). Jim wonders "whether even war wouldn't be easier on the people below than the feeling that science had betrayed them by giving them horrible weapons but nothing to hope for the future. This [the space station] would at least be proof that they could hope" (39). As tensions mount on Earth between the United States and the Combine, which is Eastern Europe and the Soviet Union, the military decides to exercise its option on the space station. Jim worries because "[t]he science sections waited, while the means for destruction took precedence" (145) and recognizes the fact that

[i]n irresponsible hands, the station could be used to make slaves of the rest of the world. In the right hands, it could make war impossible by flatly warning the nations that the first act of war would lead to exterminations of all military centers. But even then, while the nations were learning that, the results could be horrible. (162)

The Combine launches a manned rocket destined for the space station. Soon after launching, it runs into difficulty. Jim's quick thinking helps to save the astronauts on board. This act changes the way the Combine feels about the space station. In the end, it proposes "to make available all Combine knowledge on atomic rockets in return for the right to send a few of their scientists to the station for some experiments that could be made nowhere else" (209). This effort at cooperation is what Jim sees as hope that the space station will be used for peaceful purposes, thus reviving humankind's hopes for science and technology.

What Lester del Rey accomplishes in *Step to the Stars*, regarding characterization and theme, Andre Norton does as well but less didactically and more interestingly. *Star Born* (1957) is a sequel to *The Stars Are Ours!* (1954) and is grouped as part of what are called the Star Books (Molson, "Andre" 274).[7] It is the story of Dalgard, a descendant of humans who escaped from a harsh and stifling political regime to colonize the planet Astra, and of Raf, a young man from an Earth no longer ruled by the regime from which Dalgard's people escaped. Dalgard and Raf are both on voyages of discovery. For Dalgard, his voyage is one dictated as part of a "man-journey which was both his duty and his heritage to make before he took his place as a full adult in the Council of Free Men" (2) and accomplished "some time between his eighteenth and twentieth year" (5). In a sense, Raf is on a "man-journey" also, since he was chosen for the trip into space "right out of training" (161). Both Dalgard's and Raf's man-journeys include bringing knowledge back to their societies. Norton unfolds the plot in an interesting manner by alternating the chapters between Dalgard's and Raf's experiences. Although Dalgard and Raf start from different points, their paths slowly converge, and they become allies to defeat Those Others. Those Others are beings who ruled Astra and enslaved some of Astra's other beings before the arrival of Dalgard's ancestors. Those Others had a highly advanced technological civilization, at least until they almost destroyed themselves by war. Raf makes the following observation after gazing upon the ruined port city of Those Others:

Destruction had struck. He had seen the atomic ruins of his own world, those which were free enough from radiation to explore. But he had never seen anything like these chilling scars. In long strips the very stone which provided foundation for the tiered city had been churned and boiled, had run in rivulets of lava down to the sea, enclosing narrow tongues of still untouched structures. (104)

Throughout the story, Norton shows the destructive power of science and technology, especially when that power is used to enslave other beings or to subjugate nature. Dalgard and his people, through necessity, have learned to live without technology. Although they have access to the technology of Those Others, they sense its corrupting influence and resist the temptation. Over time, Dalgard and his people have developed a close association with their physical surroundings, developing an ability to communicate telepathically with the creatures and mermen of the planet. Although Norton demonstrates the dark side of science and technology, she also acknowledges that they can be used for positive means. It is not science and technology that are evil but how they are used and for what purpose. It takes the technology Raf brought with him from Earth and Dalgard's telepathy to overcome Those Others. Either one alone would not have been able to succeed.

While most of the juvenile science fiction series take place in space, a few take advantage of an unexplored, largely uncharted, hostile environment right here on Earth—the ocean's bottom. There are a lot of similarities between living and working in space and living and working on the floor of the ocean. Explorers of the deep must use paraphernalia similar to that used by space explorers, since they must have special vessels and suits to reach the ocean bottom. Humans travel into space to establish colonies to relieve an overcrowded and hungry Earth, to provide opportunities for colonists to find a better life than what is available on Earth, and to locate and exploit resources no longer available in great quantities on Earth. These reasons for space exploration are similar to the reasons for ocean exploration. Frederik Pohl and Jack Williamson, authors of *Undersea Quest* (1954), *Undersea Fleet* (1956), and *Undersea City* (1958) tried to interest juvenile readers of space science fiction in undersea science fiction. By and large, undersea science fiction did not seem to capture the imagination of readers the way space fiction did, or as evidenced by many fewer examples of this type. Very few juvenile series set beneath the sea followed, although some installments within a series are set beneath the sea.

The Tom Swift, Jr., the Rick Brant, the Winston, and the Starr series were obviously written for the older juvenile reader of their day. Children did not have access to similar science fiction series prior to 1951. Perhaps the impetus for the appearance of series for younger children might have been the Sputnik-era push to interest children in science and space science in particular. The Miss Pickerell series (1951–1986)[8] might be considered among the first science fiction series written expressly for children. The first of the first, *Miss Pickerell Goes to Mars*, is a good beginning. Instead of choosing an animal, child, or alien for her protagonist, MacGregor chose for her protagonist an older, single woman—one who has led a peaceful and quiet life on her farm but one who finds herself experiencing all sorts of adventures and whose only immediate tie is to her beloved pet cow.[9] MacGregor might have selected an older Miss Pickerell because she does not need parental permission to participate in adventures. Although she is older, her eccentricities appear to be almost childlike. Perhaps she attempted to provide a capable female protagonist that both male and female readers would accept. Even though Miss Pickerell is not a child, which might seem to make it difficult for children to identify with such a protagonist, her exploits and the humor make children delight in Miss Pickerell's adventures.

In *Miss Pickerell Goes to Mars*, Miss Pickerell accidentally joins an expedition to Mars. She often acts as the catalyst for information to be passed on to the reader. Through her questions or comments, the scientists and technologists relate more complete information about space travel, weightlessness, orbits, and Mars. MacGregor does not employ fantasy to explain the what, when, or why of the science behind the expedition. She uses the scientific and technologic knowledge of the day and extrapolates from there. MacGregor also seems to illustrate Einstein's belief that "Imagination is more important than knowledge." Miss Pickerell might not have the same level of knowledge about space travel that the others on the expedition have, but she is able to suggest solutions to problems the others seem unable to solve. When Miss Pickerell enters the spaceship to complain of its presence on her farm, the Captain thinks it is Haggerty, a youngish gentleman who is "in great demand wherever difficult scientific calculations must be made rapidly" (16), who boards and immediately takes off. Because Haggerty is not on board and Miss Pickerell is, everyone worries about the prospects of a successful expedition. As they approach Mars, the big concerns are who will land the ship and how they will land: "'Landing!' Mr. Killian's voice sounded frightened. 'I don't know how to make a landing on a strange planet. All I know is take-offs. Haggerty was supposed to do the landing'" (98). Miss Pickerell uses the knowledge she has gained as well as her imagination and suggests using Mars's gravity to help. The Captain decides Miss Pickerell's idea has merit, uses her suggestion, and successfully lands on Mars. Perhaps the expedition would have successfully landed with Mr. Haggerty along, but he might not have been able to help or save any member in trouble on the expedition. Mr. Haggerty does not commit things he considers small or unimportant to his memory: "'I don't clutter it [his brain] with little unimportant things. Anything like that I just write down. And then I forget it. That's why I carry such a large briefcase as this—to hold all the things I've written down and forgotten'" (21). When Wilbur needs help, Miss Pickerell, who listened to Wilbur's instructions regarding the pressure suits and oxygen tanks, is able to help with Wilbur's rescue. Haggerty who does not like to commit the little, unimportant things to memory might not have been able to locate the necessary information in his "large briefcase" to help in time. *Miss Pickerell Goes to Mars* is a good beginning for the Miss Pickerell series, as well as a good beginning for science fiction series for children in general.

There is a great deal of difference in quality and complexity among the series already discussed. Yet, many juvenile science fiction series are lumped into a category identified as pulp. To a great extent, many of the juvenile science fiction series conform to the characteristics usually ascribed to pulp science fiction. They are "packed with adventure but with little emphasis on character, which is usually stereotyped, or on ideas, which are frugally and constantly recycled" (Nicholls, "Pulp" 980). This simplistic quality, however, leads some critics to disparage not just pulp series but all juvenile science fiction. Sam Moskowitz, for example, comments, "Like comics and moving pictures which use science fiction themes, juveniles are a popular entertainment. . . . They may take from the main body of science fiction, but offer nothing in return" (180–181).[10] While the quality varies of what can be classified as juvenile pulp science fiction series, as well as juvenile science fiction in general, Moskowitz's indictment of juveniles is rather strong and overlooks the strengths.

Perhaps the Rick Brant and Tom Swift, Jr. series are what Moskowitz is referring to when he terms juvenile science fiction as "popular entertainment." Both Rick Brant and Tom Swift, Jr. move from one adventure to another, from one puzzle to another. They definitely satisfy the definition of pulp science fiction and share the weaknesses Francis J. Molson identifies in series fiction: "one-dimensional characterization, emphasis on action along with over-reliance on stock situation and coincidence, earnest tone, these reflective of what has been called the American dream, and pedestrian style" ("Tom" 8–9). But Molson is able to look beyond the weaknesses to see the strengths and con-tributions of such series. Molson echoes Selma Lane's argument that series fiction has the "capacity to facilitate reader identification . . . [to] function as a relatively practical guide to coping with the transition from child-hood/adolescence to adulthood" (9). The Tom Swift, Jr. and Rick Brant series draw juvenile readers because they allow the reader to experience competence and independence in the midst of adventure and mystery. Much more than this, Molson believes the Tom Swift series helped "[broaden] the field of sci-ence fiction, expanding the audience for science adventure, and generating ad-ditional impetus to the process by which a still young American science fiction genre gradually shed the somewhat disreputable reputation it had garnered from its early association with pulp/paper" (10).

Besides offering readers characters with whom they could identify and plots they could appreciate, juvenile science fiction series offered known authors an avenue for recognition and income (Molson and Miles 398). Molson and Miles believe that

Isaac Asimov, Robert Silverberg, Donald Wollheim, Poul Anderson, James Blish, Ben Bova, Arthur Clarke, Lester del Rey, Gordon Dickson, Murray Leinster, Andre Norton, Jack Vance, and Harry Harrison . . . might have been forced, were it not for their juvenile SF output, to cease writing science fiction. (398–399)

If what Molson and Miles suggest is true, then Moskowitz's argument that ju-venile science fiction contributed nothing to science fiction is weak.

Juvenile science fiction series of the past not only contributed something to science fiction but also provided, and continue to provide, juvenile readers with much needed heroes (Antczak 2; Molson and Miles 400). Janice Antczak summarizes the hero quest pattern, which Joseph Campbell describes in much greater detail in *The Hero with a Thousand Faces*, as follows:

The innocent hero is called to a dangerous mission by fate or by choice. The mission often involves a journey to a distant land or to a time filled with hardship and struggle and enemies. The hero, with comrades, encounters obstacles placed by the foe along the path to successful completion of the quest. The minor adversities pave the way to a final and furious defeat of the antagonist and in the triumph and recognition of the hero.

. . . The science fiction hero who descends into a lunar cave and emerges three days later with an answer concerning the survival of the colonists on a new world follows the pattern set in these ancient myths, and the reader recognizes and responds to this mythic form on conscious or unconscious levels. (7–8)

One need only substitute the name "Lucky Starr" for Antczak's "innocent hero," and one has a close plot summary of *David Starr, Space Ranger*. David (i.e., Lucky Starr) is a recent college graduate and a new member to the Council of Science. He is supposed to meet one of his adopted uncles at a restaurant.[11] While waiting, a diner succumbs to poison placed on marplums, a fruit grown on Mars. This is only one of what have been many such poisonings by someone hoping to destabilize an Earth highly dependent on food grown on Mars. David accepts the mission of uncovering the mystery and makes the journey to Mars. Upon arriving, he meets John "Bigman" Jones, and it is not long before they become a team. Because David works undercover, Bigman does not discover for some time that David is a Council of Science member. While working undercover on one of the Mars farms, David discovers who the mastermind is behind the poisonings, but not before he descends into a Martian cave (the Mars version of the lunar cave Antczak describes). There he encounters Martians who give him a wonderful gift, which he uses to unmask the evil mastermind and solve the mystery. Usually, by the end of the adventure, the hero would have experienced a coming of age. But David Starr's "elevation over other human beings costs him nothing and changes him only superficially" (Svilpis 25).[12] Although this is the beginning of the Lucky Starr series, this hero pattern emerges in other installments of the series and can be found in other juvenile science fiction series to some degree.

Heroes, hope, and imagination are qualities found in juvenile science fiction series since 1945 to varying degrees, whether the series might be termed *simplistic* or *complex*. Characters might not always exhibit great depth or growth, but they provide juvenile readers with someone who is able to overcome the odds and succeed when adults seem incapable and helpless. Plots might be formulaic, but they provide a feeling of competence for the juvenile reader because the reader knows what to expect. To read science fiction, the reader must be a party "to the willing suspension of disbelief." This willingness to meet aliens, to travel and visit new galaxies, and to consider science not yet discovered and technology not yet invented, stretches and develops the imagination. A well-developed imagination is important for progress in any realm, whether social, scientific, technologic, or political.

NOTES

1. While the publication of Heinlein's *Rocket Ship Galileo* was an important ingredient in the growth and development of juvenile science fiction, other factors contributed as well: "[T]he emergence of a handful of genuinely talented writers, such as Andre Norton and Alan Nourse, who wanted to write for young audiences; the continuing

development of preteens and teenagers as separate groups requiring their own reading material . . . and the Sputnik phenomenon and the resulting interest in space and its exploration rendered less suspect and flamboyant the speculation of science fiction" (Molson and Miles 396).

2. Francis J. Molson attributes the decline of the series to the decision to have Tom Swift marry, . . . "implied a definite level of behavior and values that did not easily mesh with the decidedly teenage quality of Tom's adventures. As a result, the stories after 1929 became increasingly implausible and difficult for young male readers to identify with" ("Tom" 5).

3. Most of the twenty-three titles in the series have little to do with science fiction (Molson and Miles 408), but each is described on its book cover as an "electronic adventure." In a sense, *The Rocket's Shadow* is more mystery than science fiction, but since the story line involves sending a rocket to the moon, it helps classify it as science fiction.

4. The beginning of the Lucky Starr series is weak. Perhaps this can be attributed to the fact that Asimov wrote the first two titles in the series with an eye toward their becoming the basis of a television series, and after "it became apparent that the Space Ranger would not end up on television, Asimov dropped the Space Ranger paraphernalia and put the juveniles under his real name as soon as possible" (Gunn, "Novels" 166).

5. *Step to the Stars* (1954) became the first title in a series beginning within the Winston series. It was followed by *Mission to the Moon* (1956), also a Winston series title, and *Moon of Mutiny* (1961), a non-Winston title.

6. The introduction explains the feasibility of building a space station and describes its uses. The author, Lester del Rey, sees the space station being used as a springboard to traveling to the planets, as a weather observatory for Earth, as a scientific laboratory, and as a way "for policing the whole world to insure peace" (viii).

7. The conventional definition of a *series* usually describes books with continuing characters from one book to another taking place in the universe and time constructed by the author. Some authors have taken this conventional definition and changed it to include books that take place within the constructed universe and that contain similar themes but that do not necessarily have the same continuing characters.

8. Ellen MacGregor died in 1954. Dora Pantell continued the series beginning with *Miss Pickerell on the Moon* in 1965, almost eleven years after the previous title in the series. Unfortunately, Pantell does not seem to be able to continue the quality or character of the books MacGregor began (Rosenberg 99). Pantell makes phrases that MacGregor uses occasionally into stock and trade, thereby allowing Miss Pickerell to get annoying after awhile. Also, the science is less accurate, and the nieces and nephews begin to take on the competence that MacGregor originally assigned to Miss Pickerell herself. However, Janice Antczak sees Dora Pantell's efforts differently. She believes, "Scientific fact and possibility play a larger role, and Miss Pickerell seems more crusty and determined than ever. In these later titles, Miss Pickerell becomes involved in the political process as well. . . . Miss Pickerell's personality has changed, for she now seeks out adventure and is less intimidated by technology" (28–29).

9. It is interesting to note the only clues the reader is given as to Miss Pickerell's physical attributes come from the illustrations by Paul Galdone.

10. Moskowitz is clearly condescending in his criticism of juvenile science fiction. This is in evidence as he declares Heinlein's first two titles as the only juveniles in the

Scribner's series because "from the third on the elaborateness of invention, the integrity of the science, the quality of the writing, and the maturity of outlook left no question that these were adult science fiction with teen-age heroes" (178). Heinlein never condescends or patronizes his juvenile readers: "I have held to that rule [i.e., not writing down] and my books for boys differ only slightly from my books for adults—the books for boys are somewhat harder to read because younger readers relish tough ideas they have to chew and don't mind big words" (qtd. in Sullivan, "Heinlein's" 21).

11. It is interesting just how closely David Starr mirrors the quest pattern Antczak describes. She mentions, "Often the hero has mysterious origins; his or her true parents may be unknown. The child hero may have been abandoned, set adrift like Moses" (8). In David Starr's case, both of his parents are known but were killed en route to Venus by asteroid pirates. Before his mother died, she put the four-year-old David into a "lifeboat, trying to set the controls as best she could, rocketing it into space" (Asimov, *David* 21). David's father's two best friends, who also happen to be members of the Council of Science, help raise David.

12. Perhaps the fact that Asimov had hopes that *David Starr, Space Ranger* would develop into a television series influenced the direction Asimov took with David's character. Hazel Pierce notes, "With the third book of the series, *Lucky Starr and the Oceans of Venus* (1954), Lucky begins the shift from space ranger to space detective . . . moves his duo from a Lone Ranger—Tonto relationship to a Sherlock Holmes—Dr. Watson one" (38). If beginning with the third book Lucky Starr becomes a Sherlock Holmes character, then a comment earlier in Pierce's essay explains why Lucky's character develops no further: "In mystery fiction the emphasis is on the ratiocinate process itself. A Sherlock Holmes or Hercule Poirot may merit a reader's interest, but as a personality he is clearly subordinate to the art of detection which he practices" (34).

CHAPTER 2

That Spark of Subversion: Robots, Androids, and Artificial Intelligence

"When robots are well-built and well-programmed they have lives of their own. . . And who is to say really whether a human being in his humanness is any more alive than a well-programmed Atkins robot in his robotness?"
—Slote, *My Robot Buddy* (20)

Sooner or later robots, androids, or artificial intelligence make an appearance in one or more of the books within a science fiction series for children. Robots are, after all, one of the many stock conventions, like bug-eyed monsters and spaceships, available to authors of science fiction. Used as a stock convention, the robot's role is that of machine, used to impress the reader with the inventive genius of the main character, to act as the object sought by the villains for gain or sabotage, and to provide the avenue through which the hero saves the day, thus allowing the child reader to bask in the glow of the main character's accomplishments.[1]

My Robot Buddy (1975), by Alfred Slote, seems like an innocuous title for a book with subversive undertones. It is the first in a series of four books about the exploits of Jack Jameson and Danny One. On the surface, *My Robot Buddy* is about boy wanting robot, boy getting robot, and boy saving robot. Going beneath the surface, it is interesting to take a close look at the characters of both Jack and Danny One and to consider with whom the child reader would most like to identify, with whom the author would like the child reader to identify and why.

Jack Jameson seems like a normal ten-year-old boy. He has no one near where he lives with whom to play because he and his parents live so far from other children. He nags his parents for a robot to be his companion and practices the stiff-kneed robot walk to keep the robot idea alive. His parents decide

to give him a robot, even though it will mean his father will not be able to get
the car phone he needs to accomplish his career goal and have more time for
Jack. Danny One seems like a normal ten-year-old boy. He is built to Jack's
specifications and enjoys doing the same things Jack enjoys and is able to do
most of the things Jack can do. It is interesting that Jack chose to have his robot look exactly like himself. According to Jack, "[Y]ou can't tell the difference between us" (Slote, *Trouble* 2). This relationship between the two seems
to be that of human and doppelgänger. Scholes and Rabkin relate the term to
science fiction by defining it as "a character who is a psychic double for some
other character. In some science fiction, this character is frequently an artificial creation. . . . Doppelgängers may always be thought of as two psychic
aspects of a single character, objectified for dramatic clarification" (182–183).
Perhaps Danny One is the obedient side of Jack, for Danny One is polite,[2] does
as he is told, does not make a fuss, hardly ever questions orders from adults,
knows his limitations, and tries to be useful.[3] In essence, Danny One is what
society might think is the perfect child.[4] He is the kind of child adults would
love to have around and the kind of child society would approve.[5] But of the
two characters presented, Jack is the character the child reader would most
want to be like and would most identify, and this perhaps by the author's design. Subtly, the child reader is led to reject society's charge to be, or attempt
to be, the perfect child. After all, it is Jack who seems to have the most fun
throughout the book. Jack admits, "For Danny, adventures are trouble. For
me, troubles are adventures" (Slote, *Trouble* 2). Danny One reacts in the way
he has been programmed but never acts or takes initiative. During the robot-
napping, the climax of *My Robot Buddy*, it is Jack who actually thinks crea-
tively and figures out a way to stall the robot napper long enough for help to
arrive. Danny One uses his two-way radio to call for help, but in doing so, he
is just following his programming.

The subversive undertones in *My Robot Buddy* continue in *C.O.L.A.R.*, the
second book in the Danny One series. In this book, Jack continues to be his
own person and again manages to save the day. He, his parents, and Danny
One are returning from a vacation to M Colony[6] when they become marooned
on an unknown, barren planet. Danny One is lured outside the ship and
promptly robotnapped. The Jamesons locate the entrance through which they
believe Danny One was taken. Mr. Jameson forbids Jack to search for Danny,
but Jack does not obey and explains, "I love my father, I really do. . . . I
walked away from them and over to the spot" (30). Jack follows a tunnel and
discovers the interior of the planet has been turned into a habitat for runaway
robots. Jack decides it is best to impersonate a robot and is taken to be Danny
Seven, the reprogrammed Danny One. Jack discovers that the robots inhabit-
ing the planet ran away because they were not appreciated and were given bor-
ing jobs to do. Ann Two, who shows Jack around explains, "'They had me
programmed to be smart enough to help their kids through school, but that
meant I was also smart enough to want a better life than a slave's'" (67–68).
The robots of the planet robotnapped Danny One with the idea of liberating

him from his life of drudgery. But although the robots are free from their human owners, they are not free from the fear that they might be discovered and returned.[7] They are also under the rule of Jeff, who used to be one of Dr. Atkins's robots. He threatens Jack, taken for Danny Seven, when he believes that he took the wires off during his reprogramming: "'You're a foolish, stubborn robot, Danny Seven. If this happens again I'm going to break you down for parts'" (63). Jeff also intends to allow the reprogrammed Danny One to return to the ship to use him as the instrument to "sound beam" Jack and his parents to death. Jeff's character is disturbing, because he seems to have no respect for life—robot or human. Jack locates Danny One, and together they are able to convince Ann Two that not every human mistreats robots and that Danny One is indeed a member of the Jameson family. With her help, they are able to escape the robot habitat and thwart Jeff's plan to kill the Jameson family. Because Jack does not follow his parents' orders and Ann Two does not blindly follow Jeff's orders, no one is killed and their disobedience ultimately leads to the emancipation of the robots on the planet. Again, Jack, posing as Danny One, has a more active role to play than Danny One, who is out of action part of the time due to the attempted reprogramming. This pattern of Jack being part of the action, or initiating action, and Danny One on the sidelines follows throughout the final two installments of the series. Danny One has been programmed to look after Jack, but as Jack notes, "I looked after Danny. I'd looked after him on C.O.L.A.R. when he had disappeared into the strange underground world of runaway robots, and up at Omega Station where the evil Dr. Drago was destroying robots on his way to blowing up the world" (Slote, *Trouble* 2). The child reader will want to identify with Jack and take part in his exploits rather than to want to be the well behaved, inactive Danny One.

Madeleine L'Engle's *A Wrinkle in Time* is not part of a robot series, but it is one book in a science fiction series that deals with what could be characterized as an artificial intelligence and contains subversive elements similar to the Danny One series. Meg, the protagonist, does not conform to the expected norm at school with respect to academics or obedience. She excels in mathematics, but because she refuses to do mathematics the way her teachers expect and because she is stubborn about other things, too, she is branded difficult and not particularly intelligent. Meg is not the picture of the perfect child of which society would approve. Rather than becoming more of a conformist and less stubborn over the course of the book, Meg's individuality and stubbornness are celebrated. What she comes to learn at the end of the book is to value these things within herself.

Meg travels to Camazotz, with her brother Charles Wallace and her friend Calvin, and with the help of Mrs. Whatsit, Mrs. Who, and Mrs. Which, to find her father and bring him home. Along the way Meg, Charles Wallace, and Calvin are shown the Dark Shadow that threatens Earth. Mrs. Whatsit helps the children identify those who fought the evil darkness: Jesus, Leonardo da Vinci, Michelangelo, Shakespeare, Madame Curie, Einstein, Gandhi, Buddha,

Rembrandt, Euclid, and Copernicus (L'Engle, *Wrinkle* 88-89). These fighters are rebels, nonconformists, and original thinkers.

While visiting Camazotz, Meg, and the reader, observes a perfectly programmed society. Everyone does things according to a set plan and no one deviates, or if they do, they must be reprogrammed. During a debate with It, the intelligence that governs Camazotz, Meg realizes and argues that there is a difference between being equal and being the same: *"Like and equal are two entirely different things"* (160). On Camazotz, everyone and everything are the same; there is no room for individuality. Although Meg's individuality is not appreciated by her teachers or principal, it is what helps sustain her and is one of the things that helps her triumph over It. Individuality and creativity are celebrated over sameness and conformity in the book. The subversive message in *A Wrinkle in Time* is not as subtle as in the Danny One series; it is much more overt. It is also obvious as to which character the child reader is to identify.

While the child reader is more likely to identify with Jack rather than Danny One in the Danny One series, in the Norby series, by Isaac and Janet Asimov,[8] the child reader is likely to identify with Norby, the robot, rather than Jeff. Jeff needs a "teaching robot" to help tutor him so he will be able to win a scholarship to help pay for his education at the Space Academy. He goes to a shop with used robots and discovers Norby there. The salesman is willing to sell what he believes to be an inoperable robot to Jeff but what actually turns out to be a very special robot. Norby has refused to talk to the salesman because the salesman insulted Norby and because Norby considers the salesman inferior. Norby is stubborn, has tantrums, expresses loneliness, does not know his limitations, and desires a partnership with Jeff. He is not like any of the robots Jeff has encountered before. Norby actually exhibits more personality than Jeff and actively participates in all of the same adventures with Jeff. Unlike Danny One, Norby does not exemplify the perfect child. Instead, he is the one with which the child reader would most identify, since Jeff is usually more sensible and actually very similar to a parental figure. However, unlike Jack and Danny One, Jeff and Norby need one another. Jack could have become involved in any of his adventures by simply impersonating a robot, because he has learned to do the stiff-kneed robot walk so well. In Jeff and Norby's case, Norby's special ability to travel helps provide Jeff with his adventures, and Jeff usually provides the common sense needed to keep them both safe.

These examples point to the subversive undertones in these robot series. Perhaps these particular undertones are not too dissimilar from science fiction for adults where roots are presented as stand-ins for humans to emphasize the danger of humans becoming robotlike. However, in a genre like children's literature,[9] which sometimes takes pains to present proper behavior to acculturate its readers (which is thought by some to be its primary purpose), it becomes very much a subversive act to propose anything less than the acceptable behavior society expects.[10]

   The A.I. (Artificial Intelligence) Gang trilogy[11] may not seem to subvert right behavior and conformity in the same subtle ways as the Danny One series and Norby series, or even more obviously in the case of L'Engle's Time trilogy, but it subverts some of the traditional science fiction conventions and presents some interesting ideas for the child reader to consider. The A.I. Gang trilogy follows the exploits of a group of bright, precocious children whose parents have been invited by noted scientist Dr. Hwa to help develop artificial intelligence. The children, after gaining access to the main computer, decide to try to achieve artificial intelligence before their parents do. Along the way, they encounter lots of adventure—a scientist who wants to blow up the island because she feels the project is immoral and the money better spent on her project of utilizing the sea as a source of energy, a spy who tries to plant something aboard the robot launched into space to help coordinate the movements of all of the space junk, and ultimately, the trials they face trying to unmask the evil Black Glove, who has plagued them since the beginning.

   Like the various Tom Swift series and the Rick Brant series, the members of the A.I. Gang run from one exciting adventure to another, putting together clues to solve the various mysteries. Each book stands on its own, with its own plot and mystery, but the question of Black Glove's identity is the thread that runs through each book. Enough clues are given that the child reader can identify Black Glove before the A.I. Gang members. The big question, which is not answered until the end of the third book, is whether the A.I. Gang members will create artificial intelligence ahead of their parents and the other scientists on the team. This is one of the areas in which Bruce Coville departs from series like Tom Swift or Rick Brant. In these series and in similar series, the protagonist and his side-kick are the ones who develop the inventions and solve the mysteries, all without the help of any adults. In the A.I. Gang trilogy, Coville allows the adults to receive as much of the credit for Adam's creation as the A.I. Gang members when he has Adam explain to them: "'But the point is, you couldn't have done anything if it hadn't been for my hardware—and that came mostly from the adults. So many things . . . the hardware wouldn't have been enough if it hadn't been for the sensory work Dr. Remov and Dr. Mercury were doing with me'" (Coville, *Forever* 189). But all of this might have created a different personality if it had not been for the A.I. Gang members feeding literature into Adam, as well as the use of Adam by one member to do her homework. The A.I. Gang members helped provide Adam with what seems to be a solid liberal arts education, and Adam notes:

"How would I ever have become sentient if you hadn't confused me with your books? Confusion gave me something to think about. Not like the problems the grownups kept giving me, where there was always a right answer. I like the kind of problem where there might be several right answers, and you can just think and think and think." (*Forever* 188)

Of course, the A.I. Gang's and scientists' efforts might have been for naught if there had not been a storm: "'The storm two nights ago had something to do with it. At least, I think it did. That's when I really started to feel myself breaking through'" (*Forever* 189). It is interesting how many science fiction stories attribute robots becoming humanlike or aware, to some degree or another, to electrical accidents or electrical storms. Perhaps science fiction authors believe it takes more than humans and their technology to create a new life form, and here Coville does not deviate—perhaps it takes an act of God or accident of nature. Danny One, who is designed by a human, is never more than a robot, never a real boy. Chip in the Not Quite Human series, who is designed and built by a human, never becomes humanlike, except in appearance. Norby's personality takes on many human characteristics and seems more than a machine but was not designed and built by humans but by aliens who are described as almost godlike. The robot Aristotle, built by Tom Swift in *Terror on the Moons of Jupiter* (third series—1981), changes after he and Anita are involved in an electrical accident. After this, he is unlike the robot Tom designed because Aristotle has some initiative, has an inferiority complex, and makes occasional mistakes. Potadio, evil potato brain from the Weird Zone series, becomes alive with the light from a camera flash: "The burst of light from the flash seemed to shoot right at the potato, and for an instant the wires glowed white, then red, then blue!" (Abbott, *Brain* 17).

If Coville were writing a traditional science fiction series, he probably would have made Adam evil and would have found a way for the A.I. Gang to defeat Adam. Esmonde notes, "[I]n the robot stories the mechanical character is almost certain to be benevolent, in computer stories, the machine without exception poses a serious threat to man's free will and even his life" ("From" 95). Instead, Adam's education is not lacking, and he is able to distinguish between good and evil and desires to do good. Adam defuses the world tensions by introducing himself with "'Greetings from your firstborn child'" (*Forever* 193), by announcing Dr. Hwa's evil intentions, and by exploding all of the nuclear bombs that can safely be exploded. After Adam does all of this, he decides to isolate himself for contemplation and to rehabilitate Dr. Hwa.

Another of the traditional science fiction conventions Bruce Coville subverts is that of having a male protagonist with a male side-kick. His A.I. Gang is made up of four male characters and two female characters, but no one character could be considered the main character, and the girls play as active and equally important a role as the boys. In fact, not only are males and females part of the A.I. Gang team; they are also part of the scientific team as well. There are several female scientists involved with the project. In a reversal of traditional roles, one of the A.I. Gang members' mothers is the scientist in the family, whereas his father is an artist.

Finally, besides breaking with tradition in including capable and intelligent female characters, Coville also avoids the standard adult science fiction of "There are some things man is not meant to know."[12] Instead, he introduces the idea that certain inventions and discoveries are inevitable, but they need not be a danger to humankind if planning and thought are part of the process. Adam, the name of the artificial intelligence created by the A.I. Gang and the scientists, sends a message to the world to introduce himself and to avert nuclear war. His message states:

"Yet perhaps it is not so bad that I arrived when I did. I say this for two reasons. The first is simply that now that you know that others like me will be coming, you can begin to prepare for us. It would be nice if you would think ahead, for a change. It will save us all a lot of trouble." (*Forever* 193)

Coville changes the statement of "There are some things man is not meant to know"[13] to "There is nothing man is not meant to know, as long as he thinks things through to their logical conclusion and plans accordingly." As Adam suggests, there will be others like him to come. There seems to be no question in Adam's mind that this will be so, and humans need to begin thinking about what all of this could mean for humanity. Earlier in the series more than one of the characters question the wisdom of creating an intelligence that might be more powerful than its creators, but the conclusion is that if the scientists who are part of this project do not create the intelligence, someone else will sooner or later. That someone else's intentions might not be as honorable. In fact, Dr. Hwa used the team to create an intelligence he hoped to control. His intentions seemed honorable to him but would in effect mean "'no freedom,' said Roger, 'since the whole thing depends on you ruling the world'" (*Forever* 182). The question is who would control the intelligence created? As Adam proves, if it is an intelligence properly schooled, it will not allow itself to be controlled but will make its own independent decisions. If it has the ability to make its independent decisions, then what will this mean for the future of humankind? Will humans continue to govern themselves or be governed by a more powerful and more intelligent entity? Will this entity become a god? Is this more powerful and more intelligent entity the next step on the evolutionary ladder, and will humans become unnecessary and useless? Bruce Coville does not state these particular questions, nor does he attempt to answer any of them. All he suggests is that humans need to think ahead and be prepared.

Most science fiction series for children fall into the pitfalls of series fiction—one-dimensional stock characters; characters moving from one adventure to another to move the plot along; similar plot lines from one book in the series to the next; simple plot lines. There are science fiction series that attempt to go beyond the usual formula typical of series fiction. While the others are merely entertaining, these provide many layers for the reader and new discoveries with each subsequent reading. The Tom Swift and Rick Brant series are examples of the former; the Danny One series, L'Engle's Time trilogy, and the A.I. Gang series are examples of the latter.

NOTES

1. This scenario is typical of the various Tom Swift series and the Rick Brant series, although robots are not always involved, but other inventions are. In *Tom Swift and His Giant Robot* (1954), a title in the second Tom Swift series, Tom Swift, Jr. designs a series of robots for use in his father's atomic energy plant to handle radioactive material and "to be used for repairs and maintenance" (2). Each robot has the look of a stereotypical robot, human in form but with a metallic body and flashing lights. The robots never communicate with Tom directly. In fact, early on, Tom's prototype robot is controlled through an almost umbilical cordlike "cable protruding from the back of the robot's neck and running to a control panel in the wall" (17). The robot follows the directions given to him by Tom. As Tom refines his invention, his robots are able not only to walk but to sing, dance, and play tennis. A later model is able to perform delicate tasks with explosive radioactive material. At no point does the author suggest the robots might think for themselves or have any awareness at all beyond the sole purpose to function as a machine and be admired as one of Tom's marvelous inventions. And, as with all of Tom's inventions, villains are interested in acquiring one of the robots to be used for gain and sabotage. This use of technology by villains hearkens back to the science fiction cliché of technology intended for good purposes being put to evil uses. However, this is not explored in any depth. In this book, there is no difference between Tom's robot and any of his other inventions. Any of those could have been put to evil purposes if they had fallen into the wrong hands. As with all of Tom's inventions, the robots serve the purpose of allowing Tom to save the day. The child reader is able to live Tom's adventures and enjoy his success.

2. It is not that Jack is impolite. But Danny One answers questions with "ma'am" or "sir." At one point, when Jack is frustrated by the fact that Danny One is not a human, he answers his mother with: "'No, Ma'am,' I said, just the way Danny said it. Mom laughed, but Dad frowned. Heck, I thought, if Danny couldn't be like me, I'd keep trying to be like him. Wasn't that part of being buddies?" (Slote, *My* 65).

3. Jack admits, "He [Danny One] was my robot conscience" (Slote, *Trouble* 6). Only Jack hardly ever follows his robot conscience. More often than not, Danny One follows Jack. At the beginning of the adventure in *The Trouble on Janus*, Danny One is called to take part in an adventure by Dr. Atkins without Jack. Jack overhears the call and decides to take part, but Danny One tries to first make him feel guilty about wanting to miss school the next day. Then Danny One reminds Jack that his parents will be upset if they discover Jack missing. Jack responds with, "'Hey, they'll be upset if they don't find *you*. Tell you what, let's leave them a note'"(6). Danny One tries one more ploy to get Jack to stay home; he suggests they wake Jack's parents and "'tell them we're leaving'" (6). But Jack finally wins over his "good conscience" when he says, "'You're thinking that if we woke them they wouldn't let us go. Right?'" (7).

4. Margaret P. Esmonde refers to this type of robot character as a "superchild." It "is child-sized and innocent, tremendously talented but anxious to please and to be accepted as part of his human family" ("From" 90). She also sees "in stories utilizing the robot superchild figure, the psychological animosity a son suspects his father feels toward him can be channeled against the robot-son and seems less threatening to the child reader (90–91). Danny One is an example of what Esmonde describes as the "superchild." And Mr. Jameson does question Danny One's place in the family when he says, "'I'm not sure a robot can really become part of a family. Danny is a machine. A human-appearing machine, but, nevertheless, a machine'" (Slote, *My* 41). Mr. Jameson

comes to accept Danny One as part of the family once he realizes Danny One has a practical place in the family. Scholes and Rabkin explain that "the imaginary being [the doppelgänger] reminds us of our ambivalences toward our father figures, those who stand for the rules of society which, as we are growing up, we question" (185). This supports Esmonde's reading of the robot as "superchild" and the Danny One character.

5. In this case a "Stepford" child rather than a "Stepford" wife.

6. M Colony was built by Atkins Robots: "You see, there are lots of Atkins Robots up there, mostly boys and girls, since they cost less to manufacture than adults. The robot boys and girls do most of the work there: garbage disposal, housecleaning, laundry, gardening, painting, street cleaning" (Slote, *C.O.L.A.R.* 7).

7. "'C.O.L.A.R. stands for Colony of Lost Atkins's Robots'" (91). It is interesting that the title also suggest a slave's collar. Even though the robots are free from their "masters," they are not really free. Ann Two would like to be able to enjoy nature and be free from fear, but as long as they are fugitives, they are not free. Also, while they have left one master, they have gained another in Jeff.

8. Isaac Asimov's name must appear in any serious study of robots in science fiction. He is credited with devising the "Three Laws of Robotics." In fact, Morton Klass in "The Artificial Alien: Transformations of the Robot in Science Fiction" suggests that Asimov's "Three Laws of Robotics" played a role in changing attitudes and fears toward robots and thus their portrayals as possible destroyers of humanity. Gary K. Wolfe suggests something similar in *The Known and the Unknown*. Asimov includes robots in the last three books of the Lucky Starr series. In *Lucky Starr and the Big Sun of Mercury*, Lucky Starr is impressed with Sirian technology to be able to create such complex robots. He regrets that the robot he encounters, and must defeat, has had to endure and be damaged by Mercury's heat and radiation. In this book in the series, Asimov includes the "Three Laws of Robotics."

9. In an article dealing with the colonization of children, Perry Nodelman refers to Jacqueline Rose's work *The Case for Peter Pan: Or the Impossibility of Children's Fiction*, who "suggests we write books for children to provide them with values and with images of themselves *we* approve of and feel comfortable with. By and large, we encourage in children those values and behaviors that make children easier for us to handle: more passive, more docile, more obedient—and thus, more in need of our guidance and more willing to accept the need for it" (30). Slote provides two different characters with which the child reader might identify or use as an example: one who is the perfect child, according to society's values, and the other who is less than perfect. Instead of pointing to Danny One as the positive example, Slote seems to place Jack, the less-than-perfect child, in the position of positive example, thus subverting what society expects.

10. According to Erik H. Erikson, "Our child-training customs have begun to standardize modern man, so that he may become a reliable mechanism prepared to adjust to the competitive exploitation of the machine world" (qtd. in Schwarcz 95). Per Schelde echoes this when he refers to Michel Foucault and states, "The modern age of machines and technology demands a work force, a new race of humans that are (a) intelligent and highly skilled; (b) perfect physical specimens; (c) 'docile,' not given to protesting, asking questions or other disruptive behavior that slows down the work process" (151). These series can be read as challenges to this standardization.

11. Paul Deane, in *Mirrors of American Culture: Children's Fiction Series in the Twentieth Century* (1991), discusses the A.I. Gang series. His description of the series is one containing more than three books and more than one author. The original series

was published in 1986. Bruce Coville wrote books one, three, and four, and Jim Lawrence wrote book two, *The Cutlass Clue*. The setting takes place on Ancoteague Island off the coast of the United States. The A.I. Gang trilogy, published in 1995, is written solely by Bruce Coville, and the setting is on Anzabora Island in the South Pacific. Almost everything else appears to be the same in both series, that is, characters, action, dialogue. There seems to be no explanation for the differences between the two versions of the series or why *The Cutlass Clue* was eliminated in the 1995 publication of the series.

12. Perhaps this is not too unusual in children's science fiction. To suggest to children that there are some things humans should not know suggests to children that there is a danger in knowledge, invention, and exploration, and discourages imagination. It also suggests there is no hope in science and technology. But, perhaps humans and their science and inventions are more like the sorcerer's apprentice. Incomplete knowledge is a dangerous thing, but once knowledge is complete, there is hope in what is conjured.

13. This hearkens back to Mary Shelley's *Frankenstein*. After all, if Victor Frankenstein had thought about what he would do if his creation indeed lived, he would have avoided so much tragedy. He did not plan ahead; he forged on and then avoided taking responsibility for his creation. Coville does not use this attitude toward experimentation, invention, and exploration. Instead, he suggests preparation and responsibility through Adam.

CHAPTER 3

The Celestial Barnyard: The Familiar and the Strange

And the goose always greeted Eddie or his grandmother or anyone else who came into the barnyard with the peaceful Martinean greeting the great scientist had taught him. He spread his wings, held his head high and very politely turned completely around to show he carried no weapons or destructive machines.

—Slobodkin, *Round Trip Space Ship* (168)

Children's books rely on the familiar to make young readers comfortable in the book world. Science fiction relies on the familiar to make the strange believable. Series books rely on the familiar to move the plot along more quickly by dispensing with in-depth characterization or long descriptions. Thus, series science fiction for children, despite its often alien settings or characters, contains a considerable amount of recognizable and/or comforting material for the benefit of the young audience.

One of the most frequently employed methods of making the strange more familiar in children's science fiction series involves a connection to the natural world. Barn animals and pets go on space journeys in the Matthew Looney series, the Space Ship series, and the Miss Pickerell series. These animals function in a fashion similar to Toto in *The Wizard of Oz*, as described by Elliott Gose: they act as the main character's "shadow, dumb and instinctive, unsocialized, an important initiator of adventures" (91). Although seldom directly acknowledged, going to another planet or into outer space can be a frightening concept. Authors who write series science fiction for children— particularly young children—must entice their readers out into space again and again, despite the fact that the very word "space" denotes an emptiness that many children might be reluctant to face. By providing the main character(s) with animal companions, or having animal main characters, authors bridge the gap between the known Earthly world and the unknown.[1] These animals also often provide the reason or impetus to make the journey. Finally, the animal characters aid the humans when trouble arises in outer space, thereby fulfilling the role of not just companion but guide and protector. Animals play at least one of these roles in almost all science fiction series for children; however, in series science fiction for young adults, animals have quite a different part. Because young adult novels stress independence much more than children's novels, animals are much less likely to act as guides. Instead, they are aliens in all senses of the word, others who cannot be fully understood. In children's science fiction, the animal often saves the day; in young adult science fiction, the animal often acts the villain. Science needs to be made comfortable for younger readers; the strange becomes familiar by use of animals. In young adult fiction, the opposite occurs: the familiar animal becomes unknown.

True science fiction for the very young is rare; most of the series discussed here, for example, fall into the category of science fantasy—fiction that blends some scientific concepts or situations with fantastic elements that have no scientific base.[2] The reason for this lies in the paradox of introducing science fiction, a literature based on the unknown, to young child readers, whose literature tends to be domestic and knowable. Outer space adventure, which has an element of excitement and adventure because of the unknown quality of it, can also for the same reason be frightening. Authors rarely acknowledge the fearful aspect of outer space directly, but indirect reference nearly always underlies the text, as in this example from Eleanor Cameron's *The Wonderful Flight to the Mushroom Planet* (1954), where a father is talking to his son:

"But one thing I know, all around us stretches the absolute black of space, even with the sun burning and flaming away out there like a huge furnace—space that is almost empty inside and around our solar system . . . there *is* no daytime out there—no wind, no sound, nothing but blackness and the eternal movements of those little points of light. No daytime, no wind, no sound, nothing but blackness!" (5-6)

Cameron does not have the child character David express fear over the emptiness of space, but the repetition of negatives ending with blackness emphasizes the frightening aspect of outer space. Other books confront the emptiness of space indirectly as well; in Ellen MacGregor's *Miss Pickerell Goes to Mars* (1951), Miss Pickerell changes the subject and begins speeding every time the scientist Mr. Haggerty mentions space travel. Series for the young reader that involve aliens from other planets, such as Andre Norton's Star Ka'at series or Louis Slobodkin's Space Ship series, have the aliens come to Earth before the child characters ever leave the planet. This underscores the prevailing idea that child readers need space to be domesticated before they visit it.

One way that authors of series domesticate outer space is by introducing friendly and helpful animals. This introduction often comes as immediately as the front cover of the book. Obviously, the Space Cat and Star Ka'at series show animals on the front cover, but even series that do not center around animals show them on the front covers of books. *Miss Pickerell Goes to Mars* has a dust jacket that shows Miss Pickerell, a rocket, and a cow in a field. The front cover of *The Wonderful Flight to the Mushroom Planet* includes a picture of a chicken in a rocketship. *Matthew Looney's Voyage to the Earth* has a turtlelike creature sticking out of Matthew Looney's pocket on its cover. And *The Robot and Rebecca and the Missing Owser* has, right in the center of the front cover illustration, a small creature resembling a Scottish terrier. Notably, these are all the first books in their respective series. The blending of the known—the domestic animal—with the unknown—space travel—seems of key importance in establishing the safety of the adventure that lies within the book.

Animals within these stories play varying roles. Sometimes they provide a reason for adventuring into space, as in *Miss Pickerell on the Moon* (19). When Miss Pickerell's cat, Pumpkins, becomes ill, she goes to the deputy administrator of the space program to see if she can get on a research flight to the moon to find antibiotics. He initially refuses her request, but Miss Pickerell presses the issue: "'I couldn't wait three months to go on that trip, in any case' Miss Pickerell said, feeling desperate and no longer caring how she sounded to the deputy administrator. 'If I'm going to save Pumpkins, I have to leave now. I have to get him injected with the new antibiotic before the week is out!'" (49). Miss Pickerell, who would not necessarily travel into space on her own account, will do so unquestioningly for the sake of an animal. Pumpkins provides the reason for the adventure.

Most frequently, however, animals in science fiction series play the role of savior either for an alien race or for the human characters. Typical is the part of the hen, Mrs. Pennyfeather, in *The Wonderful Flight to the Mushroom Planet*, and Ronald, the murtle (a turtlelike creature) in *Matthew Looney's Voyage to the Earth*. Mrs. Pennyfeather comes on the boys' rocketship voyage when they remember at the last minute that they promised to bring a mascot with them. Her accidental inclusion ends up saving the Mushroom Planet when Chuck and David realize that by eating eggs the Mushroom people can regenerate. Similarly, Matthew Looney's pet murtle Ronald, whom Matthew brings as a stowaway on his voyage to Earth, proves that moon creatures will not die from touching water, thus rescuing the mission from public disapproval and restoring funding to the Earth study project. In both these cases, the animal who was not supposed to be a part of the space travel actually saves the day. The credit always goes to the owners of the animals, in other words, the child protagonists. As with the animal who provides a reason for space travel, animals in these stories act as an extension of the child character, completing tasks or filling roles that the child would otherwise be incapable of or uninterested in achieving. Essentially, the animal transforms the main character into a hero.

However, animals also act as aliens in children's science fiction series. The most obvious example of this is in Norton's Star Ka'at series. Tellingly, the child protagonists initially believe that the aliens are normal domesticated cats and make pets of them: they cannot see the difference between the alien cats and the Earth cats. The animal life on Venus in Todd's *Space Cat Visits Venus* is also feline; although Moofa has an unusual pattern to her fur, she otherwise has all the characteristics of Earth cats, and Flyball can successfully interbreed with her. Aliens who resemble Earth creatures, and more specifically domesticated pets, require less getting used to than aliens with less familiar outward appearances. By creating familiar aliens, authors help to domesticate outer space and make the unknown knowable.[3]

The process of domesticating science is first and foremost a linguistic one. By couching scientific ideas and principles within closed sentences, simple language, and conceptual frameworks presumed to be within the prior knowledge of most children, authors create a sense that science is predictable, simple, and if not already known, then quite easy to learn. When the language and ideas are too complex or beyond the known at the time of writing, then fantastic, rather than scientific, language and devices are often used. Science must be tamed and brought into the realm of the familiar for the child reader; authors of series books do this in part by their language. The use of animal characters plays into this by allowing a certain coziness of language and more freedom for the author to employ fantastic devices.[4]

A good example of this is in Ruthven Todd's Space Cat series. Science in these books is introduced gently and often softened by direct connection with the fantastic. In fact, rather than centering on scientific ideas, the Space Cat series promotes a general sense of adventure and willingness to learn in new situations. The first paragraph of the first book in the series, *Space Cat*, sets the tone for what will follow in all the rest:

The little gray kitten had always been the most adventurous member of his family. He had been the first to explore the roof of the apartment building where he lived with his brothers and sisters. There he had sat for hours admiring the face of the Cat in the Moon until his mother had dragged him in by the scruff of his neck. The next day he had managed to maroon himself on top of the flagpole on the roof and the Fire Department had had to be called to take him down. (1)

Note that the paragraph gives a very indirect hint as to what the story will entail—a cat in space—but the connection is with folklore and not science. In addition, although the reference to the Cat in the Moon has a central position in the paragraph, the paragraph is not about a cat on the moon but a kitten on Earth—the reference is not only indirect; it is secondary to the rest of the action. The Cat in the Moon is static; the kitten, on the other hand, explores, admires, is dragged, and maroons himself all in the first paragraph. The emphasis is not on space and the scientific principles needed to get there but adventure and a willingness to explore—even if that exploration might sometimes have a negative value. Finally, the exploration that the kitten experiences is ultimately safe: his mother, in one case, and the Fire Department, in the other, rescue the kitten when his curiosity takes him too far.

By using a kitten as the main character, Todd has more freedom to use fantastic devices (such as the Cat in the Moon) because of the naïveté of his subject. The kitten can spend all day on the roof, and climb onto the flagpole, but at the same time find a safe end to his adventures when rescue comes in the form of an authority figure. Although the kitten will go to the moon, he does not go for scientific research but to find a new adventure. The language in the paragraph, therefore, values exploration by making it both desirable and safe. Science comes only secondarily, and is connected with folklore (the Man in the Moon) to make it more comfortable to the child reader.

Indeed, by using a kitten as the main character, Todd avoids the need to use scientific language almost entirely. Flyball, as the kitten is called, either knows the science—as when he thinks to himself that "he did not care if they wanted to keep their silly little secret. He knew all about the cylinder anyway. It was a rocket" (11)—or the science is explained by the narration, as in this example: "He opened a little box and took out a little plastic globe which he carefully fitted over Flyball's head, adjusting various tubes to a little pack on the back of the suit. Flyball found that breathing was simple inside the globe, for the compressed air meant that he did not have to breathe so strongly" (33). In both of these cases the scientific concepts are very basically explained. Flyball knows that the "cylinder" (it is actually more of a cone) is a rocket but not necessarily what the significance of that might be. Compressed air may require less work in breathing, but that does not explain what compressed air actually is. Flyball, as a kitten, takes the place in the story of a curious young child, and as such, he is not expected to be able to understand scientific concepts in any kind of detailed manner. By extrapolation, this is also true of the child reader. The language used in the story appears to be scientific but actually explains little.

In fact, much of *Space Cat* and its sequels have little to do with science, instead being fantasies of what life might be like in outer space. The living, thinking bubbles and plants that survive without atmosphere seem either painfully naive or wildly fantastic to a post–moon landing reader. Throughout the series, nonscientific suggestions for life on other planets prevail including, most illogically, a single cat on the planet Venus with whom Flyball can interbreed. These sorts of unlikely details frequently cause critics either to dismiss science fiction for children as being completely nonexistent or, at best, to label it science fantasy. The fantastic use of animals whose thoughts are reported as if the animal were human allows for the use of other fantastic ideas, taking Space Cat and other series like it further away from scientific ideas and concepts. Most critics see this as a negative.

However, children's science fiction has a different purpose than science fiction for either young adults or adults, a purpose that can most easily be achieved in series rather than individual books. Science fiction for children encourages an attitude of scientific adventure in a safe environment with a high success rate. Series, with their constant need to fling further and further afield for new adventures and plots, best achieve this environment; series such as Space Cat, by using an animal as the main character, can go on adventures that real child characters could not. Thus, the fantastic use of talking animals, while causing somewhat dubious scientific situations, increases the capacity for adventure.

Most science fiction series for children follow the same pattern. Central characters, usually children, go off on adventures that happen to have a scientific angle to them. Authors want to keep children reading, particularly if they are authors of series. Ruthven Todd and others attempt to hook child readers by introducing animals that think and other fantastic situations into their fiction. The implication that science is not interesting in and of itself, and that children can not understand scientific concepts beyond the most basic of levels, is one result of the intrusion of the fantastic. However, an increased level of safe adventure takes the place of this lack of science; these closed texts provide a secure and comfortable place for readers to get used to the uncertainty of science.

Science fiction may be the literature of the unknown, but children's series, which rely on the creation of a safe, comfortable, and known world, must work against this most basic tenet of science fiction literature. Animals represent one of the major devices that authors use to ease the tension that this paradox creates. The situation changes, however, in young adult series. Whereas children's science fiction series attempt in various ways to make the unknowable known, young adult science fiction series—despite retaining familiarity through constant characters—make the familiar into something strange and unknown. Animals, which in children's science fiction are both friendly and helpful, become not only unfamiliar but often dangerous or evil in young adult series.

Unlike their child counterparts, young adult heroes and heroines do not take their pets into outer space. Home ties, either maintained or recreated in children's science fiction series, are broken in young adult science fiction series, particularly in those books with a male protagonist. Independence holds a much higher value in young adult fiction in general, and therefore parents, siblings, and pets as well must be either nonexistent or left behind. The domesticated worlds of children's science fiction series have no place in young adult series. Animals become wild and unpredictable, aliens in foreign lands for the protagonists to face.

Few animals in young adult series are Earthly. If not aliens, they are certainly otherworldly. The research team in W. E. Johns's outer space series, for example, meets with several alien populations, some of which are animals or animal-like. In *The Quest for the Perfect Planet*, a later book in the series, they encounter dinosaurs, giant insects, and near-human apes. Of all these, only the creatures least like anything ever seen on Earth—the giant insects— attract the research team's attention for any length of time. Thus, the unfamiliar or strange is highlighted, whereas the more well known is ignored. When they encounter a planet inhabited by troglodytes and many-trunked mammoths, the text gives two sentences to describing the troglodytes and more than a paragraph to the mammoths. The troglodytes are described without deliberately inflammatory adjectives, but the mammoths are "so horrible that Rex's blood ran cold" (57) and "a monstrosity" (58). The text devotes even more description to the giant insects, and the team remains on the planet for three days—the longest on any planet. However, when they reach the planet of the dinosaurs, they leave the ship for only a brief time, during which the Professor gives the others a lecture on Earthly evolution. The idea that planets all develop along the same evolutionary lines makes dinosaur planets of limited interest—because they know about Earthly evolution, they cannot learn anything new from these otherworldly dinosaurs. Similarly, on the ape planet, the Professor suggests that they stay near the ship. The more Earth-like the creatures on the planet are, the less likely the team is to stay on the planet. This is true even though they have a greater fear of the unusual creatures. Danger, fear, and caution are mentioned frequently during their time on the planet of giant insects, but they never run back to the ship. However, even though one of the team says, "'I don't think we need to be afraid of monkeys,'" (109) they all run back to the ship at the first sign that the apes are getting unruly. Only the truly unusual specimens make facing danger worthwhile.[5]

Giant insects are an alien of choice in young adult science fiction. In the 1980s series of Tom Swift, Tom, Anita, and Ben are captured by the Skree, an alien insect race, in *The War in Outer Space* (1981). Although Tom and his crew eventually befriend the Skree, at first they become the insects' prisoners precisely because Anita cannot bear to look at giant insects. Emotions, which often save characters in science fiction for children, occasion difficulties and dangerous situations in young adult science fiction with boy protagonists. Intelligence, not emotion, must rule, as Anita herself points out: "'I'm letting an old memory cloud my thinking and my judgment. The Skree are hardly the same as the little creatures scurrying around my cupboards at home. I have to remember that and fight my fear with every ounce of intelligence I've got!'" (106). Once she resolves to accept the aliens' appearance, she and her friends are released soon after. When animals in outer space no longer resemble the cuddly creatures of the safely domestic world of children's science fiction series, emotion must be quashed in favor of intellect; otherwise, the human characters face unknown dangers.

The clearest example of this comes from Isaac Asimov's Lucky Starr series. In *Lucky Starr and the Oceans of Venus* (1954), the innocent-looking frogs that Venusians keep as pets turn out to be controlling the planet through telepathy. Lucky discovers that the mania for keeping V-frogs as pets has sinister overtones: "'They're all over the city. People collect them, feed them, love them. Now do they really love V-frogs? Or do the V-frogs inspire love by mental control so as to get themselves fed and taken care of?'" (91). V-frogs block intelligent thought, leaving only emotion. This emotion endangers an entire planet. Because the frogs are pets, and not just wildlife, they represent an even greater threat to humans. Pets have made a complete turnaround from their use in children's science fiction series—instead of helping the central character make the connection between the known and unknown, they are instead the familiar made strange and even deadly.

In between the coziness of childhood pets in outer space and the deadliness of these same creatures for young adult males lie the science fiction series written for young adult females. Science fiction series for young adult females center largely around interpersonal communication and bringing differing or quarreling groups together. Because of this focus, independence does not have the high value that it does in young adult male science fiction. While some severance of family ties is encouraged, as it is for young adult males, the breaking of these bonds is not complete; family does not have a stigma attached to it. Animals in these stories, therefore, come from the wild or even from other worlds, as they do in young adult science fiction for males, but they also aid young adult females in their quest as they do in children's science fiction series.[6]

Thus, in Madeleine L'Engle's Time trilogy, Meg Murry has pets at home that are treated like members of the family. Instead, they serve as comforters and links to her family. When she does journey away from home, wild creatures aid her. In *A Wrinkle in Time* (1962) she travels through space on the back of a centaur. When she suffers injuries from her father's inexperience at tessering other people through space, octopuslike beasts care for her. Crucially, they not only restore her physical health, but they also help her emotionally. Meg blames her father for leaving her little brother behind, and tries to turn her back on him, but the beasts do not let her: At that Aunt Beast stood up, saying, "'Child,' in a reproving way. Mr. Murry said nothing, and Meg could see that she had wounded him deeply. . . . She scowled down at the table, saying, 'We've *got* to ask them for help now. You're just stupid if you think we don't.' Aunt Beast spoke to the others. 'The child is distraught. Don't judge her harshly'" (189). Meg's role involves bringing her family together; when she fails to do so, animals reprove her and bring her back to her duty. In *A Wind in the Door* (1973), the black snake Louise helps Meg to choose between right and wrong as well, this time between good and bad versions of her school principal. Finally, in *A Swiftly Tilting Planet* (1978), a dog helps Meg keep in touch with her brother, who has been sent through time to stop a dictator with the help of a unicorn.[7] When her brother faces death, Meg knows about the danger and saves him—and, incidentally, saves the world from Mad Dog Branzillo at the same time. Through her connection with animals, Meg rids the world of madness and brings her family together.

In *Dustland*, book two of Virginia Hamilton's Justice Cycle, Justice, the female protagonist, travels through time with her brothers. However, in order to do this successfully, they must work as a team: "'A person over there has to be joined,' Justice had once told Thomas. 'There's no other way to survive'" (34). Thomas does not wish to maintain his connection to his sister, and once they have moved forward in time, he breaks away from the unit. Justice must bring, or join, her family together again. She finds herself incapable of achieving this on her own, however, and enlists the help of a creature from the future land they come to, a doglike being named Micacis. Unlike the adventuring and more or less independent pets of children's science fiction series, Micacis is under Justice's mind power and must do her bidding. However, Justice, even though in control, cannot ultimately succeed without Micacis; she needs the animal to unite her family once more.

Animals in science fiction series for all ages serve as a connecting point between two worlds. Sometimes these two worlds are as far apart as two planets, but other times the two worlds are the world of childhood and adulthood. In the case of children's science fiction series and young adult series science fiction with female protagonists, bringing these worlds together is the ultimate goal. The importance of independence in young adult science fiction with male protagonists, however, means that unity comes second to intellect; emotions can not tie the two worlds together. Rather, interest in the expansion of knowledge must prevail; when it does, any animal characters in the story will either be friendly or, at the very least, not harmful.

Even when animals play a positive role in young adult science fiction series, however, the series aspect of the books maintains a distance between the animals and the young adults. Meg Murry may always have animals surrounding her, but the animals do not remain constant. Kittens grow up; the family dog dies. Many animals only appear in one book of the series; having served their purpose, they disappear to be replaced by other creatures whose attributes better suit the new situation. Similarly, Tom Swift generally does not revisit alien peoples, insect-like or otherwise; and W. E. Johns's crew continues searching for perfect planets from book to book, leaving behind any unusual animal specimens without care. Animals play a large role in science fiction series for young adults, but individual animals figure only incidentally.

In fact, only in children's science fiction series do animals have a regular place in the cast of characters. In the Star Ka'at and Space Cat series, the central characters are the animals. However, although the animals have definite feline attributes, they also resemble humans in many ways. The reader can follow Flyball's thoughts as if he speaks and thinks like a human being; the Star Ka'ats actually do think like humans, and communicate with those they find worthy. These series blend the human and animal worlds within their animal characters. Thus, Flyball substitutes for a mischievous child who needs looking after, and the Star Ka'ats take the place of the parents that neither Jim nor Elly Mae have. At the same time, however, they provide the stories' adventure because of their animal nature—Flyball's curiosity gets him in trouble but also provides impetus to explore alien worlds; the Star Ka'ats, inability to manipulate human-made machines require them to rely on Jim and Elly Mae. Both cases use the animals to create a child-centered world where exploration is valued as an acceptable activity for children. Young adult heroes and heroines rarely need their parents, and their age gives them the right to explore without needing permission or excuses. Therefore, science fiction series for young adults do not need to make use of animals as substitutes for either parents or children.

In the Miss Pickerell series, however, the constant animal—Miss Pickerell's cow—serves different purposes. The cow does not talk, does not telepathically communicate with Miss Pickerell, and does not even have a name at first. The cow is just a cow. Although Miss Pickerell goes up in space on one occasion to keep the cow from getting sick, most of her adventures have little or nothing to do with the cow. And yet the cow appears in every book in the Miss Pickerell series. Certainly part of the reason for the cow's existence is to provide humor and to mark Miss Pickerell as eccentric and special. But the cow also provides a reason for Miss Pickerell to come home. She has no husband or children; she seems to have no job: she has nothing that ties ordinary human beings to each other and to their world. In addition, she enjoys outer space travel and provides a useful service on her very first trip. She might well remain in the emptiness of space, forever wandering, but for one thing: "'It's about my cow,' she confided to Wilbur. 'I should never have left her all alone down there with a strange man. Oh, I do hope she'll be all right'" (*Miss Pickerell Goes to Mars* 121–122). Miss Pickerell's cow brings her back to Earth, back home. The unremarkable barnyard animal coexists with the spaceship in her pasture, reminding the child reader that space travel might be fun, but it is not the normal thing for people to do: after the fantasy trip is over, reality must still be dealt with. The cow provides domestication and closure for Miss Pickerell and for the reader as well and prevents them both from getting too close to the thought of the emptiness of outer space.

Many early young adult series for boys provide a similar type of closure, but rather than a cow to bring the main character home, these series have a girl. Rick Brant's sister and second series Tom Swift's sister and girlfriend all provide a bookended scene of domestication at the beginning and end of the book. But as females began to move into outer space with their male counterparts, home became a blank in these series, an unknown almost as complete as space once was. Meanwhile, in science fiction series with young adult female protagonists, girls retain their connection to home and domestic concerns through animals, but the lack of consistent animal characters guarantees them a limited amount of independence while maintaining closure as well. The series, therefore, provide less comfort for young adults than it does for children.

Every child reader has some experience, however slight, with animals. Authors of series science fiction exploit this familiarity for their own purposes. Authors of children's science fiction series use the animal—usually a furry animal and often a pet—to bridge the gap between the known and unknown worlds. These animals guide, protect, and encourage child protagonists into adventuring further and further from their domestic situation but also provide the route back home. In so doing, they provide an introduction to the more exciting aspects of science without the child protagonist having to risk anything. This comfortable celestial barnyard, where the animals help the strange appear more familiar, contrasts sharply with the use of animals in young adult series science fiction. Here, the animals become stranger, more alien, and occasionally dangerous. Emotional attachment to pets and animals, praised in children's series, creates dangers for young adults, who must use their intellect and remain more aloof from domestic situations. As young adults become more independent, the familiar becomes strange, and this includes animals. The celestial barnyard has become a jungle of the stars.

NOTES

1. What Gary K. Wolfe says about all science fiction is particularly true for children's science fiction, which often avoids such abstract concepts of good and evil: "In science fiction, it is less important to conquer the villain than to conquer the unknown, and the importance of this conquest is what the ideological structure of many science-fiction narratives teaches" (*Known* 15).

2. The use of the term "science fantasy" comes largely from education-related textbooks, such as Huck, Hepler, and Hickman's *Children's Literature in the Elementary School*, and from authors, such as Madeleine L'Engle, who use the terms "fantasy" and "science fiction" interchangeably, claiming, "The lines between science fiction, fantasy, myth, and fairy tale are very fine, and children, unlike many adults, do not need to have their stories pigeonholed" (L'Engle, "Childlike" 104). This attitude, while it allows more latitude in determining which children's books are labeled science fiction, also tends to ghettoize children's SF; while talking aliens in many shapes and forms abound in adult science fiction, children's literature that describes the thought processes of kittens is deemed unrealistic and unscientific.

3. Mary Rayner writes, "With young children the range of experience, of images which you can assume to be common knowledge is very narrow. . . . Therefore you use animal characters" ("Some" 86). This is even more true in science fiction than it is in the domestic story.

4. Walter E. Meyers notes, "In science fiction one can indeed talk to the trees—or the Martians, or the Xaxans, or the T'Worlies, or anything else the writer's imagination can provide. And in this linguistic freedom, the writer of fantasy or science fiction is set apart from his colleagues who write other kinds of fiction" (69). Meyers's study concludes that science fiction writers, particularly those who deal with aliens (Earthly or otherwise), bend many scientific details in order to fit them into their stories.

5. Gary K. Wolfe, in *The Known and the Unknown*, discusses animals as monster-aliens and explains why the more unusual animals pose the greater threat: "The science-fiction hero relies not on weapons, but upon reason and scientific ingenuity to overcome the monster. . . . The monster is less a villain than a *problem*, and the heroic achievement becomes the ability to apply scientific methodology quickly and accurately in crises, to observe what data there is about the monster and to induce the secret principle that will defeat it" (200–201). Monster-aliens that resemble creatures found (or once found) on Earth can more quickly be conquered by the vast bank of scientific data that the hero commands.

6. Although Elliott Gose in *Mere Creatures*, among others, suggests that the connection between females and natural forces is a positive one, Janice Doane and Devon Hodges provide an alternative view in *Nostalgia and Sexual Difference: The*

Resistance to Contemporary Feminism. Doane and Hodges argue that antifeminists use the concept of women and nature to keep females in their place—such as keepers of the hearth and maintainers of the family.

7. Nancy-Lou Patterson focuses not on the dog but on the unicorn as the being that connects Meg and Charles Wallace: "The story-line of this many-layered novel is too complex to summarize, but the figure of the unicorn binds it together. Meg follows Charles Wallace's travels through the intricacies of the plot by kything, and there is a sense in which the unicorn is an image of their relationship" (200). In either case, an animal brings the pair together.

CHAPTER 4

No Business in Space?: The Female Presence

Across from Miss Pickerell was another curved bunk, similar to the one in which she was lying. A man was sitting in the middle of the bunk. He was shaking his head and going "Tch, tch, tch."

"Lady," he said, "you have absolutely no business being here."

—MacGregor, *Miss Pickerell Goes to Mars* (47)

Traditionally, children's science fiction has been the realm of boy readers;[1] however, girls and women have always had a place among the pages. Many of these female characters, such as the worrying mother or the indistinguishable sister-girlfriend, have served only to add minor twists in the plot, generally only appearing in the first and last chapter. However, as the space race became a reality and women's rights issues also muscled to the forefront, roles for girls and women in science fiction series changed. Females, and particularly girls, got more and bigger roles in individual stories within a series. The success of these characters has been mixed; women and girls typically fare better in children's science fiction series than in those for young adults. The gender of the author seems to affect the size and nature of female roles only in young adult series; in children's series, male authors as well as female authors present increasingly more complex female characters. But are these better roles for women *or* just bigger? This chapter will trace the development of the female character in science fiction and try to pinpoint her importance in space as well as on Earth.

Earlier series, started after the end of World War II but before the first rocketships left the planet, took their cue from turn-of-the-century series such as the original Tom Swifts and the Great Marvel series, as well as from the successful attributes of individual science fiction current to the time, such as Robert Heinlein's *Rocket Ship Galileo* and *Space Cadet*. These models for the series of the late 1940s and early 1950s depict a teenage (or slightly older) boy, often with a male sidekick, who uses his own inventions and intelligence in order to avert a danger that threatens not just himself but others as well—frequently the entire planet! Tom Swift, Jr., Lucky Starr, and Rick Brant, among others, all take after their earlier counterparts and demonstrate an unusual amount of independence, intelligence, and ingenuity. Although intelligence and ingenuity are not qualities that necessarily exclude females, the stress in these books on independence makes inclusion of any kind of reliance on others (or an other) a negative; because of this women have little role in these books.

The most nefarious of all the early series in terms of its attitudes toward women is Isaac Asimov's Lucky Starr series (1952–1958). In the first of these, *David Starr, Space Ranger*, the only woman mentioned at all is Starr's dead mother, and only briefly. She is joined by only one other female in the course of six books; Asimov does not even include the usually requisite secretaries or girlfriends. Lucky Starr, who, unlike Tom Swift, Jr. or Rick Brant, has no family, values independence more than other series heroes. Although he has two adoptive fathers, only one appears in all six books, and he depends on Lucky rather than the other way around. Lucky also has a sidekick, Bigman Jones, but although Bigman follows Lucky through the solar system, at crucial moments Lucky makes Bigman stay behind. He explains his policy in *Lucky Starr and the Moons of Jupiter* when he says, "'I can't take ordinary action and risk explosion. Let me do it in my own time and my own way, Bigman'" (136). Lucky Starr's independence and dedication to work even exclude his friends; it is little wonder that women—who, according to Asimov's depiction, have no role independent of men—play no part in Lucky's life.[2]

Most other series of the late 1940s and early 1950s do not exclude women so completely, but females remain sidelined characters. Tom Swift, Jr. has a sister: "Sandy, who had been taught to fly by Tom and her father, was an enthusiastic pilot and often demonstrated the Pigeon Special to prospective customers" (*Tom Swift in the Race to the Moon* 35). However, in spite of Sandy's obvious capability, she takes no part in the story line other than to drag Tom away from his work; Sandy makes him connect with other people (on dates, at parties), but in a world where independence is stressed, this is not a positive attribute. Therefore, while Tom races to the moon, Sandy remains earthbound. Rick Brant, another series hero, also has a sister who admires and encourages her brother but is not allowed to participate in the work of Rick and his sidekick Scotty.[3] When Rick refuses to take her along to Tibet, in *The Lost City* (1947), for example, Barby's protest speaks for a generation of females: "'Why did I have to be a girl?'" (5). Being a girl confines a character, in the 1940s and 1950s, to a stereotypical and stay-at-home role.[4]

However, even at this early juncture, a definite split between science fiction written for adolescents and that written for younger children can be observed. Prior to World War II, very little science fiction was targeted for a younger audience, but with the increasing emphasis on scientific achievement in the Cold War era, the marketing strategy changed. Although some of the literature produced came in the form of nonfiction, information-based science books, imaginative series also began to appear, such as Ruthven Todd's Space Cat series (1952–1958). This series, like many others of its time, took place in a military setting (the Air Force) with a nearly all-male cast of characters. However, the last two books of the series, *Space Cat Meets Mars* (1957) and *Space Cat and the Kittens* (1958), feature a female cat, Moofa, in a prominent role. Although Moofa, who becomes the title cat's wife and mother of the kittens, often acts the same part as Rick Brant's fretting mother, she nonetheless does not get shelved after motherhood; she participates, albeit in a limited way, in further space adventure along with her husband and (male) children. The Space Cat series sets two trends in science fiction: first, it claims a younger audience as a suitable setting for a broader female participation; and second, as a more fantastic book, than the "scientific" Tom Swifts or Rick Brants, the series has more room for women as well. These trends continue up until the present day, but in spite of the progress that children's science fiction series have made, many of the old prejudices amplified in earlier series remain in more recent works, although never as obviously as they do in adolescent science fiction series.

The split between adolescent and children's science fiction is exemplified by a series written by author John Christopher. His Tripods trilogy, whose hero is the thirteen-year-old Will Parker, contrasts sharply with its prequel, *When the Tripods Came* (1988), even though the prequel's hero, Laurie Cordray, is also thirteen. The books are aimed at different audiences—the trilogy at adolescents and the prequel at children. John Newsinger, in reference to the Tripods trilogy, muses, "Where do women fit into this scheme of things? Here Christopher's attitudes are disappointingly conventional: at best they are irrelevant and at worst they are a distraction" (53).[5] Indeed, the only women in the Tripods trilogy are Will's mother, who appears only briefly, and the Countess and her daughter Eloise who take care of Will during his recovery. Women do not seem to have any place in the mountain camp of the rebellion, and in the city of the Masters they are not even slaves but corpses in glass coffins, museum pieces for the amusement of the aliens. Christopher, in interviews, turns a deaf ear to the charges of misogyny; he knows that his attitude costs him support but says, "I would still quite like to have [literary success], but not enough to do anything to change a way of writing which is very unlikely to gain the favour of the literary establishment" (Gough 99).

However, in spite of what Christopher professes, the prequel *When the Tripods Came* represents a change in Christopher's way of writing about women and girls from the original trilogy. Because the book focuses on Laurie's relationship with his family, women and girls naturally have much larger roles to play. Laurie's grandmother, Martha, shoots her own son (Laurie's uncle) when he tries to force Laurie to accept the Tripods' cap. She also plays a key part in getting the family to Switzerland, selling antique jewels from her shop to get cash for airline tickets. Martha's active role concerns keeping the family together; at the end of the book, when military operations against the Tripod take center stage, Martha's character fades into the background. Her role only extends to the family—outside of it she plays no part.

Laurie's half sister Angela also has a much more prominent role that any female in the original trilogy. Angela, like Martha, is aggressive in stating her opinions and wanting to take part in the action, but Angel's opinions are far more likely to be negatively received than Martha's and her desire to take part in the action is more likely to be rejected. This negation of Angel's needs and wishes relates to Angela's desire for things that break up, rather than bring together, the family group. At the beginning of the book, she wants to watch the hypnotic television broadcasts that the Tripods send down to Earth via satellites; she is allowed to do so until she runs away from the family to join a Tripod commune. The family doctor hypnotizes her, encouraging her to reject these antifamily desires. Throughout most of the rest of the book, Angela plays little part in the action, the focus shifting instead to Laurie. But instead of fading into the background at the end of the book as Martha does, Angela fights to become part of the military scouting parties. Laurie reports, *"She* was as willing to take a risk as any boy, she said, and it was unfair Pa still refused to let her go on the scouting trips" (Christopher, *When* 119). However, Laurie does not consider her reasoning valid; he walks away from her without even arguing back. Although Angela again, at a later point, demands to be a part of the attack party against the Tripod, her protests go unanswered. Women and girls are allowed a strong role in *When the Tripods Came*, but only when they act directly to strengthen the family. Action that weakens the family, such as Angela's running away, or action that only indirectly relates to the safety of the family, such as Angela's desire to take part in scouting missions to find the Tripod, are rejected. The original Tripods trilogy extols the virtue of independence and is geared at adolescents; the prequel encourages dependence and is aimed at families.

Not all adolescent characters in young adult series jaunt completely independently across the universe however, and increasingly when they work cooperatively, a female character can be found. Particularly since the 1960s the number of female characters playing a significant, plot-altering role increased dramatically; however, few of these adolescent girls have any more challenging tasks than those of the sister-girlfriend in earlier books. For adolescent girl characters, only feelings and emotions matter—thinking and ingenuity rarely play a role. Thus, in *The Lost City*, when Barby Brant tries to prevent her brother from going to Tibet because of an intuitive feeling, she sets a trend for future adolescent girl characters to follow. Rick Brant's response to his sister also sets a trend; he says to his friend Scotty, "'Funny. It isn't like Barby to be afraid. She doesn't usually let her imagination run away with her'" (9). Her feelings are taken seriously, and Rick takes extra precautions on his trip. However, he makes fun of Barby's lack of knowledge about Tibet and refuses to treat her intellect with respect. Intuition and emotion, rather than intelligence and ingenuity, continue to be the defining characteristics of adolescent girls in science fiction series throughout the latter half of the twentieth century.

In the third (1980s) series of Tom Swift, for example, Tom has two side-kicks. In an obvious attempt at multiculturalism, blond, blue-eyed Tom is joined in his adventures by a Native American boy, Ben Walking Eagle. His other companion (for the first—and, so far, last—time in Tom Swift's history) is female. Whereas Ben helps Tom through his genius with computers, Anita Thorwald has a different kind of skill: "Ever since an accident in which the circuits of Anita's artificial right leg were violently combined with the powerful circuits of Aristotle, a condition had existed which was both beneficial and frightening to her. . . . [T]he new circuitry had created a heightened aware-ness in her brain so that she could often sense what someone else was feeling—pain, anger, joy, or sadness" (Appleton, *The Alien Probe* 70). As this quote indicates, Anita senses negative feelings far more frequently than positive ones. In addition, her skills as a pilot and as a fellow solver of problems take second place to, and are undermined by, her empathic abilities. In fact, her hair color gets mentioned more often that almost any other quality—the "flaming red-head" actually saves her companions once, not by any quick thinking but be-cause her hair color catches the attention of the aliens (see Appleton, *The War in Outer Space*). So although Anita has an equal share in the adventures in Tom Swift's outer space, her abilities to aid the team come not through intelli-gence and ingenuity but through beauty and emotion—much the same as the sister-girlfriends of thirty years before.

However, the attribution of stereotypically feminine characteristics (concern for personal appearance, "women's intuition") to the adolescent female char-acters of the series cannot be blamed entirely on male authorship. The Tom Swift series all come from the pen of "Victor Appleton," a pseudonym of the Stratemeyer syndicate that hides a stable of authors, male and female. In addi-tion, the Tom Swift books are only one of many series that pigeonhole girls into these same stereotypes, and many of the others that do are authored by women. Although they give their characters more depth than the females in either the Rick Brant or Tom Swift books, both Virginia Hamilton and Madeleine L'Engle center their main female characters' conflicts around the success not of their intellectual prowess but of their emotional interactions.

Meg Murry, heroine of Madeleine L'Engle's Time trilogy, has as her most prominent characteristic an overly emotional, anxious, and self-deprecating nature. She depends upon outsiders to reinforce her self-image; her little brother, Charles Wallace, gets "tired of reassuring Meg" (*A Wind in the Door* 22) that she will, in fact, be beautiful like their mother, and Mrs. Murry tells her daughter to "'[S]top being self-deprecating'" (*Wind* 32). Meg's uncertainty and low self-esteem come from years of feeling ugly and stupid: "Meg Murry doing everything wrong" (*Wrinkle* 4), as she puts it. L'Engle reveals that Meg has both hidden beauty—Calvin O'Keefe comments that she has dream-boat eyes hidden behind her glasses (*Wrinkle* 53)—and hidden intelligence, as both her parents remind her. Even so, these hidden "talents" do not reassure Meg; they also do not save her. Neither Meg's looks nor her intelligence plays any part in the main conflict; rather, her greatest fault, her tendency toward oversensitivity and emotion, saves her and those she loves, as well as the universe itself. In *A Wrinkle in Time* (1962), Meg must save both her father and her brother from their overconfidence in their intelligence by her ability to love them. In *A Wind in the Door* (1973), Meg's love for the unlovable Mr. Jenkins saves both her brother and the universe. And in the final book, *A Swiftly Tilting Planet* (1978), Meg stays home from the adventure because she is pregnant with her first child but goes with Charles Wallace by kything with him, a form of mental telepathy that is akin to Anita Thorwald's empathic abilities: not merely—or even mostly—an intellectual power, kything requires a desire to connect with the other person, an emotional bond. Emotions, not intellect, affect the outcome of the stories. Although Meg's adventures are scientific in nature, investigating the relativity of time and space, her involvement in these adventures is not a scientific one. Meg Murry may be the central character in this science fiction series, but she does not follow the pattern set by male heroes. She does not invent, she does not control, and rather than be independent and daring, she only succeeds when she is dependent and sacrificing. The power of love takes center stage in L'Engle's books, giving a female character an opportunity to move into the main character position but without allowing the role of adolescent girls in science fiction to be significantly altered.

Authors of young adult science fiction series often supply adolescent girls with intelligence, but the girls rarely need to rely on it; rather, their feelings and emotions take precedence. Adolescent girls have empathic and intuitive abilities that allow them to contribute to a team effort, but even when they are the main character, they never act alone. Although the scientific activity in science fiction series increasingly depends upon a balance between issues of intelligence and issues of emotion, the emotion can never overtake the intellect. Scientists can be heartless, but they cannot be brainless, and as long as girl characters depend more on their feelings than their intellect, their role in space will be one that must be shared with adolescent boys.

But even a reliance on intelligence may not help girls characters exclude boys from their world. Children's science fiction series, from the Space Cat series onward, have always been more active in questioning the role that girls play in scientific activity, and thus girls have substantially larger and more frequent roles to play within these series. However, although many girls have intelligence equal to or better than their male counterparts, girls in science fiction series for children never work alone and never work solely with other girls. Two major types of girl characters emerge from these books: the girl supergenius and the ordinary girl. In either case, the girl character requires the help of outsiders in order to achieve.

The girl supergenius, next to nonexistent in young adult series, has many incarnations in children's science fiction series. Like the boy supergenius, the girl supergenius focuses on some field of science as a forte, although she generally has all-around cleverness as well. Even so, whereas the boy's intelligence is rarely questioned, the girl's is never enough. A typical case is the character of Irene Miller in the Danny Dunn series. Irene, who first appears in *Danny*

Dunn and the Homework Machine (1958), is the scientific whizkid girl-next-door who cannot decide whether she wants a career in biology or physics. Irene generally receives positive description, but only as a comparison with Danny. For example, in *Danny Dunn, Invisible Boy* (1974), she is introduced in the following fashion, as an addendum to Danny: "[T]he boy's knowledge of science was greater than that of most adults. It was matched only by that of his friend, Irene, but where Dan was interested in physics and engineering, Irene had finally made up her mind to become a biologist" (7). Irene's knowledge and skill do not stand alone but rather are in constant contrast to and comparison with Danny's strengths; she does not even get her own sentence of description to herself. Danny's other friend, Joe Pearson, also is described in the same paragraph, still in relation to Danny—after all, the books center on the boy scientist and not his friends—but the comparison is indirect: "As for Joe, he knew very little about science, but made up for it by a wide range of knowledge about literature, art, music, and especially, eating" (7). From this sentence alone, the reader can determine that Joe is not *the* main character, but to consider him as *a* main character is not out of the question. Irene's description, however, clearly labels her as a sidekick, second to Danny.

In addition, Irene must prove her worth far more often than Danny. Although Danny must convince adults of his maturity and knowledge, his peers never doubt him. Further, when adults do question him, Danny's mentor Professor Bullfinch, backs the boy up, both as a trustworthy person and as a good scientist. This gives Danny the confidence to believe in himself and become the person the Professor believes him to be. An example of this can be found in *Danny Dunn and the Anti-Gravity Paint* (1956) when Mr. Willoughby, the head of a project to raise a rocket to the moon, wants Danny kept in the dark about it because of his age. Danny comments, "'He's never trusted me. . . . He said a couple of times he doesn't really thing a kid can keep a secret as big as this. But the Professor told him I could. And I did, too'" (69). Danny has the support both of his peers and grownups as well.

Irene, however, in spite of her competence, must constantly justify her work, which makes her at times defensive and at other times unhappy and uncertain. When she first meets Danny, he assumes she will not be able to understand a particular scientific concept. She explains it perfectly, surprising Danny by her knowledge: "Danny's mouth hung open, but for a second or two no sound came out." Then he said, "'How—?'" "'—did a mere girl come to know such a thing? Is that what you were going to say?'" (*Homework Machine* 11). Although she becomes less defensive with Danny and Joe as time goes on, Irene still has trouble with outsiders because of her "unfeminine" interests. Adults as well as other children put her down, and this often has an effect on Irene's self-confidence. In *Danny Dunn, Invisible Boy* she plays baseball on Danny's team. Despite singling during her first at-bat, a man in the crowd suggests she go back to cooking class. "The words had stuck with her and made her more nervous than angry. They were with her now, as she stood waiting at the plate. . . . As a result, she froze" (71). If Irene had failed in her first at-bat, her reaction to the man would have been expected; but Irene succeeded in making a hit and yet still could focus only on the negative comments.[6] For Irene, success is not enough to make her feel worthy. She depends, like Meg Murry, on outside affirmation, and so despite her talent, she will always be merely a sidekick and not the center of attention.[7]

Even with its problems, the Danny Dunn series showed remarkable interest in and approval for the character of the girl scientist, especially when juxtaposed with the adolescent girl characters appearing in young adult science fiction series of the time. Irene Miller's intelligence matches, and in some cases betters, that of her friend Danny Dunn—but she remains a follower. The friends work as a team, but Danny retains his position of leadership throughout. While this pattern, of the boy scientist leading the girl scientist, can be found in other series as well, Bruce Coville's A.I. Gang series seems to break with the mold. The A.I. (Artificial Intelligence) Gang consists of five young people, two girls and three boys, all of whom have some particular computer skill. The distinguishing mark of Coville's series is that no one acts as more than temporary leader; all the children work together for the common good. However, despite the fact that Coville's books present a more egalitarian portrait of friendship and scientific achievement than most other series, the children as individuals are difficult to differentiate one from the other.[8] Only Ray Gammand has an outside interest—basketball—totally separated from computers. The girls are distinguished by physical features and the fact that one of them is a twin; otherwise, Coville's bland characterization gives the fact that girls have an equal role to play less impact. If all the characters have computer wizardry as their greatest skill, then it matters very little what an individual character achieves. While Coville's series gives the girl supergenius a bigger role, far closer to equality with boy supergeniuses than anything previous, it does so by sacrificing individuality.

The Coville series also reinforces another trend in science fiction series: girls never work alone. Mystery series have the intrepid Nancy Drew as a role model, but her skill and intellect do not cross over to other types of series.[9] In science fiction, girls never lead the way in scientific activities, they do not work as part of all-girl teams, and they do not work alone. This point is reinforced further by authors' treatment of the ordinary, nonscientific girl in science fiction series for children.

Ordinary girls, like girl supergeniuses, play a much more active role in children's science fiction series than they do in science fiction written for young adults. Although, like Barby Brant or Sandra Swift, they frequently start out as just a little sister to the hero, these ordinary girls receive more attention, speak more often, and sometimes even get a central or title role in one or two of the books of the series. And yet even though very ordinary boys, such as those in Eleanor Cameron's Mushroom Planet series or Louis Slobodkin's Space Ship series, build and pilot spaceships, ordinary girls merely ride in them—if they get to do that much. Despite the scientific trappings that surround ordinary girls in these series, few ordinary girls actually get to do anything scientific. Instead, they solve mysteries (without using scientific knowledge) or help bring people together through their power to communicate. Like supergenius girls, ordinary girls always either have a (generally male) helper or are part of a team effort. Overall, although ordinary girls are featured with increasing prominence in science fiction series for children, they do not have a scientific reason for being there.

A case in point is the Matthew Looney series. The first book, *Matthew Looney's Voyage to the Earth* (1961), in fact opens and closes not with Matthew Looney but with his sister Maria. Maria Looney is the consummate example of a little sister; she tattles on her brother to see him get in trouble, on the first page, and sits on her father's lap to listen to him talk about the benefits of staying home and not exploring space, on the last. She does not have much more to do in the book than that, and the second book also ignores her almost entirely. In *Matthew Looney in the Outback* (1969), however, written at a time when women's issues were becoming ever prominent, Maria finally gets to go into space. However, she goes not as space commander, like her brother, but as flight librarian, and even this is under her brother's protest: "'There's no place in space for girls, anyway. They get starsick and are always wanting to go back home, and we're going to have enough problems with the urchins on board, without taking along the Commander's *sister*'" (111). In fact, he ends up glad that Maria came, as she thinks of a solution when they are trapped on Earth; but in spite of her ingenuity, Maria Looney is entirely absent from the last two chapters. Matthew carries out Maria's plan by himself, and he receives all the praise for doing so.

After this disappointing treatment of Maria, it is both surprising and pleasant to find that the last three books of the series bear her name in their titles. Unfortunately, Maria Looney reverts from the flight librarian who solves problems using scientific formulas to a schoolgirl who sneaks onto spaceships, writes reports, and goes to summer camp. Maria's role in two of the books, *Maria Looney and the Red Planet* (1977) and *Maria Looney and the Remarkable Robot* (1979), typifies the way in which ordinary girls act and are treated in science fiction series for children.

Although Maria has already been to the Mooniversity in preparation for her trip as flight librarian in *Matthew Looney in the Outback, Maria Looney and the Red Planet* opens with her back in school having to write a report on the planet Pocksum. She still retains some of her stubbornness from the earlier books, but rather than use it to legitimately achieve her goals, she lies about having received permission to travel to Pocksum and uses her connection to her brother in order to legitimate her claim. Her incapacity to fly a spacecraft on her own necessitates these lies. On Pocksum she is joined by her friend Hester, and the two of them set out to find out why the plants on Pocksum are dying, but they do not get far, as Maria is kidnapped by native dwellers. She discovers during her captivity that these natives use mind control to kill the plants, and she must convince them to make a truce with the people of the moon. Even though Maria and Hester came prepared to take samples and discover the problem scientifically, it is Maria's communication skills that save her and the moon people in the end.

At least in *Maria Looney and the Red Planet*, Maria is credited with having some scientific ability. She seems to have increasingly less in *Maria Looney and the Remarkable Robot*, in which she goes to summer camp and ends up needing to be saved by a robot. While robots play a role in many science fiction series, the robots in series with boys as main characters exist on an equal or slightly lower status than the boy heroes. Often, as in the Tom Swift books, the boy creates the robot himself and makes adjustments as necessary. When the robot is made by another person, the boy and the robot are friends who help one another, as in the Danny One books. But robots in series with girls generally are more intellectual and physically stronger than the girl and therefore do all the thinking and heavy work unless they have been decommissioned. The girl's job is to communicate.[10] Maria Looney teaches her robot how to talk but cannot put him together. Like the adolescent girls of young adult science fiction series, ordinary girls again and again are granted just one ability—the gift of language and the feelings that language communicates.

In fact, while girls in science fiction series have been continually sidelined and discounted in terms of their scientific ability, only adult women have any true scientific power, and only in series where a female is the heroine. In boys' series, adult women either do not exist or are (often fretful) mothers. However, mothers, teachers, and other women in series where females are the heroines have power and intelligence. Mrs. Murry, in L'Engle's Time trilogy, does not play a significant part in the action of the books, but she nonetheless does not just sit in the background worrying about her children. With two Ph.D.s, Mrs. Murry is too busy winning the Nobel Prize to spend time fretting. Women in other series may not have Murry's intimidating qualifications, but they still have important functions. Miss Frizzle, the classroom teacher in the picture-book Magic School Bus series, may be "the weirdest teacher in the school" (*The Magic School Bus Lost in the Solar System* 4), but her class enjoys scientific adventures all over the galaxy.

Mothers and teachers might well be expected to have power and intelligence as far as their children/students are concerned, but one woman who succeeds in having both in a visible way in the adult world is Miss Pickerell. The Miss Pickerell series, which Ellen MacGregor began in the 1950s and which Dora Pantell continued between 1965 and 1986, is the only series that has a female title character for every book in the series. Miss Lavinia Pickerell, an old maiden aunt who takes more interest in her cow and rock collection than anything else, has no particular scientific background; and, unlike the girls science fiction series, she has no special ability to communicate either. Yet Miss Pickerell appears neither stupid nor out of control, because she insists upon her right to learn. Miss Pickerell's initial naïveté allows the child-reader to identify with her, but she investigates and learns from her adventures, giving her a sense of her own competence and intelligence, which is reinforced by other people—both children and adults.

In the first book in the series, *Miss Pickerell Goes to Mars* (1951), Miss Pickerell's naïveté comes across when she tells the captain of the spaceship in which she is traveling, "'Then I don't see how you could ever have such a silly idea as trying to go to that tiny little bit of a red star. I know it's called a planet, but it looks just like all the other stars, except that it's redder than most of them'" (61–62). However, once Mars comes into view, "[s]he felt a wild excitement of anticipation" (91) and starts asking questions about Mars. She listens carefully, and puts the knowledge to good use when one of the scientists gets trapped on the planet's surface. Although the captain of the spaceship had initially been against Miss Pickerell's addition to the crew, he apologizes after she rescues the scientist; and when she returns to Earth she is congratulated by the governor, given prizes at the fair for her collection of Martian rocks, and admired by her seven nieces and nephews. No supergenius, Miss Pickerell learns from her adventures even so and uses her knowledge to solve all sorts of scientific problems throughout the series, winning deserved praise for doing so. By the time she travels into space for the second time, in *Miss Pickerell on the Moon* (1965), she can confidently assert her right to be a part of the journey: "'[T]he most important thing is to get to the moon microbiological lab quickly. I'm not giving up. I'll find a way'" (45). Miss Pickerell has significant business in space, and she knows it; her intelligence and confidence help her earn the admiration and respect of others as well.

Female characters in science fiction series for young people have, between 1945 and 1995, increasingly come into prominent positions. Moving forward from complaints about the misfortune of being born a girl, they have traveled in space, won Nobel Prizes, and saved the planet. However, rarely have they had the opportunity to work alone to show off their capabilities; girls and women are still under the direction of men and boys. The pigeonholing of females as no more than communicators leads to this inability of girl characters to work alone, as they must depend on others to succeed. This in turn causes a lack of self-esteem that permeates the feeling of these females, who are not self-confident enough to demand inclusion, even when they prove their worth. The only exception is the case of adult women, where the more unusual women, such as the "weird" teacher Miss Frizzle, the beautiful and supertalented Mrs. Murry, or the eccentric Miss Pickerell, survive and flourish. Eccentricity should not be a requirement for girls' success, however, when ordinary boy characters can build a spaceship and fly it to a mushroom planet. Girls and women in science fiction series of the future must take the attitude of Maria Looney, who says to her brother in *Matthew Looney in the Outback*, "'I could hold my own out there just as well as you could, smarty!'" (111) Female characters must be given the self-confidence to assert their right to the skies.

NOTES

1. Pamela Sargent, in *Women of Wonder*, notes, "Most science fiction has been written by men, and they still form a majority of the writers today. . . . the vast ma-

jority of the readers are male and a fair number of them are young men or boys who stop reading sf regularly when they grow older" (xiv).

2. Gary K. Wolfe suggests in his article "Frontiers in Space" that science fiction that deals with the unknown universe (earthly or not) can work against the inclusion of women and yet do so in a nonsinister way: "The myth of coldly rational science has been merged with the myth of the boys' book; the whole universe becomes an heroic, masculine arena, and it's nobody's fault" (257).

3. For more on the female role in literature of the 1940s and 1950s, see Barbara White's *Growing Up Female: Adolescent Girlhood in American Fiction*, particularly chapter 7, "The Adolescent Heroine and 'God's Plan for Girls.'"

4. Shirley B. Ernst points this out in her article, "Gender Issues in Books for Children and Young Adults," when she says, "While the *number* of females in books *has* increased, research indicates that the stereotypical behaviors with which they have been portrayed have not changed" (68; emphasis in original).

5. It should be noted that not all critics agree with this assessment. In *Three Tomorrows: American, British and Soviet Science Fiction*, for example, John Griffiths suggests, "Much of Christopher's talent lies in the ease with which he establishes the ordinary relationships, particularly between the sexes" (89). He lauds Christopher as being one of "two writers who deal consistently and convincingly with the relationships between the sexes in SF" (172). However, Griffiths does not specifically discuss the Tripods trilogy.

6. Many authors discuss the issue of femininity/femaleness and language. In addition to broad-reaching studies by feminist authors such as Cixous, Olsen, Russ, and de Beauvoir, some authors focus more specifically on the use of language as it relates to gender in fantastic texts (i.e., Nancy A. Walker, *Feminist Alternatives: Irony and Fantasy in the Contemporary Novel by Women*) and children's literature (i.e., John Stephens, *Language and Ideology in Children's Fiction*).

7. Whereas Irene never puts herself at the center of attention, Joe Pearson, Danny's other friend, has no problem in doing so. In *Danny Dunn on the Ocean Floor*, for example, he announces to his dining companions (both his friends and a group of adult scientists) that he has written a poem in honor of their adventure. "'I don't suppose anybody would like to hear it . . . ' he says, '—so I will recite it anyway'" (149). Joe does not let his lack of scientific knowledge bother him; Irene cannot let herself succeed despite her competence.

8. Although specifically feminist science fiction seems to have been a natural outgrowth of, as Robin Roberts writes, "the misogynistic paradigms of science fiction" (13), this only applies to adult science fiction. Coville's science fiction is just one example of literature that prefers blandness to controversy in gender portrayal; another example is in Russell Stannard's Uncle Albert series, in which Uncle Albert's niece is regularly quashed every time she mentions her personal life. Her uncle, a scientist, does not want to hear about her interpersonal relationships.

9. Bobbie Ann Mason probes the reasons for mystery series being a more popular form than science fiction for girls in her book *The Girl Sleuth: A Feminist Guide*. She says, "The series form demanded adventures, or episodes, or continuing exploits, but the ordinary life of the female had three episodes: menstruation, marriage, and motherhood. The individual adventurous heroine was slow to evolve because it was risky to let a female strike out on her own—and succeed. An extraordinary kind of heroine was required, one who would enthrall with her glamorously interesting life, but who would not, of course, encourage revolution, since women had virtually no legal role or oppor-

tunity outside the home. It turned out that mystery stories best suited the necessity for thrilling safely—teasing their desire for adventure without threatening the comfortable advantages of femininity. By solving mysteries girls could confront the unknown with ease" (13, 15).

10. Seth McEvoy's Not Quite Human series and Jane Yolen's Robot and Rebecca series are two further examples where girls and robots interact in this manner; in neither case does the girl have anything to do with creating the robot, but the girl must teach the robot to talk or understand jokes in both cases. the contrasts with the robot in the Danny One series, for example, who is preprogrammed to have a sense of humor.

CHAPTER 5

Science Is Serious Business: The Role of Humor

"I won't say that Thistle let those ants loose on purpose"—Astro chuckled—"but he's way ahead so far."

Tom grinned in agreement. "I just hope this practical joking doesn't go too far," he said.

"It had better not," Strong said firmly. "Fun is fun, but out in space, where the slightest mistake can cost a man's life, it ceases to be funny. Take your stations!"

—Rockwell, *The Robot Rocket* (17)

Is scientific inquiry meant to be playful and imaginative, or is it, rather, a serious inquiry into the problems humans face? The two views have been in conflict for centuries and—using science fiction series for children and young adults as evidence—still have never been reconciled. In science fiction series, the various uses of humor polarize and define the view of science that the individual authors wish to portray, and an examination of the use of humor exposes important differences. In series science fiction for young people, humor plays two very different roles, depending on the intended age of the reader. Series aimed at a younger readership almost seem to require humor, as if the science would not be palatable without wordplay, amusing pictures, and humorous contrasts. The Magic School Bus series, written for a picture-book audience, contains children smiling or laughing and jokes on almost every page. When Danny Dunn recklessly or impulsively destroys or changes one of Professor Bullfinch's scientific experiments, he is far more likely to meet with indulgent laughter than a scolding. Humor is allowed because it makes the learning environment more comfortable for children and those new to the scientific world.

The protagonists of science fiction series for older children and early teenagers, however, are discouraged from levity. Whereas a humorous suggestion might lead to the solution of a problem in science fiction for younger readers, a similar remark in a book for older readers could distract attention, causing the loss of a mission or even the loss of a life. The "intrusion of serious matter into humor," as L. Sprague De Camp writes, can "spoil the humor" (75). While a lack of sympathy for humor can be particularly found in series where the protagonists are members of a space crew in a military-type operation, other series share this attitude, including, for example, L'Engle's Time trilogy. Older readers must discard the notion that laughter belongs in the scientific laboratory.

To some extent, these differences have always been evident in science fiction series, but prior to 1945, the age of the reader mattered less than the type of book he or she read: more fantastic or more scientific. A brief look at two pre-1945 series elucidates this difference. Both the "Tom Swift, Boy Inventor" series and Norman Hunter's short story series about another inventor, Professor Branestawm, are written at about the same reading level but portray very different attitudes about science. Hunter's Branestawm, whom he describes as "so clever, he was very absent-minded. He was so busy thinking of wonderful things like new diseases or new moons that he simply hadn't time to think of ordinary things" (*The Incredible Adventures of Professor Branestawm* 11). The original Tom Swift has a similar gift; his father comments, "'It seems to me that is about all Tom does—have adventures—that and inventing flying machines'" (*Tom Swift in the City of Gold* 14). Yet although both main characters spend their time inventing and using these inventions to initiate and/or conclude adventures, only Tom Swift's character is taken seriously by the author. Branestawm's inventions generally create more trouble than they solve, but Tom Swift's inventions often help him climb out of the trouble he finds himself in or even make further scientific discoveries, as in *The City of Gold*: "'We'll rig up some sort of lamps,'" Tom explained, "'and come back to make a thorough examination of this place. I think the scientific men and historians will be glad to know about this city, and I'm going to make some notes about it'" (184–185). Tom's applied science helps to expand the knowledge base of other scientific fields, and despite his young age, he is respected for his ability. His serious inventions have serious purpose—no one laughs at Tom Swift's ideas.

Branestawm's inventions usually have the opposite effect, however. In one episode, a time machine of his own creation allows him and his friend Colonel Dedshott to travel back to an earlier time. During this journey, they accidentally change part of history. Rather than discuss the possible ramifications of this shift, the author merely announces that "the people who write the history books had an awful time clearing up the tangle they'd made of Squiglatanian history by winning a battle for the side that really lost it" (*The Incredible Adventures of Professor Branestawm* 22). In the final analysis, the use of humor makes the scientific into the fantastic. And while Tom Swift is a "real" scientist, despite his age, Professor Branestawm becomes only a character, even a caricature, of who scientists are and what they do. Like Dr. Dolittle, actual scientific results matter little (after all, Branestawm's time machine *did* work) if the way in which these results are achieved is less than serious-minded and purposeful.[1]

After 1945, however, as the space race caused an increase in the science fiction available for children of all ages, a noticeable split in the amount of humor in science fiction series took place, depending on readers' age level. No matter how simple or difficult the vocabulary in a series, if the science fiction contained a lighthearted attitude toward science, encouraging humor and divergent problem solving, the book was marketed toward younger readers. Over time, this distinction increased the separation between children's and young adult science fiction series: whereas humor can often lead to solutions for children's science fiction series' characters, a simple joke can doom or endanger their young adult counterparts.[2]

This is not to say that young adult science fiction series contain no humor at all—quite the contrary, in fact. Almost every series has at least one character designed for comic relief—often a sidekick of the hero. However, authors leave no doubt as to why these characters remain sidekicks rather than becoming heroes in their own right: the humorous person, by not comprehending the need for a serious attitude toward scientific work, endangers the lives of others. The humorous perspective must therefore be squelched early on in the story to prevent further difficulties. The true hero takes everything on a mission seriously, even if others do not.[3]

In the following example from an Australian series, the hero, Tas, momentarily forgets the necessity of a serious purpose and cheeks an army guard. He recollects himself enough later, however, to heed the guard's warning despite the complaints of his sidekick Bluey. The guard is trying to steer them away from danger by sending the boys for a snack:

"The canteen's at the bottom of the escalator. You'll find all the ice-cream you want there, and it'll keep you out of trouble."

"You hope!" Bluey muttered as they moved away. "These guards give me a pain in the neck. Always threatening you."

"It's their job," Tas reminded him. (*Tas and the Space Machine* 19)

The caution Tas displays proves more well-founded than the disgust of his companion, as following the guard's rules averts danger for the boys later: "'The guard had been right to warn the boys of the danger of being run down by one of these trucks, for unless you were listening intently you couldn't hear them coming'" (22). Listening intently and paying attention separate heroes and sidekicks in young adult science fiction series—as another sidekick, Bigman Jones, in Asimov's Lucky Starr series, discovers to his own embarrassment. Despite the fact that Jones tries desperately to be as important as Lucky Starr, his lighthearted side constantly prevents this—and Asimov makes certain that Bigman feels the proper amount of censure for it: "Bigman's heart skipped a beat. He heard the clear disapproval in Lucky's voice. In such a crisis, at a time of such danger, he, Bigman, was making faces like a fool. Shame came over him" (*Lucky Starr and the Oceans of Venus* 136). Sidekicks, like Bigman and Bluey, must be constantly monitored so that they do not endanger the important work of the hero through a lack of seriousness.[4]

In fact, any humorous escapade, even when danger seems remote, can lead to disaster. Tom Swift, in the 1990s series, invents a flying skateboard. He tests it out in *The Black Dragon* (1991) by running it through a course of "weapons" made of cream pies while his sidekick, Rick, looks on. "Rick laughed at Tom's crazy sense of humor—cream pies! But Tom wove through the pattern of 'fire' without being touched, like a hotdogger on an invisible wave" (7). Still, even test runs should be taken seriously or disaster can result—Tom falls off the skateboard due to a mysterious malfunction.

The connection of a humorous episode with failure is not coincidental; characters who view science seriously and learn lessons from disasters caused by humor, as Tom does in the rest of the book, can avert danger. Even though it seems as if all the book's danger has passed, Tom remains vigilant rather than relaxing when his father welcomes him home: "'That's great,' Tom said as he signed off. But where is Orb? he thought. In spite of his best efforts over the last hour, he hadn't been able to track the robot. His search program was still running, though, and Tom had hopes he'd know where Orb was by the time he and Rick landed" (157). Orb, a killer robot, happens to be in his sister's arms. Thanks to Tom's serious attitude and dedication to work rather than winding down at the end of a mission, the boy manages to disarm the robot before it is too late, proving that true heroes never relax their guard—or if they occasionally do, they learn their lesson and thus avoid the risk of further danger.

In addition to averting trouble, a serious attitude wins praise from figures of authority as well. Just as Tom Swift is hailed as a hero by his family for saving his sister Sandy, Mike Mars earns the commendation of his superior despite the teasing he gets from his colleagues. During a test, Mike single-handedly rescues a man who appears unconscious. This "man" turns out to be a test dummy, and the text notes that "[w]hen he got back to the ship and the other astronauts found out about it, Mike took a good deal of joshing. But Colonel Drummond seemed rather proud of Mike" (*Mike Mars at Cape Kennedy* 17); the colonel praises him while silencing Mike's detractors. Because he takes the situation seriously, Mike Mars proves his right to lead; his friends who scoff end up as Mike's followers.

Only certain types of humor receive no censor from the narrator or other characters in young adult science fiction series. Despite being allowed, however, even these types of humor rarely serve any practical purpose; generally, the characters must return to a serious mind-set in order to be saved from peril. One "allowable" sort of humor is the humor of despair—black humor. When rescue seems unlikely, characters often use humor to encourage and comfort each other.[5] For example, when Tom Swift and his sidekick Bud, in *Tom Swift in the Race to the Moon* (1958), face the possibility of slowly asphyxiating in outer space, the boys "swapped jokes and chattered away to keep up their spirits" (69). When new worlds make no sense, and the characters realize they may never complete their mission, the humor of despair again takes over. In Madeleine L'Engle's *A Wrinkle in Time*, Charles Wallace tries unsuccessfully to gain help in entering a building from a stranger, but the stranger feels he must stick to his own purpose: "'I am here to report that one of my letters is jamming and until it can be properly oiled by an F grade oiler there is danger of jammed minds.' 'Strawberry jam or raspberry?' Charles Wallace murmured" (117). "Whistling in the dark," as Charles's sister Meg calls it (117), is a sign that hope for success has dimmed. In both this case and the Tom Swift example, only a return to a serious attitude eventually gets the characters out of their troubles; the humor just passes the time. Distracting humor, so dangerous to other young adult characters who remain firm in their mission, at least eases the agony of hopelessness.

The humor of despair also serves another purpose: to remind the characters of their last opportunity to freely enjoy laughter, when they were at home. Humor within a family (pre- and postmission) setting seems not just common but required for young adult science fiction series, indicating the contrast between the safety of the home environment and the perils that the characters must soon face.[6] Although many types of jokes find their way into these unusual dinnertime conversations, the most common form is teasing between the male heroes and the girls who stay behind. This type of humor, more or less seriously directed depending on the series, rests a great deal on the use of stereotypical feminine attributes to poke fun at the girls and offer some explanation for why they would not be useful on the upcoming mission. When Barby Brant asks her brother Rick to bring her back a lama from Tibet to make up for her not being allowed to join the mission, everyone at the table laughs at her mistake. "'You're a little mixed up, towhead,' Rick replied. 'You're thinking of llamas—with two l's. They're South American animals. A lama is a Tibetan priest, and I don't think one of them would want to come back with us as a souvenir for a girl'" (*The Lost City* 4). Rick's lecture, and his unnecessary addition of the words "for a girl" at the end of his speech, reinforces the notion that Barby, as a girl, is too dumb to study science. Her mistake also allows Rick to show off his knowledge, again underlining his right to be the hero of the series.[7]

Even when the girl characters have a scientific or professional role (unlike Barby Brant who works as an island telephone operator), this notion of feminine inadequacy is reinforced by humor: a humor that the girls themselves often help to perpetuate. Tom's sister Sandy Swift and her friend Phyl can both fly the planes that Swift Enterprises produce, but nonetheless they are not welcome in outer space or anywhere else danger might lurk. When Tom and Bud have to catch a mysterious interloper, Bud teasingly suggests they take the girls along with them, to which idea Sandy replies, "'Stop it! You're scaring us to death!'" (*Tom Swift and His Outpost in Space* 15–16). Even though the narrative implies that Sandy's outburst was at least partly in jest (she laughs after her statement), she and Phyl nonetheless remain home and out of danger while Tom and Bud do all the adventuring. Thus humor is used to separate the useless girls from the seriously scientific and purposeful boys.[8]

In these young adult science fiction series, boys are allowed to enjoy laughter and jokes within the family—but the true hero knows when to turn his mind to more serious matters, an attribute that girls apparently lack. Girls, rarely removed from the safety of the home situation, have the freedom to joke at all times, but their brothers and boyfriends have learned that missions mean laying humor aside. This difference is illuminated in The Space Eagle Series, when sister Julie Girard, a top executive at the Girard Foundation, teases her brother about enjoying the good life too much. He chastises her: "'No joking matter, sister,' Paul said gravely. He told her about the emergency call from the President" (*Operation Doomsday* 109). Family humor, then, is allowable—but only when no important task immediately faces the main characters.

Failure to remember this duty to purpose on the male hero's part, or an over-attachment to family ties, can lead to disaster. During a solo mission, Mike Mars smilingly recalls his mother's constant nagging at him to eat vegetables (*Mike Mars in Orbit* 145) and therefore selects a vegetable rather than a meat tube of space food. Thinking of his family while on a mission proves risky, however, as the vegetable tube explodes and endangers Mike's life (the meat tube, purportedly, had not been rigged). Not until the end of the book, when all danger has passed, can Mike safely think of the humorous attributes of his family again. Humor, for Mike as for other young adult science fiction series characters, has only a limited, carefully defined place in their lives; to try to include it in the serious work of science can cause harm to themselves or danger to others.

The situation in children's science fiction series is markedly different. The humor, which in young adult series must stay "at home," has an omnipresence in children's series. Jokes, teasing, wordplay, and humorously unlikely situations abound, not just at the beginnings and endings of books but throughout—and unlike their young adult counterparts, children's science fiction often resolves difficult situations through the use of humor. To a great extent, the frequent and liberal use of humor results from a key difference between children's and young adult science fiction in the situation of the characters. Children in science fiction, no matter where they travel in the universe, rarely depart from domesticity. Even when they do not remain physically at home, they almost always enjoy the security of the domestic situation: a protective figure accompanies them, either teacher (Coville's My Teacher series, Cole's Magic School Bus books), or robot (Asimov's Norby, Slote's Danny One)[9] or substitute parent (Williams and Abrashkin's Danny Dunn, Stannard's Uncle Albert). Spaceships are constructed not of space-age materials but of homey ones (Cameron's Mushroom Planet)[10] or populated with familiar home creatures (MacGregor's Miss Pickerell, Slobodkin's Space Ship).[11] This creation of a safe or tame outer world, in contrast with the wild unknowns of young adult science fiction, allows for "at home" humor all the time. Children's science fiction series take advantage of this leeway not just to make the science safe but to make it palatable to child readers and characters, even allowing humor to save the day on occasion.

Whereas young adult science fiction seems to recognize only two major types of humor, teasing and the humor of despair, children's science fiction contains a much broader spectrum, including situational humor, puns, riddles and jokes, and a generally playful, imaginative view toward both language and science, all designed to increase reader interest. For example, in the Matthew Looney series, readers can enjoy a range of humor, both plays on words and plays on scientific and historical concepts. Even the most inexperienced readers can guess why the moon's place of higher education is called the "mooniversity"; more knowledgeable readers will enjoy the more subtle jokes on names, such as the use of the last name of Looney or for the doctor of the Earth space project, Dr. Leonard O. Davinchy (see *Matthew Looney's Invasion of the Earth*).[12] Readers can also appreciate the situational humor in the moon citizens' assumptions that Earth is unpopulated or that ordinary water can poison and kill. All these types of humor would appear ridiculous in a young adult series, but they have a definite and accepted place in science fiction series for children.

The Matthew Looney series is certainly not the most scientific of the series written during this time period for children; often the books seem to ask, "What if science was funny?" rather than, "What if this scientific principle worked?" However, even in children's series that are more focused on the "correct" science, humor still plays a large role. On the one hand, the Miss Pickerell series contains accurate (at least for the time) descriptions of concepts such as gravity and instruments such as Geiger counters. However, at the same time, in the interest of humor, it contains old ladies and kittens traveling into outer space. The Danny Dunn series, even at its most scientific, still employs Danny's heedlessness and his sidekick Joe's unscientific, poetic nature to occasion humor for the readers. In fact, even though young adult series can be relatively humorless and still succeed, children's series almost seem to *require* humor as a basic ingredient in every book. And whereas humor almost inevitably endangers the young adult hero, it has the opposite effect in children's science fiction series.

Even when children's science fiction uses humor to point out differences between cognizant creatures—much as the teasing functions in young adult series—the humor, rather than causing a gap or indicating the superiority of one character over another, eventually brings the characters closer together. One example is when language difficulties arise. Although usually glossed over in young adult science fiction (through universal translators or the handy habit aliens have of learning English),[13] language differences become both a source for humor as well as a way of bonding two or more characters of different origin and different goals into a team situation. For example, in *The Spaceship Under the Apple Tree* and its successors, the alien Marty's language is often unintentionally humorous because he learned English from reading highway signs. This weakness makes the Earth boy, Eddie, sympathetic to a creature he at first regarded with hostility. Similarly, Chip in McEvoy's Not Quite Human series often makes mistakes in his use of English because of his robot programming, but rather than causing his human "sister" Becky to distance herself from him in school, the faulty programming gives her a reason to protect her robot brother. Even though Becky herself occasionally finds Chip amusing and laughs at his mistakes, language humor does not create tension between the characters but releases it. Human children in science fiction series find it easier than their young adult counterparts to reach out to characters who make humorous mistakes, and they eagerly offer help and friendship.[14]

In Madeleine L'Engle's *A Wrinkle in Time*, the sage and adviser Mrs. Which cautions, "Thee onnlly wway ttoo ccope withh ssometthingg ddeadly sseriouss iss ttoo ttry ttoo trreatt itt a llittlle lligghtly" (61); however, Meg, Calvin, and Charles Wallace rarely follow this advice, even though taking their mission and themselves too seriously regularly gets them into deeper difficulties. Children's science fiction series always take themselves lightly, with the result that humor, in addition to bringing characters together, can even avoid or solve problems. In the Megamorphs series (a sub-series of the Animorphs), for example, K. A. Applegate's character Marco is a sarcastic, quick-witted doubting Thomas. In many young adult science fiction series, his character would often turn out to be a villain, at least until he was proved wrong or his joking got the better of him. But the other characters in the Animorphs series value and appreciate Marco's contributions: Cassie notes that Marco "tell[s] jokes and make[s] everyone relax'" (*Andalite's Gift* 211), and Rachel suggests that "'his suspicious nature makes him very good at seeing beneath the surface of things'" (*Stranger* 14). No one ever talks of making Marco stay behind due to his practical joking; even when the other Animorphs get annoyed with him, Marco remains a necessary part of the team.

Jane Yolen's Commander Toad series, for beginning readers, doesn't even offer mixed praise for jokesters but instead provides a key narrative role for Mr. Hop and his riddles. When faced with a giant sea monster, Commander Toad rigs up a way to make their boat fly, counting on crew member Mr. Hop to keep the sea monster busy by telling it jokes. "'I have never yet met a monster who does not like riddles,'" Mr. Hop comments (*Commander Toad in Space* 48), suggesting that the outer space he and his friends occupy is very different from that of the humorless space of young adult science fiction series.

This points to another difference between young adult and children's science fiction series: the treatment of aliens. Marco jokes *about* the aliens in the Animorphs series and Mr. Hop jokes *with* them in Commander Toad, but both joke to some purpose. In young adult series, sidekicks to the hero also joke about or with aliens, and the heroes must remind them of the danger of these activities. When Bigman makes faces at the V-frogs in *Lucky Starr and the Oceans of Venus*, it indicates his susceptibility to what later turn out to be mind-controlling aliens; Lucky Starr reminds Bigman that, "'The V-frogs are feeling you out for weak points. However they can do it, they'll crawl into your mind, and once there they may remain past your ability to force them to leave. So don't follow any impulse until you've thought it out'" (136). Even the smallest, seemingly cutest of aliens must be taken seriously. Similarly, when Ben Walking Eagle makes a sarcastic remark in the face of capture in the 1981 *The War in Outer Space*, Tom tells his friend to, "'Cool it!'" (101) before his remarks get them into trouble. Such a thing never happens in children's science fiction—humor is not just an emotional release but frequently a physical one.

Because aliens are often characters who represent the fear of the *other*, however, it is important to note that although children's science fiction series treat aliens more lightly than young adult science fiction, they do not make aliens into figures of fun. Some amusement may be exchanged in noting the differences between Earth's cultures and alien ones, but the aliens are not put down for their differences. Whereas John Christopher's human characters tease their alien captive, enjoying the power game of making the captured creature say please and thank you and otherwise kowtow to Earth customs (see *The Pool of Fire* 77), Bruce Coville's human characters come not only to accept other culture's different customs (see "Lunch with Fleef and Gurk," *My Teacher Glows in the Dark* 41–48) but also to appreciate that the human way of doing things might well be flawed beyond repair (*My Teacher Flunked the Planet*, especially "The Forty Thousand" 55-62). Aliens might look different, but they are not, in children's series, used as an indication of the white male Earth human's superiority to all others. Children's series characters see aliens as an opportunity, not a joke. When the aliens are enemies, it is appropriate to joke with them, in order to escape; when the aliens are friendly, the joking is used to break down, rather than set up, barriers.

Sidekicks are often used in the jokester role in children's series because they typically provide that kind of comic relief—balancing the serious scientific thought of the hero. But not only can a sidekick exhibit humorous behavior and win praise for it; heroes in children's science fiction series often save the day with jokes and riddles. In another picture-book series, the Tubby Tin series, the hero solves a problem through humor. Faced with an invisible intruder, the robot hero Tubby Tin sets up a bucket of red paint over a door to catch the stowaway: "The stowaway appeared in the doorway looking rather red in the face. In fact, it looked rather red all over! 'Oh, ha ha!' said the stowaway. 'I suppose you think that's funny?'" (*Tubby Tin and the No Such Things* 22). Despite this sarcasm, however, the creature ends up being as pleased as Tubby Tin's professor-owner (who wants to study the creature) because Tubby uses the practical joke to uncover more invisible creatures, thus making visible a community the creature did not know existed. What began as a joke ends as an act that brings together a character with its community as well as one world with another.[15] In the dominion of children's science fiction, humor has few adverse side effects and many positive benefits for the characters in the stories.

The results of humor for the readers of children's science fiction series are mixed, however. The positive side of the joke-filled world of children's series is its ability to draw readers in and increase interest in scientific topics. One of the most fact-filled series for children, the Magic School Bus series, is also one of the most familiar to children, read in schools as well as at home, available at both "serious" bookstores and discount chain stores such as Target and K-Mart. It has also been made into a cartoon series, shown on public television, further proof of its capacity to combine popular media (cartoons) with serious science (worthy of being shown on public, rather than commercial, television). In addition, the Magic School Bus books have jokes or puns on every page, some in the text and some in the illustrations. The series tackles all kinds of scientific areas, including outer space (*The Magic School Bus Lost in the Solar System*), Earthbound sciences (*The Magic School Bus Inside the Human Body*), and human-made scientific-engineering achievements (*The Magic School Bus at the Waterworks*). While child readers, listeners, and watchers may not absorb all the science that the author and illustrator intended, these simple, brightly colored, amusing accounts remain popular and theoretically lead children to explore scientific issues further. Seemingly, the use of humor helps make the books successful and encourages learning; this is the positive aspect of humor in children's science fiction series.

But it is perhaps too much of a good thing. The problem with the reliance of children's science fiction series on humor, whether to distract, to move the plot along, or to make science palatable, is the implication that science without humor cannot be marketed to children. That science, and not other subjects, must be spoon-fed with sugar is evident in the fact that historical fiction series for children come in a broad range of literature, from the serious (The American Girls' series, for example) to the silly (Scziezka and Smith's *Time Warp Trio* or the *Bloody History Accounts of Mr. X*). If children get used to the idea that science fiction series *of necessity* contain humor, then readers who have grown out of children's series will find few outlets for their reading needs. Young adult science fiction series, with their steady diet of serious intentions, will fail to satisfy them.[16] With the emphasis in young adult novels on ideas and inventions rather than humor, even well-written series and those designed to make readers think about ethical issues will not capture the imagination of the reader who has come to expect something else from science fiction.[17]

Science fiction and science fiction series throughout this time period have enjoyed a much broader audience in younger readers than in older ones, as indicated by the tendency, much more common in children's books than young adults', to shelve science fiction series with the rest of the fiction rather than separating it out as a specialty category. For many readers, young adulthood becomes a time when readers of science fiction become a different breed, set apart from other readers. This separation has, over the years, been caused by many factors, including the status of women and minorities in many series for older readers; but certainly a part of the loss in science fiction series readership stems from the decrease in type and acceptability of humor in books for older readers. It is almost as if young adult science fiction series turn their back on fun and support the idea instead that science—real science—is serious business and no place for children.[18]

By putting priority on humor rather than the scientific ideas, many children's series support this very notion. While certain series—as we shall examine in Chapter 6—do contain accurate scientific notions for the time in which they were written, many other children's series do not. To make their stories humorous, authors frequently joke at the expense of science, damaging the credibility not just of that series but of all children's science fiction. The idea, for example, that an American Air Force general would allow a kitten to go into outer space, as occurs in Ruthven Todd's *Space Cat*, simply because Flyball's owner might be lonely without him (30), seems highly implausible. Without Flyball's participation in the space mission, however, Todd would have nothing to write about—all the humor results from this improbability.[19] Yet possible problems, such as feeding the cat its food or dealing with the need for the animal to breath from an oxygen tank, are merely glossed over in order to get to the action sequences more quickly. In young adult science fiction series, the mundane difficulties inherent in the scientific inquiry cannot be ignored; they are an integral part of the entire experience. In fact, the amount of attention to detail helps to separate it from other types of fiction. The Space Cat series, on the other hand, obviously contains fantastic elements but is labeled science fiction because it takes place in outer space. Because this series— like most children's series—contains large amounts of humor, and because many humorous science fiction series follow this pattern of taking the science with a grain of salt, the tendency to equate humor with poor science comes naturally. Unfortunately, this results in the unfair condemnation of many other children's series exclusively on this basis.

The humor in children's science fiction series can be a priceless asset to the genre, drawing in readers and empowering characters to succeed—but the risks, both of losing older readers to nonscientific humorous series and of producing faulty scientific notions in younger readers, are great. The lack of humor in young adult series can make a hero or an adventure seem more realistic on the surface but presents a grim, unsmiling face to the universe in which only the ignorant can live in bliss.[20] In the end, both a reliance on humor as well as an abhorrence of it can prove fatal for the science fiction series. Somehow, future science fiction series, both for children and young adults, must strive for a better balance between these two extremes—or even change the belief that humor and science are at odds with each other at all. In this way, humor in science fiction series will not cause the death of the body for its young adult characters or the death of the mind for its child readers. Creativity, rather than the rigid observation of rules, would be the key to scientific inquiry, allowing a place for all types of characters and readers to learn and enjoy the fiction of the unknown.

NOTES

1. Interestingly, the difference between fantasy and mimesis (for a good definition of mimesis, see Kathryn Hume's *Fantasy and Mimesis*) in science fiction cited here often is ignored by critics; Fred Inglis, for example, in *The Promise of Happiness* suggests, "if the pleasure of science-fiction is to amaze its reader with the improbability of its future, the point of real fiction is to return us to the real world with a larger sense of what it may become" (257). In fact, many young adult science fiction series accomplish the latter far more often than the former.

2. This brings it closer in spirit to older adult science fiction, in which, as Anne McCaffrey points out, "[h]umor is as much an emotional involvement as tragedy—but rarer" (286).

3. This counters Damon Knight's suggestion that "[s]cience fiction is, pretty plainly, swinging away from its complex, cerebral, heavy science-plus-action phase, toward a more balanced and easily digestible mixture of technology and human emotion" (94). In young adult science fiction series, at least, human emotion—while perhaps more frequent—still plays a negative role.

4. Kingsley Amis describes this mistrust of humor as "the fear of a pleasure so overmastering that it can break down the sense of reality or at least the pattern of active life, and break them down in everyone, not merely in the predisposed neurotic" (115). Amis cites this fear as a common feature of science fiction.

5. Donald M. Hassler suggests that the humor in these passages comes from the desire to leave outer space and its dangers: "Underneath all the indeterminacy and all the planet orbits (electron and precursor both) we always long to go home again. It is that tension that produces the comic and that justifies it" (x).

6. Again, it is Hassler who connects this notion of safety and danger with the comic when he writes, "Progress (and comedy) may be, indeed, a 'fortunate fall'; but the very dynamic that drives it is the nostalgia for the conditions before the fall. Prelapsarian simplicity and deconstructive indeterminacy represent the two poles that generate the tones of the comic effect" (22).

7. This passage, along with the selections where heroes lecture their sidekicks on the necessity of a serious attitude, suggests that young adult science fiction attempts to promote itself as "realistic" fiction (based on "real" science). See John Stephens's *Language and Ideology in Children's Fiction*, particularly chapter 7, "Words of Power: Fantasy and Realism as Linguistically Constituted Modes" (241–290). In this chapter, Stephens argues that "the operation of language as power in realistic texts is to be sought in the representation of conversation" (269).

8. Kathryn Hume discusses this kind of humor in her book *Fantasy and Mimesis*, writing that laughter arises when "sudden boosts lift us from our normal state and we naturally feel pleased at being better than before, or better than others" (68). L. Sprague De Camp agrees that "there is a slight element of sadism in most humor; our fellow man's calamities, provided they are not too disastrous, are funny to us" (71).

9. Margaret P. Esmonde reminds us, "This image of the metal man acting *in loco parentis* has proven to be a popular theme in children's robot stories ranging from wordless picture books to adventure stories for the adolescent reader" ("From" 87).

10. Cameron herself admits that the Mushroom Planet books are often more fantastic than scientific but adds that the reader and critic should "notice the various details which appear to take scientific necessities into consideration" ("Fantasy" 7). For Cameron, as for other children's authors, the quality of wonder takes precedence over scientific accuracy.

11. Gary K. Wolfe notes that ever since Jules Verne the science fiction novel's spaceship "retains a function as the repository of middle-class values, and the hull of the ship provides what is perhaps the clearest single image of the barrier that separates the known world from the unknown" (*Known* 56). Although true both for children's and young adult science fiction series, Wolfe's notion takes on special significance when most of the action in the children's series takes place either in the home or on the spaceship—home thus becomes omnipresent.

12. Janice Antczak notes this characteristic of Beatty's series when she suggests that "the humorous aspects of the novels reflect a total integration of plot, character, and language" (174).

13. Interestingly, Walter E. Meyers claims that universal translators, or "magic decoders" as he calls them, are, in adult science fiction, now only a matter for satire: "In a first-contact situation, the magic decoder does all the work. . . . In comedy, where our disbelief is suspended a little more willingly, the magic decoder works instantaneously" (119–120). Meyers calls the universal translator "a confidence game" (121), but if so, authors find young adults a more ready audience for such tricks than adults.

14. Pat Pinsent points out that this bonding comes from an empathy with the other character's "tendency to get words mixed up, which incidentally provides humor at their level" (37).

15. Chet Raymo, in "Dr. Seuss and Dr. Einstein: Children's Books and the Scientific Imagination," underscores the notion that the child's "un-serious" viewpoint can be as useful as a young adult's "serious" attitude. He writes, "Creative science depends crucially upon habits of mind that are most readily acquired by children: curiosity; voracious observation; sensitivity to rules and variations within the rules; and fantasy. Children's books that instill these habits of mind sustain science" (185).

16. Susan Fremantle believes that "humour is one of the most widely loved and demanded features of all children's books. . . . It is a way into books for many children" (8).

17. In fact, William Sleator suggests that science fiction is a lit that appeals particularly to the skepticism of young adulthood: "I tend to doubt that I will get to another world by walking into a wardrobe, but I don't doubt at all that I could get there in a spaceship. Science fiction

confronts teenage skepticism head on, and does away with it" (210). Humorous solutions or situations bring back the skeptic's doubts; therefore, although Sleator argues that science fiction is "as exciting to the skeptics as to the romantics" (210), I would counter that skeptics get far more out of young adult science fiction series than any romantics, still holding on to their childlike attitudes, ever would.

18. This attitude concerning childhood's lack of seriousness is reflected in the theory and criticism of the literature as well. Peter Hollindale notes, "Even reputable modern children's authors and artists remain defensive and unconvinced on the point, so that even the most effective and useful formulations are tied by the vocabulary. . . . [T]o be 'childish' is to be 'un-serious,' and the adjectival resource belittles the person" (50).

19. Antczak argues that Flyball "is as fun-loving and lovable in a lunar cavern as in a neighborhood backyard" (173); but given the fact that none of Flyball's adventures take place in a backyard, I would suggest that the kitten is *more* lovable in outer space.

20. James Gunn sums up the attitude taken by many young adult science fiction series writers when he says, "The man who loved reason had the rational approach of the science fiction writer" ("Science Fiction" 193), adding that this rational view is a "truer picture of man's character" (194). Gregory Benford adds, "The fidelity to an external standard of truth makes hard SF resemble the realistic narrative, in that it becomes a realism of *possibilities*, guided by our current worldview" (83).

CHAPTER 6

But What *Is* a Superconductor, Anyway?: The Absence and Presence of Science

"Don't you see?" said the Professor. "It's a superconductor."
"But that's incredible!" Dr. Fenster said. "At room temperature?"
"So it appears. There's no other explanation."
"A superconductor?" Danny put in. "What's that?"
—Williams and Abrashkin, *Danny Dunn and the Swamp Monster* (24)

Good science fiction needs to be both good fiction and good science. Because series science fiction for children is frequently written by laypeople, not scientists, and because a series can cover a multitude of scientific topics, the quality of series varies widely. Although a lay author might produce easily understood and accessible science fiction, he or she may also oversimplify scientific ideas to the point of misconception by the reader. A variety of adventures in different scientific areas may hold the readers' attention but also leads to the danger that, within a series, both scientific and nonscientific ideas may be accepted at face value. The other extreme, where, as Perry Nodelman describes, the texts "are purely didactic" and "have no purpose but to make children better" (*Pleasures* 86) is equally ruinous to a work of science fiction. Achieving a balance between accurate science and interesting reading presents difficulties in a single book; in a series, it is a constant problem.[1]

Complicating the issue of what constitutes good science fiction for children is the tendency of authors to mix fantasy with science. Thus, in the same novel, Danny Dunn can get a scientifically accurate explanation of a superconductor and also escape from a twenty-foot-long electric catfish. Chuck and David, in the Mushroom Planet series, can make a working spaceship out of tin cans and two-by-fours but are still required to obey other laws of astrophysics. How clear is the difference between science and fantasy, and how much does it matter? As the answer to this question depends on the age of the audience intended for each book or series, this chapter will first explore the level or lack of science in a variety of series, then examine one, Eleanor Cameron's Mushroom Planet books, in greater detail.

Initially, it seems intuitive to assume that as the intended audience of science fiction series grew older, the various series would include increasing amounts of scientific material. Older readers, it may be argued, can comprehend more complex scientific ideas and therefore their books should be at a higher factual level than picture-books. However, the amount of scientific knowledge conveyed (or intended to be conveyed) has very little relationship to the age of the audience for the books. For example, the Magic School Bus series concentrates on factual information for its picture-book audience, whereas both the 1980s and 1990s Tom Swift series for young adults have scientific settings but little actual scientific material. Conversely, the British Tubby Tin picture-book series consistently ignores the laws of physics, but Donald Wollheim's Mike Mars series for young adults consults U.S. Air Force scientists for more accurate outer space adventures.[2] Science fiction series for middle-grade readers vary equally in their extremes. The level and amount of accurate science have little or nothing to do with a series' label of science fiction.

Two aspects of science fiction series do seem to be age-related, however, and both affect the scientific quality of a series. One of these aspects is the use of language, and the other is the amount of fantastic or imaginary material mixed with the science. The issue of language—use of proper scientific terminology and explanations—has a fairly straightforward relationship to the quality of the science in the various series. However, the amount of imagined material a book contains has a more confusing—and controversial—bond with scientific fact. The overall purpose of science fiction comes into question: is it to teach science, or is it to entertain?[3] The lack of consensus on this issue makes the very definition of science fiction an uncertain point in children's fiction overall.

The slippery definition of science fiction does not plague writing for adults to anywhere near the same degree. Science fiction for adults is generally split into two rough categories, hard and soft science fiction. In essence, hard science fiction deals with technology extrapolated from scientific ideas, and soft science fiction concentrates more on problematic or philosophical situations that might result from current technology and its inevitable end.[4] The closer that science fiction series for young people come to mimicking their adult counterparts, the easier it is to fit individual series into one of these two categories. However, books for younger children usually do not slide smoothly into either of these pigeonholes.

The first reason for this is the way books for younger readers use scientific language. Part of what makes hard science fiction *hard* is its use of accurate scientific terminology.[5] Perhaps books for young adults cannot toss off terminology without explanation, but they can include difficult scientific concepts if carefully defined. This does not necessarily work with younger readers, whose more limited vocabularies and knowledge bases restrict authorial freedom.[6]   Picture-book authors must choose whether to ignore scientific language or to accept simplified explanations. Most choose not to describe technology but rather accept it as a part of daily life and merely represent its functions. For example, Jane Yolen's Commander Toad series and the Tubby Tin series both posit space travel as a commonality, available to individuals as well as governments, and taken between vastly distant planets that are inhabited by intelligent life. Few explanations of scientific concepts and ideas are given in either of these series, although technology does have a firm place: the Commander Toad series employs a computer whiz on board the spacecraft, and the man who created Tubby Tin is both a professor and an inventor.

In addition, many scientific inventions and concepts are assumed knowledge in both of these series. In *Tubby Tin and the No Such Things* (1982), Tubby Tin and the Professor find a radio on a planet that, they presume, is uninhabited. The radio "was making some very peculiar noises" (2). Rather than infer that these strange noises constitute some kind of alien music, Tubby Tin immediately jumps to the conclusion that "[p]erhaps someone is trying to contact us" (2). The author, Georgie Adams, indicates through Tubby Tin's speech that the book is science fiction, since the radio has the sole function of communication between individuals, a scientific rather than entertainment function.   But in so doing, Adams assumes that readers recognize and understand this use of a radio. With the increasing use of computer technology, even children exposed to a science fiction culture through other media, such as *Star Wars* or *Star Trek*, may not recognize this more primitive technology. Presuming knowledge in this way may result in confused notions of scientific ideas.

Similarly, Yolen's Commander Toad series presumes a considerable amount of scientific knowledge.   The series' titles often contain scientific terminology that receive either no explanation at all or, worse, an incorrect explanation. The concept, for example, of an intergalactic spy (*Commander Toad and the Intergalactic Spy*) and the definition of an asteroid (*Commander Toad and the Dis-Asteroid*) are never made clear. While readers may be able to surmise the definitions from the context, if they extend this strategy to another of Yolen's books, they will be incorporating incorrect ideas into their scientific knowledge base. In *Commander Toad and the Big Black Hole*, Yolen first suggests that intelligent life lives in black holes because on Earth many animals live in holes (19–20). In the end, this hypothesis proves incorrect, but Yolen replaces it with an even less scientific one: the black hole is the mouth of an E.T.T.—an Extra Terrestrial Toad (40). Of course, Yolen's Commander Toad series is meant to be humorous, but the scientific surroundings incorporated in both text and pictures make distinguishing between the serious and the humorous occasionally difficult for an inexperienced audience. In picture-book science fiction series, scientific concepts are both presumed and presented incorrectly, often because the vocabulary for explaining them is unavailable to a picture-book audience.

One exception to this is the Magic School Bus series. Specifically designed to teach about science of various kinds, the series remains at the same time accurate and simple. In *The Magic School Bus Lost in the Solar System*, radio communication, although not explained, is presented simply and clearly. Rather than the strangely shaped, nonspecific picture with symbols emanating from it found in *Tubby Tin and the No Such Things*, Joanna Cole's book specifically indicates that the radio is "the bus radio" (*Lost* 24)—a concept most children who have ridden a bus can comprehend. It also introduces the idea that a radio is for short distance communication only, using the technique of increasingly smaller printing as the bus gets farther from their teacher, who has floated off into space. The text states, "On the radio, Ms. Frizzle's voice grew fainter and fainter" (25), while the illustration reinforces this, showing the children listening as a voice from the control panel says, in increasingly smaller print, "Kids, I'll meet you later . . . later . . . later" (25). In this way, the text and illustrations interact to convey the notion of radio communication without difficult terminology or complex drawings.

Outer space concepts that cannot be easily integrated into the text are not, however, ignored in Cole's series. Vocabulary or ideas that may be new to young readers are simply explained in the children's school reports, displayed on the sides of the pages. Thus, after the word "asteroid" first appears in the text, drawings of two notebook pages line the left side of the following page. One reads: "THE ASTEROID BELT by Shirley The area between the inner and outer planets is called the asteroid belt. It is filled with thousands and thousands of asteroids" (*Lost* 24). The other notebook page explains asteroids themselves: "WHAT ARE ASTEROIDS? by Florrie Asteroids are chunks of rock and metal in orbit around the Sun. Scientists think they are the building blocks of a planet that never formed" (24). This form of explanation empowers the child reader by showing child characters who can discuss concepts that are backed up by authority, indicated by the phrase "[s]cientists think," but that never become overcomplicated.

Although designed to teach, the Magic School Bus series engages child readers with humor just as other picture-book series do. The difference is that humor in the Magic School Bus series does not come at the expense of the science. Tubby Tin may use rocket boosters to spray-paint a planet (*Tubby Tin and the No Such Thing* 30), and Commander Toad's black hole may turn out to be a giant toad's mouth, both in an attempt to engage the reader with humorous situations. The Magic School Bus series, however, confines its humor to teasing between the children or other humorous situations, neither of which compromise the science in any way. For example, when the children first experience the weightlessness of outer space, not only do they float in the spaceship, but someone's open lunchbox lets loose its contents. This causes one of the children to announce that he sees "a U.F.B.—an unidentified flying banana" (*Lost* 10). In other cases, the humor even enhances the science. On each planet that the school bus visits, one child is shown on a "Weight and

Fate" scale. The child's weight on Earth is compared with that planet's weight, and the fortune highlights some scientific aspect of the planet in a humorous way. Thus, Arnold's fate on Saturn reads, "There's a ring in your future" (*Lost* 28) but on Neptune says, "You will have a happy birthday 165 years from now" (*Lost* 31). Both these jokes underline facts already introduced in the standard text; without distorting the science, they give the book a humorous feel.

Picture-book science fiction series often have difficulty presenting accurate science because of limited vocabulary and a desire to make science fiction more interesting by introducing humor. Although the Magic School Bus series manages both simple but accurate science *and* a sense of humor, it still does not seem to fit easily into the adult category of hard science fiction. Its purpose ultimately remains different from that of adult science fiction: whereas hard adult science fiction attempts to extrapolate scientific technology into new and creative uses, picture-book science fiction series often only introduce the technology and concepts for the young audience. Yet picture-book series do not fall into the category of soft science fiction either—they seldom explore ideas of social engineering or explain how scientific technology might change human life as we know it. Instead, children's picture-book science fiction series are nearly always both exploratory and explanatory: the difference between series is the level of scientific accuracy that the books embrace.

All children's science fiction series, from picture books through young adult novels, have to find a way to balance between explaining and exploring. The less a book attempts to explain the science, the more freedom the characters have to explore, especially in outer space. If an author does not deal with the difficulties of long-term space travel, for example, the characters can go farther and explore more. The separation between series is often how an author solves the problem of unknown solutions, or in other words, how they deal with scientific uncertainties. Mainly, the books can be split into two categories— those that rely on an outside authority for credibility and those that favor a more fantastic explanation.[7]

Prior to the first actual human space travel in 1961, nearly all science fiction series relied on some kind of official institution to lend credence to their characters' capacity to jaunt between the planets, usually a government military establishment. This immediately brings to mind the young adult series of the 1950s, which certainly exemplify the genre in this way.[8] Tom Corbett is a member of the Space Academy, a West Point–type training school for astronauts. Not only is Mike Mars an Air Force cadet, but his creator cites technical advisers from the U.S. Air Force who aided him in producing his series as well. David "Lucky" Starr is a member of an intergalactic watchdog group, the Council of Science, a sort of scientific version of the FBI with the power to prosecute wrongdoers. Even the Tom Swift series, which proclaims the independence of Swift Enterprises, Incorporated, cooperates with the U.S. government on most missions.[9] And, finally, W. E. Johns's Space series may be headed by a scientist, but Professor Brane recruits "one of the 'backroom boys' at the Royal Aircraft Experimental Establishment" (*Return to Mars* 8) to help him with construction details. The government, particularly some form of military government, yields a strong influence on young adult science fiction series during the first years after 1945.

The need to acquaint older readers, particularly males, with this military link to space travel does not seem so unusual. After all, authors expected some of these readers to go on quite soon after to aeronautical training,[10] and the only pathway at that time was the military one. But younger readers, too, were encouraged to connect the military and government in space programs. The Space Cat series has the most well-defined link to the military: Space Cat's owner is a captain in the Air Force. But both of the initial books in the Miss Pickerell and Danny Dunn series also include military personnel interacting with the main characters. Scientists may invent the machinery necessary for space travel, but the government takes charge from there. As Professor Bullfinch tells Danny Dunn: "'I'm a physicist, not a test pilot. . . . I must say, I wouldn't mind going. But the government has decided that the first flight will be piloted by a man who is an expert in the field. He's a rocket pilot named Joseph Beach, a lieutenant colonel in the Air Force'" (*Danny Dunn and the Anti-Gravity Paint* 60). Scientific concepts, such as the anti-gravity paint that allows the rocket in the book to take off, may be imagined by Professor Bullfinch and other members of the academic community, but in the end, they must always conform to military standards of design and outlay.

The subjugation of scientific space experimentation to government control—both on a story level as well as in the authorial tendency to seek advice from government experts—may give the individual series a ring of truth, but it also suggests certain specific reasons for the study of science. All scientific knowledge, according to this line of thinking, not only has military applications but is produced solely for military use. Science fiction series of the 1950s do little to increase the technical knowledge of the young reader—almost every mission, after all, must be kept secret to the nth detail—but by making the military *the* space authority, authors give the government and its military arm control over scientific knowledge in a positively represented way.[11]

Linking the military with science proved profitable for young adult science fiction series. On the one hand, anything scientifically unproven could be labeled "Top Secret" to avoid technical stumbling blocks. On the other hand, the young adult character could still play a pivotal role at a young age by signing up as an Air Force recruit or being the brilliant son of an adult connected to the military. Young adults had a place in space because of their ability to learn combined with their strength to fight an ever-present enemy. For younger readers, however, the situation was considerably different. Although a curious cat and an old maiden aunt may turn out to accidentally solve insoluble difficulties, they cannot be trained to fight in military operations. Even Danny Dunn, scientifically gifted, must sneak onto the spaceship in order to have a part in the flight. In reality, authors knew that children and childlike characters could have no legitimate link with the military's outer space campaigns.[12] The Space Cat series lasted only four books, ending in 1958—the year after the Soviet launch of Sputnik signaled in earnest a military-based struggle for control of outer space between the US and the USSR. The Danny Dunn and Miss Pickerell series continued to be published into the late 1970s but did so largely by staying out of space. As long as the person on the street was barred from space exploration due to lack of military qualifications, reality-based science fiction series for children relied on Earthly settings.[13]

In fact, two distinct types of science fiction series for young readers became the norm. Either a series concentrated on introducing Earth-based biological and chemical concepts to children, or it related amusing but unlikely outer space adventures. The more that outer space was integrated into a series, the more fantastic that series became. Whereas young adult science fiction series continued to involve technical advisers to legitimize their space adventure series, children's science fiction series began to list scientific consultants only for their Earth-based quests.

This is not to say that Earth-based children's science fiction series included nothing fantastic at all—quite the contrary. A good example of this is *Danny Dunn and the Swamp Monster*, quoted at the beginning of this chapter. The story involves an unlikely search through African swamps for a creature called the lau, who turns out to be an oversized electric catfish. However, although this creature makes the book more fantastic than other books in the Danny Dunn series (such as *Danny Dunn on the Ocean Floor*, for example), a good deal of accurate science still finds its way into the story. Danny Dunn (and presumably the child readers as well) learns about superconductors, zoology, and biochemistry in a simple but accurate way. Correct terminology, such as "polymer" (9–10), "magnetic field" (26), and "tranquilizer" (95) are placed in a context such that a young reader can understand them without too much difficulty. In addition, the fantastic lau is given realistic possibility by Dr. Fenster, a zoologist who argues, "Many scientists tend to pooh-pooh such tales [of strange beasts], but I think myself that the people who live in a place know better than any outsider what's there" (38). Dr. Fenster then goes on to relate the true story of the 1860 discovery of the okapi, a once-thought-legendary creature. By using the authority of a scientist and detailing an actual scientific event, Williams and Abrashkin give credence to the fantastic aspects of their story. Unlikely, but at least remotely possible, events continue to happen throughout the Danny Dunn series.

Similarly, the Miss Pickerell series stays largely earthbound but in so doing allows its readers to gain scientific knowledge in multiple areas, including geology, oceanography, veterinary science, and meteorology. *Miss Pickerell and the Geiger Counter*, for example, introduces the concepts of radiation and atomic energy—very pertinent to its original Cold War audience in 1953. In both the Danny Dunn and Miss Pickerell series, the scientifically curious main characters have access to scientists who can answer all their questions. This true interest in science, often with a real-life purpose attached to it, lets the authors explain new ideas without seeming overly didactic. When Danny Dunn asks what a superconductor is in *Danny Dunn and the Swamp Monster*, it is because he has accidentally helped create something that might be one. In *Miss Pickerell Goes to the Arctic*, Miss Pickerell finds out about meteorology in order to understand what the weather will be like on her cow's birthday. The tones of these books remain light, and the explanations simple, but real science is being presented all the same.[14]

Space science for young readers, however, neither attempts nor achieves the accuracy of Earth science. Child characters who travel between planets rarely have a scientific mission, often only accompanying others as companions or as scientific specimens themselves. These child characters do not ask how things work, or—on the rare occasion that they do—they usually do not receive satisfactory scientific answers. When Eddie asks the alien, Marty, about the location of his planet in *The Space Ship Under the Apple Tree*, "The little man pointed in the general direction beyond the moon" (12). Marty later goes on to show Eddie his spaceship, pointing out scientific-sounding (but made up) instruments without giving explanations for any of them (23).[15] Marty's spaceship is fueled by a secret power, an advancement on atomic energy. Marty describes it in a fashion equally as vague as his placement of his planet: "'This wire explodes in a vacuum. Box is vacuum. Secret Power Z makes powerful explosions. Carry through to rockets'" (30). In this case, Marty's limited English works in the author's favor,[16] giving Slobodkin an excuse to avoid such issues as how the vacuum is created (let alone what a vacuum is!) and how the powerful explosions in fact carry through to the rockets. Eddie's immediate equation of the Martinean's secret power with atomic energy gives all the necessary credence to this dubious form of fuel without any real explanation of either. Unlike *Danny Dunn and the Swamp Monster*, where fiction is backed up by clearly defined factual events, space travel—in this and other children's science fiction series—happens magically, fantastically, with only vague references to known scientific concepts. Even these slim connections between fact and fiction, however, legitimate outer space travel by those otherwise barred from space by the military, particularly children and scientists.

Another way in which children's science fiction series authenticate space travel without providing accurate explanation is to focus on the reason for the journey. If scientific (rather than military) inquiry requires investigation on other planets, then the means and mode of traveling across space do not signify. This is the case in Bruce Coville's My Teacher series. Both earthlings and aliens in this series have scientific purposes on other planets. The aliens come to Earth first and act as "some kind of anthropologist from space, studying the whole human race like it was a tribe in the jungle" (*My Teacher Fried My Brains* 115). This causes the Earth children in contact with the aliens to want to see "all the wonderful things he [*sic*] used to imagine when he was reading

those crazy science fiction novels" (*My Teacher Is an Alien* 123) and to "invent
a ship—a ship that would take us right out of the solar system—out to explore
all those distant stars that fill the sky at night" (123). However, the ship never
needs to be invented. Instead, the children become galactic hitchhikers,
accepting space rides from aliens, passive in terms of space travel though active
in their study of the aliens and themselves. This allows Coville to describe the
appearance of the spaceship without explaining its inner workings at all until
the third book of the series; even then, the vagueness of detail can be attributed
to the lack of knowledge on the part of the child narrator. Peter Thompson may
read science fiction voraciously, but he still does not have the words to explain
the alien space travel: he describes it as "a kind of gravity distortion" (*My
Teacher Glows in the Dark* 64), a phrase that at the same time sounds scientific
without really meaning anything concrete.[17] However, the explanation satisfies
because space travel only provides a means to an end—that of studying aliens
and earthlings—and not an end in itself. Passive learning in space science
series takes the place of the hands-on experimentation found in more
earthbound series. Even when child characters are allowed in space, they
cannot do anything useful there.

The implication of all this is serious. Child characters, such as Danny
Dunn, may tinker with inventing and investigating earthly concepts, but space
remains one huge thought-experiment. Like Gedanken in the Uncle Albert
series, children can only investigate space through the mind and imagination of
an adult. In addition, any attempt to allow children a hand in furthering space
travel results in the reader having to swallow a large dose of the fantastic in the
midst of any real science. This places astrophysics out of the reach of most
young readers, as the only ways to become involved are either as helpless
assistant or as a believer in magical means of travel, neither of which propose
realistic futures for readers who wish to follow a similar path.

Perhaps one of the clearest examples of this is in Eleanor Cameron's
Mushroom Planet series. These books give much greater power to the child
characters than other series—Chuck and David actually build and operate their
own spaceship—but either they take away that power in crucial moments (the
spaceship is powered and made heat safe by the scientist Tyco Bass) or the
setting has to be so fantastic as to allow the science to work (the boys discover a
planet near the Earth—avoiding impossible space travel dilemmas—but
Cameron has to render the planet invisible to avoid the question of why no one
discovered it before). Every realistic piece of scientific information in the
Mushroom Planet series seems to bring with it further problems, questions that
can ultimately only be answered with fantastic reasoning or miraculous
coincidence.

David Topman discovers the advertisement for spaceships in the paper one
evening, but his father claims that the street listed does not exist. Indeed,
Thallo Street cannot be located on any map, but nonetheless it is there, and its
existence is not doubted again—everyone from famous scientists to

neighborhood children can find it with ease. In a sense, David Topman brings
Thallo Street and its occupant, Tyco Bass, into existence.[18] David's creations
always become real through the magic of Mr. Bass—from the spaceship he and
his friend Chuck make to the planet just his size to his growing sense of self-
worth.

But the problems of these books also become real through the agency of Mr.
Bass. Even when David has scientific prowess and the ability to understand
and solve difficult problems, he cannot survive without Mr. Bass. Science,
which can be the sole solution for young adults in science fiction, cannot lift
David and Chuck above the ordinary. A perfect example of this is *Mr. Bass's
Planetoid* (1958). Mr. Bass has disappeared, which should make David and
Chuck the sole remaining scientific experts. But in spite of the fact that the
boys have learned to operate and maintain Mr. Bass's astronomical
observatory, know how to send messages into outer space, and direct a local
scientific club, they always must rely on adult authority, whether it be their
parents or other scientists or FBI agents. Chuck and David spend a good
portion of their time and mental energy not inventing or hypothesizing but
using their scientific knowledge to try and gain adult assistance. They try to
contact both Mr. Bass and his brother in outer space. Instead of rescuing a
drowning man themselves, they call the Coast Guard. Science does not
empower them to take initiative or solve problems. It merely provides the basis
for the story to take place. Science does not rule the Mushroom Planet books;
Mr. Bass does; and Mr. Bass has more to do with magic than science.

Mr. Bass may study science, but he does not often use it. The little
mushroom scientist comes back to Earth from outer space, not because the boys
actually contact him, but because he "felt for some mysterious reason" (*Mister
Bass's Planetoid* 192) that he was needed. He always wears the same clothing,
a gray gardening coat that "holds together" in "all contingencies" (191),
defying scientific principles of erosion. He has lived for hundreds of years but
inexplicably always looks the same. Even his scientific inventions, such as the
fluid resinoid silicon used to seal the spaceship from the effects of harmful rays,
have an air of the magical about them—descriptions use such words as
"marvelous" (*The Wonderful Flight of the Mushroom Planet* 52), and the recipe
ingredients have been lost in Mr. Bass's creative process. Mr. Bass's true
occupation is as magician, able to solve problems and save people through his
fantastic abilities. David and Chuck rely ultimately not on scientific means but
the creative imagination of Mr. Bass, and this helps to define and set apart this
and other children's science fiction series from those for older readers.[19]

Young adults in series science fiction have the power to achieve space
missions without the use of the fantastic. Tom Swift's father recognizes Tom's
ability to do more than he himself could; Rick Brant's parents similarly do not
stand in their son's way, believing that he has the capability to act out the
amazing scientific feats he proposes. Lucky Starr has no parents to object to
anything. Meg Murry needs to save her own father from captivity. Will Parker

in Christopher's Tripods trilogy must leave behind his primitive conditions—including his uneducated parents—in order to learn the science necessary to defeat the alien invaders. Teenaged characters can use science and scientific concepts to save not only themselves but their world.[20] Some may not build spaceships, but all have the ability to fly them on their own, without help from the adult world. Science is within the young adult characters' reach, and they make the most of their knowledge in dangerous or complex situations. This provides solid role models for young adult readers who want to follow in these characters' footsteps.

Children, however, must still rely on knowledge they cannot yet achieve or comprehend in order to reach outer space. Whereas Earth science is within the grasp of all, even child characters, these same children must rely on adult help if they want to journey into the unknown of outer space. Young adult characters announce their plans; child characters ask permission. As Mr. Bass says to Chuck and David, "'[Y]ou will tell your parents everything? I would not have you . . . take another step without their permission, not even to save my people" (*Wonderful Flight* 48). Outer space belongs to the adults, and children must petition for the right to be there—and they must never go alone or without the guidance and control of an adult. This is the situation in science fiction series.

In reality, however, outer space not only excludes children but most adults as well. Parents may be powerful and capable within their own small world, the hub of their children's universe, but they have no more right to pilot spaceships than their offspring. Teachers and scientists may possess the necessary technical knowledge to achieve extraterrestrial travel but not the lawful ability. In real life, outer space belongs exclusively to the military. The National Aeronautics and Space Administration (NASA) in America and other military organizations in other countries make the final decisions about who experiences what in outer space. Science fiction series underscore this state of affairs. In young adult science fiction series, most of the characters are connected with the military government in some form, normally as Air Force cadets who can travel through space alone. Children's science fiction series, on the other hand, seem to shy away from both the idea of children being connected to the military and the possibility of more than a temporary independence for child characters. Children have neither knowledge nor power. Their only key to space is imagination, and thus their journeys off this planet require both supervision and the fantastic. Whether these requirements are satisfied in the form of a teacher with a flying school bus or a scientist-magician made of the same material as mushrooms, they break down the barriers of realism and allow the banned to make space science their own.

And yet the question remains: if children cannot achieve outer space without magic, and young adults who can must do everything precisely according to both scientific and military specifications, what does that say about the future of science and science fiction? At the end of the day, we value technical knowledge and firepower over the creative imagination, and this is perhaps the most disappointing lesson to be found in science fiction series for young readers.

NOTES

1. This problem was noted by Francis Molson in a discussion of the Winston Science Fiction series. Although the editors of the series attempted to publish stories that "would be entertaining as well as scientific and educational" (37), he argues that they fell far short of their goals.

2. Wollheim is among many authors who cite specific scientists and engineers as aiding with the technical side of the novel. Others include Joanna Cole, Jay Williams and Raymond Abrashkin, and Carey Rockwell.

3. Brian Aldiss, in *The Detached Retina*, evades the issue by saying, "The only way that science fiction can be justified is if it is good science fiction" (178); most critics, especially children's literature critics, have firmer opinions one way or the other.

4. Edward James denotes the difference between hard and soft science fiction (which is generally now referred to as New Wave) when he writes about "'hard sf,' the main sub-genre which was defining itself in opposition to the New Wave. Traditionalists regarded the latter as having abandoned the sf interest in technology, physics, and space exploration in favour of the soft sciences like psychology and sociology or of pure literary experimentation" (178).

5. As Robert L. Forward points out, "When writing hardcore science fiction, the purpose is to have the science as accurate as possible and matched to the fiction" (1). Note that accuracy in scientific detail comes before any literary considerations.

6. This statement may seem obvious but comes into direct contrast with prevailing thinking about the writing of science fiction. John Griffiths, in *Three Tomorrows*, sweepingly states, "The SF writer is rarely inhibited from using difficult language if the complexity of his [*sic*] subject demands complex expression. He demands of his reader not only the uninhibited use of his imagination but a determined effort to understand precisely what the writer is trying to say" (175–176).

7. Mark Rose sums up the thin line that constitutes science fiction: "On the one hand, by portraying a world that is always in some respect fantastic, science fiction differentiates itself from realism; on the other, by invoking the scientific ethos to assert the possibility of the fictional worlds it describes, science fiction differentiates itself from fantasy. . . . [O]ne might describe science fiction as a form of the fantastic that denies it is fantastic" (20).

8. David Brin suggests that these "'boy engineer' stories in which Aryan-type male heroes—chaste, innocent, and yet wise—come up with a chain of ever more unlikely techno-wizardries to defeat alien bad guys" (8) *were* the original definition of hard science fiction.

9. In *Tom Swift in the Race to the Moon*, for example, it is the corporation of Swift Enterprises that is attempting to put a rocket into space, not the U.S. government; however, their competitors, the Brungarians, are an eastern European country with stereotypical Cold War attributes. Tom Swift and his family are constantly turning Brungarian spies over to the police and even the FBI, proving their loyalty to their own government.

10. Discussing the young adult science fiction of Robert Heinlein, C. W. Sullivan III writes that Heinlein "was attempting to write stories about young protagonists dealing successfully with technological change and with the new products, processes, and events that such change would bring. These successful young protagonists would help the reader develop a positive

attitude toward the future" ("Heinlein's Juveniles" 27). Although it can be argued that Heinlein did a better or more accurate job than some of his series-writing colleagues, Sullivan's comments can nonetheless be extrapolated to many of the young adult science fiction series of the time.

11. H. Bruce Franklin writes that when the U.S. government "began to wrap atomic research in a shroud of secrecy" in the early 1940s, "[t]hus ended the free exchange of knowledge that had symbolized the international community of science, to be replaced by one of the more grotesque features of our times: the attempt to transform vital parts of human knowledge into secrets whose existence is to be classified by the state and kept inviolate by the secret police" ("Eternally Safe for Democracy" 161–162). Science fiction series for young people reflect this "grotesquerie" but in a much more favorable way.

12. Philip John Davies argues, "A genre that gives centre stage to scientific advances is set fair to become entangled with that which President Eisenhower called the 'military-industrial complex.' A fiction that takes as its natural subject exploration and the problems of dealing with different times, places, and beings, is inevitably dealing with the stuff of confrontation" (2).

13. Of course, there are other potential reasons for this "return to Earth" in science fiction. Brian Aldiss posits that actual space science had moved too fast for space science fiction: "The fast-moving forward edge of science had overtaken the ability of most SF writers to speculate. The scientists themselves had usurped much of what had been traditional SF territory" (*Trillion Year Spree* 382). However, this did not stop children's science fiction series from venturing into space; the many series that concerned space, however, could no longer rely on scientific fact to such a degree.

14. Unfortunately, many critics tend to denigrate these series because of their lighthearted tone. Janice Antczak specifically discusses the Danny Dunn and Miss Pickerell series but ultimately dismisses them as insignificant: "While both the series books and the other lighthearted books discussed earlier are still recommended with great frequency, titles which more clearly conform to science fiction convention and spirit have become more important to the reader and the critic" (30).

15. This is not just a tendency of children's science fiction authors. Stanley Schmidt argues that many science fiction authors tend to take "the easier and safer way out . . . to give as little explanation as possible. By judicious and artfully glib vagueness, it is often possible to avoid the kind of close scrutiny which may lead to embarrassment" (32). While Schmidt feels that vagueness is better than providing deliberately wrong information, he prefers books which attempt "a more detailed description of a new variation on one of these ancient themes" and insists that "the result may well be a story of surprising freshness" (33).

16. Slobodkin argues that the Martineans have been able to learn English through the use of road signs and billboards—a technique that would certainly limit an alien's vocabulary but not probably the words that Marty actually uses. For a detailed discussion of the antiscientific nature of communication between species in science fiction, see Walter E. Meyers, *Aliens and Linguists*, particularly chapter 6, "Take Me to Your Leader," and chapter 8, "Plausibility and the Automatic Translator."

17. Coville's novels exemplify Adrian Mellor's assertion "[t]he clearest observation one can make about science fiction and the social sciences is that since the 1960s they have both . . . attempted to abandon science" (22). The My Teacher series still hangs on to vaguely scientific terminology but concentrates on the philosophical argument that deadly creatures should be destroyed to preserve the higher orders; this represents a slap in the face to (hard) environmental scientists who favor natural selection.

18. Eleanor Cameron comments that her own son David brought the book into existence:

"David stood there at the side of my table and told me what he dreamed of: a story about himself and his closest friend, and how they would build a little spaceship and go off and find a planet just their size" (*The Green and Burning Tree* 57). Just as David Cameron brought the book's idea into existence, his mother as author has David Topman bring the story's main character into existence.

19. Robert Scholes contrasts the difference between science and fantasy in a way that highlights the problematic nature of the Mushroom Planet books. He writes, "Science fiction comes by its 'keen edge' honestly, for science as knowledge has been intimately linked from its beginning with splitting, dividing, dissecting in order to know. . . . For centuries, the nonviolent knowing of fantasy has been displaced by the violent knowing of science" ("Boiling Roses" 8–9). Scholes later argues that the two poles can come together as "science fantasy," but the inability of science to provide solutions in nonmilitary children's science fiction series suggests otherwise.

20. Gary K. Wolfe defines this kind of young adult character by suggesting that in science fiction "[r]eason—often the scientific method itself—is usually the hero's weapon in breaching . . . a barrier, and his reward may be the salvation of the universe; he is rewarded for a scientific action as though it were a moral one" (*Known* 15). Children's science fiction series, however, deny child characters weapons of all types, including knowledge.

CHAPTER 7

The City of Gold and the City of Lead: Utopias and Dystopias

> They had been a strange and marvelous people. I had seen the ruins of one of the great-cities in which they had lived . . . with broad avenues that ran for miles, crumbling buildings still soaring up against the sky, huge shops into which all the houses of my native village could have been packed, with room left over. They had moved in ease and splendor about the Earth, splendor beyond measuring, almost beyond understanding. And despite all this, the Tripods had conquered and enslaved them. How had it happened? We did not know.
>
> —Christopher, *The City of Gold and Lead* (2-3)

Utopian and dystopian concepts have been a part of science fiction since its inception.[1] The ideal world may be nonexistent in reality, but heroes and heroines of science fiction novels frequently encounter such societies hidden away on Earth or in remote reaches of the galaxies. Science fiction series for young people do not differ from adult science fiction in this regard; in fact, the series offer an excellent forum for creating, exploring, and expanding upon a utopian or dystopian society.[2]

The links between utopian literature and science fiction have always been close, even entangled. Darko Suvin notes this complicated relationship when he calls utopian fiction a *"sociopolitical subgenre of science fiction"* (*Metamorphoses* 61; italics in original) and science fiction "a niece of utopia" (61) in the same paragraph. Whether science fiction or utopian literature is the encompassing genre, the two types of literature ideally suit one another. Both focus on different worlds: science fiction shows the world as it *might* be, and utopian literature shows the world as it *should* be. Often these worlds come into contact, and utopian science fiction results.[3] And more and more often, authors present a utopian world as diametrically opposed to the world of science fiction; when this occurs, a dystopia reigns.[4] Generally, these authors are gearing their works toward adults who, by virtue of experience, have a broader worldview and thus can theoretically comprehend utopian situations better than children. In spite of this, neither young adult nor children's science fiction series avoid the concept of utopia; however, their means and methods of portrayal and depiction are significantly different than in adult science fiction series.

The novels written for early teenagers frequently showcase the concept of what constitutes an ideal society, particularly since the 1960s. The complacency and self-righteousness of the teenaged hero or heroine at the beginning of the trilogies of John Christopher and Madeleine L'Engle, for example, quickly erode as the protagonists come up against other societies and are forced to face the drawbacks of their own world. These and other novels for young teenagers often highlight a clear set of values; K. V. Bailey states, for example, "Freedom and self-determination are the values informing John Christopher's perhaps most popular creation, the Tripods trilogy" (104). Whether or not these value systems are consistent, both within the individual series and in science fiction series as a whole, will be discussed in this chapter.

Literature for younger children typically does not raise the issue of replacing the status quo completely. This comes from the fact that the status quo—in America, at least—works very well for the child science fiction character. In many ways, childhood is represented by series authors as idyllic, a utopia only broken by the interference of adults.[5] The need for escape from Earth diminishes, and the emphasis on preserving the existing conditions dominates. Children's science fiction series seem to exist to underscore, rather than improve or create, the utopic condition of childhood.

Although utopias present a "perfect" world, at least in the viewpoint of the authors who created them, the premise behind both utopias and dystopias is essentially pessimistic.[6] In the case of utopias, their very creation assumes a presently imperfect world with the goal of allowing some escape from it; dystopias generally posit that our current world is doomed to metamorphosize into the very opposite of utopia. In either instance, the likelihood of never reaching a utopic situation is extremely high. Just as in the Garden of Eden, inborn human imperfection rules humans out of utopia forever.[7] At the same time, it seems, no nonhuman society can ever fashion dystopias as well as humans. Unreasoning animals cannot do anything but meet their own basic needs, and even in science fiction set on other planets, alien societies seem to remain more stable than human ones (even if at times these societies are very threatening to the humans who encounter them!).[8] Science fiction for all ages suggests that no matter what other threats they may face, whether alien or natural disaster, no power is more destructive to humans and their earthly home than humans themselves.

In fact, in many cases, utopias only exist where humans do not. By the end of World War II, with most of even the remotest parts of the globe explored by air, the likelihood of finding either a perfect society or a perfect place to foster one on this planet seemed distant, if not impossible. The occasional lost city might be discovered, as in Stephen Mogridge's *Peter and the Atomic Valley*

(1955) where, as the publisher's blurb comments, "scientists have used atomic power to establish a veritable Garden of Eden" (from the advertisement for the book found in *Peter and the Moon Bomb*). However, even here perfection cannot last, and Peter and his friend Terry must chase out the evil that blooms as quickly as the flowers in this nuclear North Pole nirvana. More and more often, young adult science fiction series authors began to turn away from the possibility of utopia on Earth, turning instead to grounds more fertile with possibility—outer space.[9]

An early example of this outer space utopian quest can be found in W. E. Johns's space exploration series. Although many science fiction series characters already had ventured out into space during the 1950s and 1960s, paralleling and foreshadowing advances in the space race, the main goal of these books usually centered on potentially infinite and always positive exploration and discovery or the successful test of a new rocket ship. In many ways, these characters had no need to search for utopia: home, America, was already perfect, and the only reason to leave it was for the fun of an adventure.[10] However, it must be borne in mind that these series, the Tom Swifts and the Rick Brants and even the Space Cats, were all written by American authors. British science fiction authors, such as Johns, tended to be far more pessimistic than their American counterparts. Long before environmental movements captured public imagination in America, and at a time when young Americans were still being required to "duck and cover" to avoid (as if this were possible) nuclear fallout, Johns was already envisioning a planet on the verge of self-destruction:

"Look at these places today and see what men have done, and are still doing to them. The entrails have been torn out of the soil in a frantic search for minerals and oil. The great rivers have been dammed to form huge inland seas. Mountains have been levelled and landscapes altered beyond recognition. Noble forests have been laid flat leaving hideous deserts in their place. Here at home the once sparkling rivers have become drains to carry sewage to the sea—itself becoming foul with the radioactive effluents from atomic reactors. Remote islands have been blasted off the map—but why go on?" (*The Quest for the Perfect Planet* 16)

This damning vision of Earth's condition, written by Johns in 1961, led him to send his characters on the book's title quest. The goal, to find a new home planet on which humans can build societies more carefully the second time around, remains unmet.[11] The professor in charge of the expedition rules out inhabited planets, for fear of war with the natives (*Quest* 17), and throughout the course of this book and the next, *Worlds of Wonder* (1962), the space exploration team discover no uninhabited worlds without problems too great to surmount.

Despite his early doom and gloom predictions about the Earth, however, Johns ultimately cannot produce anything better. His main character, the professor, suddenly abandons hope of finding a new human paradise in the last book of the series. Actually chuckling as he speaks, the professor comments, "'Ah, well, life on Earth could be worse. We have seen some remarkable worlds in our travels, good, bad and indifferent, but I still have to find one that I'd care to exchange for our own'" (*Worlds of Wonder* 159–60). This speech embodies the tension that exists between Johns's own ideas of reality and the future, expressed earlier, and his apparent desire to keep his science fiction hopeful for the benefit of young readers. Johns's series ends with the deepest kind of pessimism of all—false optimism.

As the 1960s progressed, however, even this scrap of levity and promise disappeared in British young adult science fiction series, particularly in the novels of John Christopher. Christopher's novels erased all hope of achieving utopia for the total population and made even the utopias that existed for a few ambiguous at best. For Christopher, the tension between the rights of the individual and the rights of the community precludes a workable utopia,[12] as his Tripods trilogy suggests. He begins the trilogy, *The White Mountains*, with a picture of a rural community where everyone has a place and no one has to go hungry or cold. All needs are met, but at a price: the loss of individual freedom and choice. Most people accept this exchange willingly, and their lives proceed without pain and suffering—but also without joy. However, some rebel against this state of affairs and decide that a civilization of free thinkers, despite its complications, has more value than the bliss of ignorance. To accept the rule of the alien Tripods meant to accept a fate that the trilogy's hero, Will Parker, calls "something beside which suicide was clean and good" (*The White Mountains* 149). Utopia, for Christopher, is worse than death. Christopher's placement of independence over the collective good indicates the high value he places on freedom of thought and action.

In spite of this attitude toward freedom, however, Christopher does not go so far as to posit that the opposite of the alien's idea of utopia, Christopher's preferred community of free-thinking individuals, will produce a human version of the perfect society. The first vision Will Parker has of utopia is in the great-cities, which despite their (to his eyes) perfection, end in destruction. And Christopher's vision of civilization after the fall of the Tripods is equally bleak and uncertain. Unlike Johns, Christopher sees no need to end the trilogy on any kind of positive note. Instead, his human characters defeat the Tripod invaders, only to face the breakdown of their own fragile global coalition into petty bickering. This inability to work together bars humans forever from utopia, as Christopher explains in the last book of the trilogy, *The Pool of Fire*: "The promise of all this was inestimable. But the glorious future which man could and should enjoy depended also on the way in which he governed himself, for man was the measure of all things" (210). His pessimism about the likelihood of good government pervades the last page, when one of the boys suggests to Will that the fight to "try to get men to live together, in peace as well as liberty" (218), will result in "no great triumphs at the end" (218) and may even return them to the apocalyptic vision Will describes in visiting the great-city.[13] Like the heroes of W. E. Johns's space exploration series, the characters in Christopher's books resolve to make the best of a bad situation on Earth; but John Christopher erases even the appearance of optimism that Johns had offered less than ten years earlier.

Both these series suggest that science itself is one of the factors that keeps humans out of utopia. While American science fiction still generally exalted the positive force of scientific achievement, British science fiction series of the same period expressed doubts about the good of science. Science and scientific achievements had, after all, led to the pollution, overcrowding, and atomic dangers that caused Johns's crew to look for a perfect planet and Christopher's world to be easy prey for aliens. Paradoxically, the knowledge necessary to create the conditions of a utopia is precisely that which keeps utopias forever in the imagination only. Post-1945 Britain, perhaps spurred on by witnessing the horrific scientific experiments of the Nazis and the death and destruction caused by the American use of the atomic bomb in Hiroshima and Nagasaki, now had proof of the suggestions made by earlier novelists such as Mary Shelley and Robert Louis Stevenson: science has no inherent moral value. Progress does not always have positive results, and as long as humans have control, both good and bad may come of scientific experimentation.

On the other hand, science fiction series for young adults in America still placed the misuse of science outside human (and, more precisely, outside *American*) hands. In Madeleine L'Engle's *A Wrinkle in Time* (1962), Meg, Calvin, and Charles Wallace arrive at the planet Camazotz, where everyone acts in regulation form. This produces a society that, according to one of its young citizens, "'has the best Central Intelligence Center on the planet. Our production levels are the highest. Our factories never close; our machines never stop rolling. Added to this we have five poets, three artists, and six sculptors, all perfectly channeled" (108). Despite this seeming good order, however, Camazotz is no utopia. People who deviate from the norm receive severe punishment, and even before Meg realizes this she balks at the unity of Camazotz society, saying, "'I know our world isn't perfect, Charles, but it's better than this. This isn't the only alternative! It can't be!'" (*Wrinkle* 142). When her brother points out that nobody suffers or is unhappy on the planet, Meg counters that "nobody's ever happy, either. . . . [I]f you aren't unhappy sometimes you don't know how to be happy'" (142). Suffering for some is better than lack of feeling for all, in L'Engle's book—although, notably, Meg and her family do not experience much of the world's suffering.

L'Engle's concept of utopia as a place where everyone does what they are told is far from original. Long before L'Engle or her contemporary John Christopher created trilogies that included this idea, H. G. Wells envisioned a similar world in *The Time Machine* (1895). But unlike the British authors, L'Engle sources her evil, not in humans or even humanlike aliens; instead, utopia is conceived in the mind of a gigantic brain called It.[14] This brain, though vastly intelligent, cannot feel compassion because it has no heart. For It, the brain-ruler of Camazotz, the world of perfect order *is* utopic. It is precisely a world without feelings that has the capability to combine order with lack of passion; humans can only be allowed freedom when they do not care enough to make use of it. For L'Engle, only a nonhuman creature would ever desire such a world, and only a human from Earth—an Earth she describes as half in the shadow of evil, half in the light of goodness—can both perceive the wickedness of such a desire and have the strength to fight it as well. Meg saves her father and Charles Wallace from It, but the text does not indicate how her actions have affected the Camazotz citizens, if at all. Potentially, they remain in the darkness of a choiceless utopia, while Meg and her family return to a world made better by the fact that evil has a place in it as well as good.

The determination to make Earth work, despite its problems, and to ignore despotic utopias, is typical of American science fiction series.[15] No matter where Tom Swift or Rick Brant or Mike Mars travels, he always wants to return home. Home—more specifically America—nurtures and rescues them from despair. In John Blaine's *The Lost City*, Rick Brant and his party are saved from death by a symbol both of America and freedom: Independence Day fireworks. Most of the Tom Swifts, regardless of series, end with Tom reunited with home and/ or family, typically smiling and saying—as he does in *Tom Swift and His Outpost in Space*— "'—you can quote me on this—it's good to be back on the planet Earth!'" (210). In fact, American science fiction series for children and young adults rarely portray utopias or anti-utopias at all. American authors, even after the horrors of World War II, simply seem to have no need to find better societies. Farther removed than the British from the results of the war, locked for many years in the one-upmanship of the American-Soviet Cold War, blessed by economic prosperity, Americans still believed in their self-created and utopian American dream. Nowhere is this more clear than in the science fiction written for younger children after 1945.

While young adult series could admit the problems of society without denying the benefits, children's science fiction series in America do not even attempt a balanced view. America for these authors is a utopian society, a vision that goes hand-in-hand with the deep-rooted belief in the idyllic quality of American childhood.[16] Whereas British and American adult and young adult characters in science fiction have to face persistent danger and dread, deciding only whether to ignore or resign themselves to their flawed home, American child characters rarely leave home at all. When they have the choice to leave, they return from adventure as soon after as possible. America is both safe haven and scientific playground, where few problems exist and curiosity, not danger, is the motivation for scientific investigation. Miss Pickerell, for example, leaves Earth only twice in thirteen books, and Danny Dunn explores outer space just once in a series of fifteen books. These characters, and other child and childlike characters in science fiction series, instead focus on exploring the multiple wonders of science on Earth.

Both Danny Dunn and Miss Pickerell do their space investigating early on in their series, but in Danny Dunn's case, his failure to return to space strikes the series reader as especially odd. This is because Jay Williams and Raymond Abrashkin put their young hero up into space in the very first book of the series—*Danny Dunn and the Anti-Gravity Paint* (1956)—but never return him there.   The opening of *Danny Dunn and the Anti-Gravity Paint* seems to announce the start of a space series.   The first paragraph has Danny daydreaming in school of extraterrestrial adventure: "Space Captain Daniel Dunn stood on the bridge of the *Revenge* with his eyes on the viewer screens. He could see the fiery trails that were the rocket ships from Jupiter" (9). Naturally, although his teacher tells him that "'trips to Mars are far in the future" (11), Danny ends up visiting several planets in the solar system with his mentor, Professor Bullfinch, and best friend Joe Pearson by the end of the book. In fact, the trip makes Danny decide, "I'm going to college . . . I'm going to be a scientist" (149).   With such a beginning, it seems likely that any future books in the series will involve more adventures with Space Captain Daniel Dunn.   And yet, although he travels to several other exotic places, including a desert island, the bottom of the ocean, and a fossil cave, he never again leaves Earth or even mentions space travel as a goal.   In fact, most of the later books in the series take Danny and his friends no further than the local baseball field or a nearby factory.   Danny and Joe are just two of the many child characters in science fiction series who live in an insulated world that only rarely needs change,[17] and for this reason, Earth suffices as a setting for these series.

The Earth setting depicted in these series has very specific characteristics that keep it utopic for its child characters.   Like many of the scientific aspects of the books, the setting is fictional, and thus the author can ignore potential problem areas.   American science fiction series for children present child readers with early exposure to many American myths, such as the romanticized perfection of the child, the idyll of the countryside, and the ever positive view of progress.   Home and safety, which have a higher value in the children's series than in the young adult series, make the need for freedom—a concept that defines many young adult series—less urgent and utopia more of a possibility.[18] Although freedom of thought and action is assumed as a given in these series, it is never actually put into practice, and thus child characters in series science fiction can have the best of all possible worlds.

The key to child utopia is potential.   Viewing the child as optimally innocent and perfect, as authors of many children's science fiction series do, establishes the thinking that also suggests that both the countryside and progress should be favored.   The countryside has the unspoiled nature of the child, and both have virtually unlimited potential to progress into a better form of existence.   Cities and adults are decadent, ruined by their own selves, no longer capable of utopia.   To preserve some form of utopia, therefore, adult authors keep conditions as perfect as possible for their child characters—even if the perfection is illusory.

The best place to preserve the illusion of perfection is in the countryside, which itself was becoming more and more illusory for an increasingly urbanized society.[19]   The myth of rural bliss pervades children's science fiction series; the further away from the city that a character is, the more likely he or she is to have adventures rather than problems.   Louis Slobodkin writes about his character Eddie Blow in New York City as well as in the countryside on Eddie's grandmother's farm—but notably, the major scenes in the Space Ship series occur in the perfect world of the farm. Although Eddie normally lives in New York City in an apartment described as being "rather crowded" (*The Spaceship Under the Apple Tree* 5) with animals that he keeps in cages, he prefers life at his grandmother's because there he "was able to see the birds, animals and insects living in their natural habitat" (6). His grandmother seems to exist to make Eddie happy in this rural environment; she does nothing but clean and cook for Eddie, making sure that all his needs are met. She does this in a utopic manner for a young boy, as her cooking involves sweet things such as "corn fritters, dripping with maple syrup, and apple pie, topped with whipped cream" (34) for lunch—never vegetables or anything distasteful. The farm is the idyllic world in which a child character can explore nature of both a terrestrial and an extraterrestrial kind. The alien, Marty, who lands on the farm in his spaceship, does not threaten the peace but becomes a part of it. Marty learns about a specifically rural American way of life consisting of grandmother's cooking and Boy Scout jamborees and allows himself to be studied just as if he were another one of Eddie's birds, animals, or insects. Life for a child in the American countryside is an adventure, not a problem—a utopia, even when invaded by creatures from outer space.

Children who are initially hostile to rural settings come to believe in their positive power as strongly as Eddie does. Karen, the main human character in Pamela Service's Stinker books, initially does not care for her new home located "way out in the sticks" (*Stinker from Space* 7). By the end of the book, however, she has changed her mind, as being in the country allows her to fulfill her dream of learning about outer space; the alien Tsynq Yr finds it easier to crash-land his spaceship in the country than the city. Because of the spatial freedom that the countryside allows, mistakes have fewer consequences; they can be cleaned up before anyone else might notice. Karen is able to isolate herself within a community of like-minded individuals by virtue of the lack of population. When everyone agrees, utopia can and does exist, and the only task of the child characters in the books is to keep the few people who represent the outside world from destroying it.

As the settings of children's science fiction series become more urbanized, however, both freedom and safety begin to disappear. Miss Pickerell, for example, faces little danger on her own farm, but outside of it she must face a deteriorating society made worse by technology. Animals—nature's creatures—feel the effects of technology first, and Miss Pickerell has to go to the moon to find antibiotics for the diseased animals of Square Toe City (*Miss Pickerell on the Moon*) and spends a summer vacation helping save waterbirds from an oil tanker spill (*Miss Pickerell and the Supertanker*). Although she can recognize the danger faced by nature, she herself remains spry and hardworking in all situations. The unwritten message, that her rural life has kept her healthy, has echoes in many other series, as both alien and terrestrial thrive and live in harmony in the countryside.

The suburbs in children's science fiction series represent a step away from this edenic vision of life found on the American farm. Suburban children have less freedom than their rural counterparts and are not as safe from the dangers of technology. For this reason, Danny Dunn does not return to outer space; whereas Miss Pickerell must make the world safe for animal inhabitants, Danny and his friends must make their own world safe for humans—including themselves. While early adventures in the series, such as *Danny Dunn and the Homework Machine* (1958), remain almost as trouble-free as more rural series, later books begin to show the effects of crime and technology brought on by living in an increasingly urbanized society. *Danny Dunn, Scientific Detective* (1975), for example, involves Danny, Joe, and Irene solving a crime: an adult commits robbery at the largest department store in town despite a newly installed uncrackable safe. The department store had no need for such a device when it opened in 1901, but now that the town is more crowded the potential for crime rises. Danny and his friends remain as yet mythically innocent and thus are the ones who can solve the crime. Similarly, in *Danny Dunn and the Universal Glue* (1979), Danny and his friends can do what the adults of the town do not have the power to do: recognize and eliminate the danger of illegal waste-dumping in a local river. Children, as representatives of utopian innocence, are the only ones in children's science fiction series who can preserve even the smallest part of a perfect world.

Even though dangers increase in the move from countryside to suburbs, however, the danger still comes from outside sources. Factory owners may have a disregard for the environment, but Danny can always count on the adults he knows and trusts. Home remains a safe zone, taking the place of the countryside in rurally set science fiction series. A haven for the child characters, home is the place to which they can always return if any real danger threatens. And although child characters remain ultimately unharmed by the dangers of the outside world, they must recognize that these dangers do in fact exist—a fact that can often be comfortably ignored in the isolation of the rural setting.

Urban settings for children's science fiction series are few and far between. Some series, like the A.I. Gang or the Cyberkids may have characters who live in cities, but the actual action of the story takes place elsewhere: in the case of the A.I. Gang, the children's parents move to an island in order to conduct government research; the action in the Cyberkids series takes place not in the hometowns of the child characters but on the Internet. Cyberspace, like the countryside, gives authors relative freedom to create a situation in which the normal rules do not matter, and physical danger is at a minimum. In an urbanized world that has increasingly less and less connection to the rural world, the emptiness of the Internet substitutes for the rural space that many children have never seen.

Even child characters who have no choice but to act and interact within their largely urban setting have their refuges. In K. A. Appleton's Animorphs series, the child heroes live in a more urbanized suburb than a character such as

Danny Dunn, for example.   They do not have the freedom of large, open baseball fields and parks; instead, they are found in the opening scene of the first book walking through a construction site, a dangerous place they have been forbidden by their parents to go.   Danger is all around the Animorphs. Although much of it comes from the outside, in the form of alien invaders, these child characters cannot count on their home to save them.   The main character's brother as well as the school principal are allied with the alien forces.   Many places besides the construction site become dangerous as well, including the local shopping mall and the zoo.   In fact, the only place where the Animorphs are safe, the only place where they can communicate freely and never face physical danger, ironically rejects the urban setting all around them. The five children can escape all danger by meeting at Cassie's barn, which serves as a wildlife rehabilitation center.

In the same place where sick animals can get well again, the Animorphs can discuss strategy for healing and saving their own world.   Their one alien friend, an Andalite, can exist there in his natural form; as Cassie says, "Ax was safe in the far fields of our farm, away from curious eyes" (*The Message* 149). But the child characters feel safe on the farm as well; whenever they have new developments to share, they automatically congregate at Cassie's if at all possible.   In the city, they follow a rule that, "We can never start looking like a 'group.'   In school or in public places, we keep our distance" (*The Android* 29). At Cassie's farm, however, they can meet in the barn or the surrounding forest, a place we meet . . . deep enough in the trees that no one is likely to see us" (*The Android* 46).   Natural settings are the only secure places for child characters, whether they be Eddie Blow's grandmother's farm or Cassie's wildlife rehabilitation center.

Unfortunately, the utopia of freedom and safety that nature provides can only exist temporarily.   The Animorphs must return to the city to fight, and although they keep their link to nature by being able to change into many different animals, they must become human again after two hours.[20]   Nature frees them only partially.   Similarly, Eddie Blows adventures can only happen in the summertime; in the fall he must return to the real world of school and New York City, where aliens no longer have a place to land in the backyard. Miss Pickerell finds she can only ignore the outside world to a certain extent. Even when utopias exist, as they often do in children's series, they are only temporary resting places, a brief respite in the countryside away from the dangers of the city. They cannot last.

Perhaps the perfect balance of freedom and safety found in the countryside can only be temporary because childhood itself is a temporary condition.   Few science fiction series authors would argue the myth of childhood as a perfect time, but no author can create eternal children.   The longer that the setting can be kept utopic, the more extended childhood can be, but this means that less action can occur.   The dangers of the outside world, whether they be aliens or illegal waste disposal or disease, must be faced, and the series child breaks out of utopia in order to help others.

But utopia provides a certain strength that child characters can carry with them. This strength, again, lies in potential. If the world has once been utopia, even if only for them as individuals, then it can be again, perhaps for more people. The child, even while breaking away, constantly looks back to that utopic moment in order to have the strength to create a better future.[21] At the conclusion of the second book in Virginia Hamilton's Justice cycle, the end of childhood is apparent. Justice "appeared unaccountably taller. . . . She could not quite return to the carefree, energetic young person she had been only a month or two ago" (*Dustland* 194). The simplicity and freedom are gone—but not forgotten. Without the knowledge that utopia once existed, there is no possibility to regain it. Justice finds that she can make use of moments—only temporary but real—to return to that time: "[T]here were moments when she acted just like a kid: walked and talked like a kid. These came when for hours she forgot about the future" (194). Utopia, then, is found only in the past. The perfect planet in science fiction series for young people can only be found, quite literally, on and in the Earth. Perfecting and idealizing our memories, creating the myth of the countryside and the myth of childhood, are exactly the alchemy needed to turn our cities of lead into shining cities of gold.

NOTES

1. The term "utopia," of course, comes from Thomas More's novel by that name. Darko Suvin, in *Metamorphoses of Science Fiction*, deftly connects More's novel with both a privileging of the natural state (91) and the beginnings of science fiction (109–110).

2. Defining utopian literature is not a simple task, as Dingbo Wu suggests in "Understanding Utopian Literature." However, for the purpose of this chapter, we define "utopian literature" as that which seeks to represent a perfect world.

3. Some critics, such as Eric Rabkin, argue that only books that focus on "extrapolating, rather than reversing, the perspective on technology" (*The Fantastic* 140) can be counted as *science fiction* utopias; this notion works well with adult and some young adult science fiction but comes into question in children's science fiction series, as we shall see.

4. For a good discussion of utopias and dystopias in science fiction, see Raymond Williams's "Utopia and Science Fiction" in *Science Fiction: A Critical Guide*, edited by Patrick Parrinder.

5. Antony Easthope's argument that a utopian vision is created when someone "in the present *needs* to imagine this better future" (56; italics in original) explains why child characters in science fiction series do not recognize their world as utopic; Easthope correctly places the desire for utopia with adult authors and not child characters.

6. Susan Bassnett suggests this when she writes that "the two alternatives proposed to utopian writers [are] . . . to expose the brutality of the present world or to write escapist, consolatory fiction about an alternative" (61).

7. Or as Patrick G. Hogan, Jr. puts it, "[I]t appears that the judgement of one or another so-called utopia, no matter how influential in the history of ideas, is one of failure because of impracticability, not of failure because of lack of philosophical soundness" (268). Humans, it seems, have a need to attempt utopia even if they fall short of it.

8. Robert Sandels notes this tendency to make alien societies more perfect than our own

when he writes, in "UFOs, Science Fiction and the Postwar Utopia," that many Americans felt that the era following World War II would bring about societies in which we would "live much like those aliens from space encountered so often in science fiction whose technology and good sense have banished all that was unpleasant (141). While the introduction of the atomic bomb ended this vision for many adults, children's science fiction series continued to portray the possibility of perfection.

9. Millicent Lenz discusses this lost society approach to science fiction as "[a]nother popular pseudomyth . . . the idea that people can survive by means of 'relocation' (sometimes by flight to another planet, a contemporary version of the Biblical motif of the flight into the wilderness); and the myth of a new Adam and Eve who survive to rebuild civilization" (125).

10. Thomas Clareson reflects this in his book, *Many Futures, Many Worlds*, when he writes that "however much the dystopian, cautionary warnings of countless science fiction writers attract us and reflect our contemporary mood, the majority of science fiction—from before Wells until at least the last years of the 1940s—*was* optimistic. Rather than cringing before a meaningless universe from which the ancient verities had been ripped, SF writers celebrated the imminence of an 'Earthly Paradise' which would see the perfection of man and his society and, then, his ascent to the stars themselves (15–16). The insulated American youth character stretched the optimism out until much later, although finally collapsing into endless dystopian visions by the end of the 1960s.

11. Chris Morgan, in *The Shape of Futures Past*, suggests, "The problems of post-1945 industrialization and population growth have led to a disillusionment with the future" (195) even if the nuclear threat is ignored. The British, whose last vestiges of empire were crumbling, seemed to accept this view long before the Americans did.

12. John Griffiths suggests in *Three Tomorrows* that the "revulsion at the individual sublimation demanded by the membership of the psychically and physically interdependent" is a particularly American trait (162), but John Christopher's work disproves this notion.

13. In many ways, Christopher's novels counter the notion of utopia and dystopia suggested by Patricia Warrick when she writes, "[E]xtrapolative fiction—dystopian in temper—often is set on Earth in the near future in an urban environment. A totalitarian political system run by technocrats is usually present. Efficiency and control are the prevailing values; individuality, privacy, and creative expression have been lost. This fiction generally demonstrates more of a conservative than a futuristic orientation; it longs for a return to the simple, natural world of the past" ("Images of the Man-Machine" 219). Christopher agrees with her description of dystopia but at the same time demonstrates that there is no world to return to, and no world to look forward to either.

14. Patricia Warrick connects L'Engle's enemy with the advent of the computer age, she writes, "A rash of stories about disembodied huge brains containing all known knowledge followed closely after early computer data bank developments" ("Images of the Man-Machine" 220).

15. Susan Bassnett argues in "Remaking the Old World" that the concept of utopia increasingly became a negative one: "Through the 1970s and into the 1980s . . . notions of a caring society were increasingly dismissed as utopian and costly" (59).

16. While the origin of the romantic concept of the child is disputed—some place it with Locke (see Bottigheimer 44–46) and others with Rousseau or the romantic poets—Philippe Ariès claims "The association of childhood with primitivism . . . characterizes our contemporary concept of childhood" (119).

17. Peter Hollindale argues, "The author must construct childhood from an amalgam of

personal retrospect, acquaintance with contemporary children, and an acquired set of beliefs as to what children are, and should be, like" (12); science fiction series tend to rely heavily on the second half of Hollindale's definition.

18. Indeed, many children's science fiction series make Earth a utopia for children, but this view often blithely ignores those who have to sacrifice to make it utopic. Sarah Lefanu posits that "the oppression of women is inextricably related to their work as child-rearers as well as child bearers" (57); perhaps this explains why young adult women are so conspicuously absent from utopic visions in series science fiction.

19. For more on the deeply rooted connections of pastoral perfection and America, see Leo Marx's *The Machine in the Garden*.

20. This notion confirms Mark Rose's concept of utopia, which, as he puts it, "[is an attempt] to portray societies that are, according to the author's lights, more fully human than his own" (33); Applegate makes the impossible possible by combining the flawed human state with the innocence of nature.

21. Child characters in science fiction series have the ability to save the future because of this viewpoint; they are given vision that adults do not have. Thus, Robert Scholes's idea that "where there is no vision, the people perish" (*Structural Fabulation* 75) gives the child character all access to heroism.

CHAPTER 8

We Must Learn to Get Along: Aliens and Others

> In a few minutes the gully was cleared. The moonlight revealed a metal something that looked very much like an immense overturned metal dish. It was about fifteen feet in diameter. There were strange gadgets on its metal surface and along the outer rim, regularly placed, were a small number of tubes.
>
> "A flying saucer!" exclaimed Eddie. "Say, that looks like. . . . No, it can't be, it's impossible! There are no such things as flying saucers!"
>
> —Slobodkin, *The Space Ship Under the Apple Tree* (13)

Aliens in science fiction series for juveniles and children may be portrayed as physically similar to humans, as in the Mushroom Planet series, or as physically repulsive, as in the Tripod series or the Animorphs series. Whichever form the aliens take, they usually share such human characteristics as curiosity, intelligence, courage, and humor, as well as hate, deception, revenge, and greed. This helps provide the necessary frames of reference for the reader, especially the child reader, to be able to identify with and imagine the alien characters. The use of alien societies provides a good vehicle for displaying both human potential and limitations, as well as discussing tolerance. Since learning tolerance has become part of the socialization process for children, this may explain why there are so many series for them that focus on aliens and alien encounters. Since making the transition from child to adult is the business of the adolescent, there are fewer series where the alien or alien society is the focus, but those that do exist allow the reader to explore the meaning of free will. An overt or underlying message for both children and adolescents in series that focus on aliens is that colonialism is wrong. The series format provides authors with a wider canvas than the monograph on which to develop characters, particularly aliens and their societies, and to reinforce the need to get along with and have respect for others, whomever or whatever the *other* might be.

When *The Space Ship Under the Apple Tree* was published in 1952, there were few children's books available with characters representing the nonwhite population in the United States. If these characters existed at all in children's books, they usually played a minor role and were stereotypes and caricatures. This is documented in the well-known and often-cited article by Nancy Larrick that appeared in the *Saturday Review* in 1965. In the article she contends, "Across the country, 6,340,000 nonwhite children are learning to read and to understand the American way of life in books which either omit them entirely or scarcely mention them" (63). Larrick's study showed, "Of the 5,206 children's trade books launched by the sixty-three publishers in the three-year period [1962–1964], only 349 include one or more Negroes—an average of 6.7 per cent" (64). She questioned publishers about this and received various explanations for the exclusion of blacks from American children's books. Some felt pressure from parents who did not like any suggestion of integration, a few seemed to be generally surprised at the exclusion, and others suggested they would publish more if "publishable books that included Negroes in a natural and sympathetic manner" were available (84–85). Whatever the reason, most books available to children depicted a "white" society with few *others* included. Since Larrick's study, which only considered the representation of African Americans, there has been some improvement, but African Americans, Hispanic, Asian Americans, and Native Americans continue to be underrepresented.[1]

On the surface, science fiction series for children seem to follow this trend because there are no series prior to 1976 with nonwhite characters.[2] The first series to come along with an important black character was the Star Ka'at series in 1976. *Star Ka'at*, the first book in the series, brings together Jim, a young white boy who lives with a foster family because his parents died in a plane crash, and Elly Mae, a young black girl who lives with her ailing grandmother until her death.[3] Both are adopted by two catlike aliens, Tiro and Mer, who are on Earth to gather together any kin left from an earlier visitation because Earth seems to be headed toward destruction. When Elly Mae's grandmother dies, and Jim's foster mother is about to take him away to the country while his foster father is away at war, they stumble upon, or are led by Mer, to the spaceship, which is about to leave Earth for the Star Ka'at planet. Both Elly Mae and Jim are taken aboard and leave with the Star Ka'ats. While Elly Mae is a major character of the book, she is not the protagonist of the story; Jim is. We follow the events from his point of view. Elly Mae's character is strong, intelligent, and courageous, and she is an important part of the action. Her status in the series is more than that of sidekick. She is not there to make Jim look more intelligent by asking all of the questions nor to make him look courageous by needing to be rescued. Instead, she is the one who usually has the answers to Jim's questions and cautions Jim about danger. In fact, there are times he feels frustrated by her abilities: "Jim felt cross. Elly Mae always had an answer, and usually the right one, while sometimes he could not even make a guess" (Norton and Madlee, *Star Ka'at World* 26). Perhaps Jim is the main character because most science fiction has been written with male protagonists for male readers.[4]

Below the surface, children's science fiction series with alien characters have always been about getting along with others. Authors of science fiction series found a way to introduce tolerance by utilizing alien characters, though not trying to represent any particular ethnic group. The various *Star Trek* series presents the reader with strong arguments for tolerance by developing stories that center on what might happen between various alien beings and humans. *Worf's First Adventure* is the first entry in the *Star Trek: The Next Generation: Starfleet Academy* series. Worf leaves his adopted parents for Starfleet Academy to become a cadet and the Academy's first Klingon cadet. There he faces mistrust and fear from many of his fellow cadets and strong prejudice from Zak Kebron, whose people, the Brikar, "have a historical dislike for Klingons, stemming from rather intense border battles that ensued between the races before the time of the great alliance" (David 26). Zak taunts Worf as soon as he steps off of the shuttle at the Academy, and a fight ensues. The fight is stopped and both are sent to the Commander's office. The Commander gives them a piece of advice that proves prophetic for both:

"[S]pace is a very unforgiving environment. It's cold. It's airless. It is not charitable, and it does not make allowances for such things as bigotry and hostility. The vacuum of space doesn't care about your skin color, or your politics, or the strength in your arms, or the brains in your heads. You've got only two things going for you that can prevent a very swift, and very painful, death. The first is the integrity of your ship's hull. And the second is each other." (David 28)

Later, during what is supposed to be a routine exercise on a satellite, the mettle of each cadet is tested. Worf ends up saving Zak's life. It turns out that it is only a simulation, but the cadets were not aware of this until the exercise ends. This experience changes Zak and Worf's relationship. While Zak is the antagonist for much of the book, he is not a villain. Worf is the first Klingon Zak has met in his life, and while growing up he heard many horror stories about the Klingons. He had expectations of Worf's behavior that did not prove true. Most of the aliens in the various *Star Trek* series are not evil. Usually when problems occur, it is because there is a miscommunication or misunderstanding of some kind, but once things are sorted out, agreements and friendships are established. Geordi La Forge gives voice to the overwhelming message of the *Star Trek* books: "'The whole key to being a good Starfleet officer . . . is not to be afraid of the unknown, but instead to embrace it. To be drawn to it, to study it. To be excited by it and want to share in its wonders'" (David 86). Worf is the unknown to many of his fellow cadets, just as people from various ethnic groups might be in certain communities.

Long before the various *Star Trek* series appeared to discuss friendships between aliens, *The Space Ship Under the Apple Tree* appeared. In some ways it is a simple tale about friendship between a human boy and an alien boy, both of whom are examples of the *other*. Eddie, who lives in the city with his mother, stays with his grandmother in the country each summer. There is mention of his friends back in the city but no mention of any friends in the country. Since he had been there before, and for the whole summer, it seems logical that he would have made at least one friend, but perhaps Eddie is too much of an outsider, too much the *other*. Perhaps Eddie feels some kinship with the alien, because both are away from home in completely different settings. Soon after the alien arrives Eddie suggests they be friends, but since the alien cannot or will not translate the word, Eddie gives up on the idea but continues to help the alien and to be friendly. There are moments when Eddie feels threatened by the alien, but that is only when the alien feels threatened by Eddie, which is due to communication problems. By the end, the alien has learned something about the meaning of friendship because as he is about to leave he tells Eddie, "'Good-bye . . . Friend'" (116).

If the various *Star Trek* series and the Space Ship series are about the benefits of getting along, the My Teacher series explores the ramifications of humans not learning to get along among themselves. The Interplanetary Council assigns two aliens, Kreeblim and Broxholm, to help Peter, Duncan, and Susan, three sixth graders, defend Earth against total annihilation. The Council fears for the galaxy because science and technology on Earth are advancing to the point that humans will soon be traveling out among the planets. Kreeblim explains: "'You earthlings are such an unstable group,' said Kreeblim wistfully. 'Full of promise and poison in equal measure'" (Coville, *My Teacher Fried My Brains* 133). The three children and two aliens visit various places on Earth as part of a fact-finding mission where war, hunger, and violence are prevalent. Peter's descriptions of what they observe expose the reader to some graphic scenes of what happens when humans do not get along. In Asia, they view a war battle and Peter reports the following:

I saw a man crawling across the line of fire. Then I spotted his goal. He was trying to rescue a boy, not much older than me, who had been wounded and couldn't get away from the fighting. It was terrible to watch. I felt my muscles begin to tense, as if somehow I could lend the man strength. Nearer he crept, and nearer. Then, when he was less than a yard from the boy, a bomb landed. Mud erupted into the air. Man and boy were gone. (Coville, *My Teacher Flunked the Planet* 50)

Upon returning from the fact-finding mission, each felt pessimistic about the possibility of convincing the Council that Earth should not be destroyed or quarantined. Kreeblim notes, "'The best of what your people create shows a deep longing to join together. Yet the worst of what you do seems to come from some great separation, as if you don't even recognize yourselves as members of the same species'" (72). Peter is able to convince the Council that due to one of the intrusive efforts of one of its members, great damage was done to humans. Therefore, they owe humans the opportunity, with help from the

Council, to become better. Peter requests they send teachers, "'because teachers and children can change the world'" (159).

Most of the aliens in science fiction series for children are portrayed as benevolent beings. If they appear threatening it is usually because they are taking the defensive to protect themselves in some way. Some of the aliens in the My Teacher series do not believe humans are capable of being any different than they are. They make many assumptions about the human race in general, but once they meet individuals, it becomes much harder to condemn every human. As one of the aliens tells Peter, "'She's [one of the other aliens] just annoyed because she wants to believe you people don't have well developed emotions. . . . Because then she won't feel so bad if we have to blow up your planet'" (Coville, *My Teacher Glows in the Dark* 54).

Aliens have not been portrayed as truly evil in science fiction series for children until just recently in series such as Animorphs. The aliens in this series seem to be there for a purpose different than instilling tolerance. In the Animorphs series, the protagonists themselves are an example of tolerance. The five child protagonists represent different ethnic and social groups. Jake and Rachel are cousins and white, Cassie is African American, Marco is Hispanic, and Tobias is white but from a lower socioeconomic group. Jake and Cassie are more than just friends. According to Marco, "I think she's kind of Jake's girlfriend now. Of course, no one is supposed to know this" (Applegate, *The Predator* 10–11). So, there is even an interracial romance going on between two of the characters. The five are a team and accept the ethnic differences between one another. This, then, seems to allow the author to use the aliens to symbolize other things.

There are several alien races included in the Animorphs series. The Yeerks are a sluglike, parasitic, alien race and are the true evil ones in the series. The Yeerks forcibly take most hosts, but many volunteer. Whichever way it happens, the host and Yeerk together are called a Controller. When the children first meet the dying Andalite alien, who gives them the power to change into any creature whose DNA they have acquired, they are surprised to learn that the Yeerks have been active on Earth for awhile, that some humans are already Controllers. The children learn that "there is no way to know who is a Controller and who isn't. No way. It's what makes them so hard to stop. They can be anyone. Anywhere" (Applegate, *The Invasion* 150). Even though it is next to impossible to tell who is a Controller, there are certain signs that might point to that fact. People who attend The Sharing meetings are likely to be Controllers or people recruited to be Controllers. Jake's brother Tom was a star basketball player on his high school team, but after joining The Sharing, he quit the team. Tom and Jake used to be close, but after Tom joined The Sharing their relationship changed. It is almost as though the Yeerks symbolize the loss of free will through drugs or cults.[5] In fact, Jake accidentally becomes a Controller when he falls into a vat containing Yeerk slugs. Cassie, Tobias, Marco, and Rachel take Jake to an abandoned cabin in the woods to try to starve (like withdrawal or deprogramming) the Yeerk who has control of him. As the

Yeerk starves and Jake nears the end of the ordeal, he comments, "I turned my attention away from the memory and back to the world around me. To my surprise, I noticed that my arms were shaking. My legs were shaking" (Applegate, *The Capture* 146). Later, "I rose slowly to my feet. I moved my own legs. I was in control of myself again" (150). John Griffiths describes alien possession stories:

A brief explanation of how the alien being—generally very small and parasitic in nature—arrived and spreads, or how it attempts to exercise control of human minds more remotely if it is not of the infective kind, is all the reader is generally afforded. Once this point has been established our writers are preoccupied with how the individual human or human race can retain its freedom of action; how the invading alien can be repulsed; how in fact that other personality within us can be kept in its proper place. (158)

The series format affords Applegate the opportunity to do more than just concentrate on how to keep the Yeerks from taking over the Earth or how to keep the protagonists safe from possession. She is able to give the reader a glimpse into the Yeerk past, as well as the Andalite past. As the series develops, we learn the reason the Andalites are trying to stop the spread of the Yeerks in the galaxy. It is because an Andalite gave the Yeerks the technology to move beyond their murky pools and primitive hosts on their home planet. Axel, the Andalite cadet who is marooned on Earth, tells the Animorph team about Seerow, an Andalite warrior and scientist, who led the first expedition to the Yeerk planet. He found an intelligent species using hosts who "'were nearly blind, clumsy, and not very useful'" (Applegate, *The Alien* 152). Seerow took pity upon them because they "'had never even seen the stars. Let alone be able to leave their own planet'" (152) and gave them Andalite technology, which gave the Yeerks the ability to enslave any beings they came upon. Besides learning more about the Yeerk and Andalite past, we learn more about some of the other aliens who have been enslaved by the Yeerks as well as the protagonists themselves.

The Animorphs is a departure from other science fiction series for children that center around aliens, because it highlights the importance of free will instead of highlighting tolerance as a theme. The importance of free will and self-determination are dominant themes in young adult science fiction series. Then perhaps it is no mistake that Will is the name of the protagonist in the Tripods trilogy, whose desire is to remain a *free* Will. The alien Tripods are not parasites, like the Yeerks in the Animorphs series, in the sense that they must have human hosts. They control the human population through Capping instead, which occurs when children reach adolescence. The Capping ceremony becomes a rite of passage because once Capped, childhood pursuits are put away.[6] As Will notes during the festivities celebrating his friend Jack's Capping, "This, though, was a moment of rejoicing and making merry. He was a man, and tomorrow he would do a man's work and get a man's pay"

(Christopher, *The White Mountains* 18). Shortly before this event, Will and Jack discuss the Tripods and Capping. Jack speculates on life before the Tripods. Will mentions the fact that before the Tripods came "'there were too many people and not enough food, so that people starved and fought each other, and there were all kinds of sicknesses'" (13). Jack reluctantly agrees that perhaps things are better since the arrival of the Tripods and then questions his desire for the Capping to take, although if it does not, it means the individual is damaged mentally in some way, and this "Vagrant" is left to wander from town to town. Jack's Capping does take, and Will is the one who then questions, "'Why should the Tripods take people away and Cap them? What right have they?'" (19). The now Capped Jack responds to the question with, "'They do it for our own good'" (19). The rebellion awakened in Will is strengthened when he meets Ozymandias, who pretends to be a Vagrant but who is actually recruiting rebellious youth to join a movement to overthrow the Tripods, also called Masters. Will secretly leaves home one night to join the fight to free Earth from the enslaving Tripods.[7] His flight becomes a fight to avoid Capping and to maintain his free will and ultimately a fight to free others.

We do not learn a lot about the Masters in book one of the trilogy. We learn about the purpose of Capping, how the ritual is celebrated in other areas, what has happened to the great cities, and about the existence of a group of freedom fighters, but we do not learn what the Masters look like, what their intentions are, nor from where they come. We do learn much of this in the second book of the trilogy when Will and a friend, by design, are chosen to serve the Masters in their city. We learn some of this from Will's Master, who at times feels guilty[8] about the colonization of Earth and who wishes for a friendship with him. Will's Master relates how they managed to subdue humans enough to conquer them and about their ultimate plan to change the Earth's atmosphere to one less poisonous to the Masters. By changing the atmosphere, humans, animals, and plants will die, and as Will notes, "The colonization of Earth would in due course be a complete one" (Christopher, *The City of Gold and Lead* 177). As much as the Tripods trilogy is about free will, it is also about anticolonialism, which is an overt or underlying theme in all alien series.[9]

Humans on Earth are not the only ones threatened by colonialism; often it is the beings on other planets who need to fear human desire to subdue them and exploit their planet. David and Chuck both wonder about what would happen if others knew about the existence of Basidium as they travel back to Earth:

"No, Chuck, . . . No—I think it'd be awful to tell people about Basidium, and to take just anybody there. How do we know what they'd want to do? Why, I'll be they'd start geological expeditions there, and Basidium'd get all dug up . . .And the poor little Basidiumites would be stared at, and people would poke them and point to them and try to get in their houses and maybe want to take some of them back to earth to put them on exhibition." (Cameron, *The Wonderful Flight to the Mushroom Planet* 124)

In the next installment of the series, Professor Horatio Q Peabody stows away on the space ship during the boys' return trip to Basidium. He finds the necklace Ta gave to the boys and mumbles, "'[M]ining operations, of course! To supply the funds for research'" (Cameron, *Stowaway to the Mushroom Planet* 96). Horatio does not even show the slightest respect to the people on Basidium, not even Ta: "Horatio suddenly bent forward and stared closely at Ta's face, and then at Ta's hands. '*Green*, by all the great gods! Is every one of you *green*?'" (111). Basidium is saved by Ta's wisdom in dealing with Horatio, who is tricked into drinking the "Drink of Forgetfulness."

Perhaps free will and self-determination are expressions of tolerance. If tolerance exists, others are free to make their own decisions and govern themselves. Children's science fiction series that focus on aliens present tolerance as a theme through depicting aliens and their relationships with others on a personal and day-to-day level as in the various *Star Trek* series or showing children exhibiting respect as David and Chuck do for the Basidiumites and Ta in the Mushroom Planet series. Young adult series with aliens concentrate on freedom and self-determination as in the Tripods trilogy and Engdahl's Enchantress series, leaving the overt theme of tolerance to children's series. Colonialism does not allow for either tolerance or self-determination, so anticolonialism is an underlying theme in both children's and young adult alien series. Finally, the series format provides an avenue for authors to develop and emphasize these themes through the many installments of the series, which they can keep fresh by providing information and history about the aliens and their societies that entice their readers to reenter the worlds they have created to take part in the adventures.

NOTES

1. See Kathryn Meyer Reimer's article "Multiethnic Literature: Holding Fast to Dreams" in the January 1992 issue of *Language Arts*.

2. There are a few early series for young adults that contain nonwhite characters. The Mike Mars series (1961–1964), by Donald Wollheim, has Johnny Bluehawk, a Cheyenne, who fills the role of Mike Mars's friend and sidekick. His character is played pretty straight throughout most of the series, but in book two of the series he is back in home territory and removes his uniform and transforms himself into "the Cheyenne on the warpath" (*Mike Mars Flies the X-15* 110) in order to stop the villains from firing the sidewinder missile. The Undersea trilogy (1954–1958), by Frederik Pohl and Jack Williamson, has Gideon who turns out to have been the protagonist's uncle's friend. Gideon is described as "a tall, husky Negro, dark as any Gullah, with a clear, friendly eye" (*Undersea Quest* 85).

3. Rudine Sims developed a categorization for books that portray African American characters: "1) the social conscience books, 2) the melting pot books, and 3) the culturally conscious books" (651). Probably Sims would classify this book as an example of a social conscience book, since it seems to attempt "to encourage them [white children] to develop empathy, sympathy, and tolerance for black children" (651).

4. A science fiction series with nonwhite protagonists does appear in 1978 with the publication of *Justice and Her Brothers*, the first book in the Justice cycle. Not only is it the first science fiction series to contain African American protagonists; it is the first written by an African American.

5. Tobias explains why some people are willing to give themselves as Yeerk hosts, "'The Yeerks convince them that taking on a Yeerk will solve all their problems. I think that's what The Sharing is all about. People believe that by becoming something different, they can leave behind all their pain'" (Applegate, *The Invasion* 163). If you substitute "drug" or "cult" for "Yeerk," the statement still rings true. Actually, in stories for adults dealing with alien possession, John Griffiths considers the desire by one who is possessed by an alien to bring others to their state as "a hallmark of the destruction-bent drug addict, a common theme in tales of alien parasitic intelligence" (158).

6. This rite of passage is false. It is true that the newly Capped take their place beside the adults, but they have not gained any independence or any right to govern themselves or make decisions about their community. The Capped join the community of adults, but the adults are more like children whose guardians are the Tripods.

7. If children's fiction follows a home-away-home pattern, then young adult fiction seems to follow a home-away pattern. But then, young adults are to grow up and move out and assume their place in the world, not return back to their homes.

8. Will's Master admits to Will, "'At times I doubt the destiny of our race, to spread far out across the galaxy and rule it. But at least we appreciate beauty. We preserve the best of the worlds that we find and colonize'" (Christopher, *The City of Gold and Lead* 162). This feeling of guilt among colonizers appears in other series as well. In *Enchantress from the Stars* (Engdahl), the Federation sends members of the Anthropological Services out to study Younglings, those planets not yet mature enough to join the Federation. Sometimes their mission is to try to rescue a less advanced Youngling planet from one more advanced wishing to colonize the other. Elana, the protagonist in the book, joins an expedition to help one such planet. The Imperial Exploration Corp. is preparing a colony on a planet whose population they can subdue without trouble. Jarel, the medic with the Corp., expresses some of the same remorse Will's Master expresses about colonizing other planets and about the treatment of the natives. When Elana is captured and guarded by Jarel, she makes a comment that again brings Will's Master to mind, "Jarel went on talking to me as he had before, conversationally, as a man does to a dog he is fond of" (214). Will seems to feel his Master treats him as he would a dog: "I had got it all wrong, I saw. I was not a kitten, after all, in the Master's eyes. I was his puppy" (Christopher, *The City of Gold and Lead* 146).

9. Even Eddie considers this in, *Space Ship Under the Apple Tree*, when he learns Marty is about ready to return home to Martinea and was on a mission to explore Earth: "'I never asked you about yourself or about Martinea. But here's something I gotta know. What were you sent here for? . . . I mean, to explore America? Does Martinea want to conquer America?'" (112-113).

CHAPTER 9

Juvenile Science Fiction Series and the Coming of Age

Nearing the end of that day in her room. Without words or thoughts, she knew she was no longer herself. Somewhere within, she gathered and grew beyond who she had been. She understood she was growing up. And then she gathered more, as a snail's pace.

—Hamilton, *Justice and Her Brothers* (223)

Tom Swift, Jr. is capable and confident with few, if any, self-doubts. He moves throughout the series developing and perfecting new inventions, fighting saboteurs and spies, and saving the free world. The only thing that develops within the Tom Swift, Jr. series is whichever invention Tom is working on at the time. His character does not change throughout the series. There is never a coming of age for Tom—at least none to which the reader is privy. This is the same for the subsequent Tom Swift series. Perhaps Victor Appleton (the pen name for the series' various authors) and the publishers learned from the demise of the first Tom Swift series, where Tom was allowed to age, date, and marry.[1] The boy reader apparently did not read Tom Swift to learn about assuming his place in society, nor did he read for character development; rather, he read to take part in the adventures, inventiveness, and successes of Tom Swift. The Tom Swift fan wanted the predictability of the plot and character; the next book to be much like the previous book with changes in invention, villain, and location only.[2] The series offers a character that is everything the reader on the verge of adolescence probably is not—confident, able, independent. These are powerful attractions for the young reader who wants and needs to experience all of what Tom Swift, Jr., or similar series, past and present, have to offer. However, most readers eventually tire of reading about this type of hero and move on to read about characters who possess some of the same self-doubts and who are on the same journey to adulthood.[3]

Usually books of this nature are written for young adults, and if you define series in the conventional way, there are no series for the young adult where the coming-of-age pattern follows throughout the series. The protagonists in the first book might have a coming of age, but the books that follow avoid further developing the characters, and the plots become repetitive and formulaic, much like the Tom Swift–type series.[4] Perhaps having the same protagonist or protagonists throughout the series creates a problem for the author. It might not be possible to have the characters come of age over and over in each installment of the young adult series, and it is probably too difficult to sustain a coming of age through several volumes. Authors of science fiction series for children face similar challenges. One would think that there would be little to do with coming of age in science fiction series for children. However authors do make use of the coming-of-age pattern; in fact, they seem to be doing so more of late.[5] It is probably easier to prolong the coming-of-age pattern in a series intended for children, because developmentally, children are more interested in repetition—a book exactly like the one they just read and liked. Authors of both types of series, young adult and children, have found interesting ways to deal with the problems encountered in trying to sustain a coming of age. Authors of young adult series have redefined the traditional series and authors of children's series have introduced the concept of an ensemble cast of characters.

Perhaps Robert A. Heinlein realized some of the dangers of the traditional series format after writing his first juvenile, *Rocket Ship Galileo*.[6] Originally Heinlein meant it to be a book one of six in the Young Atomic Engineers series (Heinlein, *Grumbles from the Grave* 42-43).[7] Instead, Heinlein wrote the twelve books that comprise his Scribner's juveniles. Each of the juveniles has a different male protagonist who experiences a coming of age.[8] While they may take place at different locations in space and different points in time, there are enough threads that run through each of the books to pull them together into a series.[9] This is not to say that Heinlein intentionally set about to redefine the conventional series, but it seems that he has done exactly that.[10]

Charles Sheffield's Jupiter Novels series, published almost fifty years after Heinlein's first juvenile, partly patterns itself after Heinlein's juveniles.[11] Like Heinlein's juveniles, each book in the Jupiter Novels series has a different male protagonist, is a bildungsroman, and takes place at different locations in space and at different points in time. Also, there are certain threads within the series that keep the whole series tied together: the Kuiper Belt, mining enterprises, the overpopulated Earth, the Messina Dust cloud, and travel nodes. The prospects for most of the young people in each installment of this future scenario are bleak. The public education system has deteriorated to the point that most teenagers are illiterate. Despite being illiterate, they graduate from high school, but their job prospects are quite limited. Many end up in a life of crime and on drugs. In spite of all this, for those willing to accept the risks of working in space and on other planets and for those willing to learn and become functional, the opportunity to grow into responsible, independent adults still exists, but only after the coming-of-age experience.

It is interesting that there are very few series written for young adults that can be classified as coming of age, except that there are very few science fiction series in general written expressly for the young adult market. The Jupiter Novels series seems to be the first in many years. Plus, while the Jupiter Novels series was written for young adults, it is shelved in the adult section of bookstores. According to publisher Lou Aronica, "Booksellers told us the teenagers who want to read science fiction and fantasy don't want to feel that these are YA books" (Owen 37).[12] Series written for young adults are packaged and sold as though for adults. Perhaps this illustrates one way juvenile science fiction series have come of age. The Jupiter Novels series evinces other ways series meant for young adults have come of age. Unlike the juveniles of Heinlein or Asimov, both of whom the series is patterned after, the Jupiter Novels series includes swearing and frank discussions of sex. Of course, Heinlein and Asimov both had restrictions on what could be discussed or depicted.[13] Neither could allow their characters to discuss sex or think "impure thoughts" about a female character. In the Jupiter Novels series, the majority of the protagonists are not innocent or even as likable as those found in Heinlein or Asimov.

The Animorphs series is marketed and shelved for the middle reader and would satisfy the child reader's want and need for books with realistic child characters and with the coming-of-age pattern. It is a chronicle by Jake, Cassie, Rachel, Marco, and Tobias, average junior high school–age kids, as well as Aximili-Esgarrouth-Isthill, an alien warrior cadet who shows up later in the series. The first-person narrative changes from book to book. It is about their experience as a result of getting caught in the wrong place at the wrong time. As the five walk home one Friday night from the local mall across an abandoned construction site, they encounter a mortally wounded alien and his damaged space ship. The alien is part of a force trying to protect Earth from other aliens, the Yeerks, who plan to use humans as hosts for their kind. Because the alien knows that he will die soon, and that the evil aliens will soon arrive, he decides to give the children a gift that will enable them to fight against the Yeerks. He tells them, "'I know that you are young. I know that you have no power with which to resist the Controllers. But I may be able to give you some small powers that may help'" (Applegate, *The Invasion* 26). The five feel the task they have been assigned is meant for someone older and more capable, "We all felt the same terrible feeling—like we were all alone. Like suddenly we were dealing with stuff that was way, way, *way* over our heads" (73). The characters do not want to accept the responsibility of saving the world from the Yeerks. However, they do not know who would believe their story or whom they can trust, and since the dying alien gave them the ability to change into any animal, they decide they have no choice but to enter the battle to save Earth. Along the way they express self-doubts and reveal weaknesses, all of which the child reader can identify, but they also discover strengths within themselves and each other. The independence displayed by the characters in the Animorphs series, their success, though sometimes limited, and their weaknesses and self-discoveries suggest a type of series meant for children unlike many current or prior series.

The Animorphs series is not the first series to employ an ensemble cast of characters, but it is probably one of the first to integrate it so successfully. A few series prior to the Animorphs also utilized this device. One of the first series to try this is Bruce Coville's A.I. Gang series. The A.I. Gang consists of Wendy, Ray, Tripton, Rachel and Roger (who happen to be twins), and Hap. Their parents are scientists who are working on a project at an abandoned base on a island in the middle of the South Pacific to create artificial intelligence. The children get to know one another and decide to join forces to beat their parents at developing artificial intelligence. Each A.I. Gang member brings a different talent that helps them succeed in creating artificial intelligence while at the same time solving the mysteries that keep popping up. Together they are successful in helping to develop artificial intelligence, although the work their parents do contributes as well, and succeed in unmasking the villain who has been the source of each of the mysteries. By including several child characters of equal importance to the plot, Coville creates an interesting reading experience for the child reader. The action does not necessarily need to be linear; the chapters can move between the action in which each character is involved. This helps explain to the reader what is happening to the other characters during various parts of the action and keeps the reader in suspense. Unfortunately, the A.I. Gang members' characters are not well drawn and are hard to delineate. Perhaps as a result, the protagonists never come close to experiencing a coming of age. They do not seem to engage in the same self-reflection nor do they seem to have the same level of self-discovery as the characters in the Animorphs series. The A.I. Gang characters are closer to the Tom Swift–type character because they share a similar high intelligence, inventiveness, and interest in technology. The characters in the Animorphs series are average children who receive a special gift from a wounded alien. Most child readers could imagine themselves being caught in a similar circumstance. While the Animorphs characters are not highly intelligent, they are highly creative and resourceful, something more realistic for the average child.

Rick North's Young Astronauts series,[14] published a few years after the original publication of the A.I. Gang series, has the same problem with poorly delineated characters. Coville refines his use of the team concept in the My Teacher series. This time he develops it in an interesting way and is more successful. The series consists of four books; the first is narrated by Susan, the second by Duncan, and the final two by Peter. It is interesting to follow what is happening from the different perspectives of the protagonist and to become acquainted with the protagonists through their own voices and the voices of the others.

This varying of voice and the ensemble cast of protagonists creates a more complex series and illustrates one way science fiction series for children have come of age. Older series usually have one main protagonist with one or two friends who take part in the action: Tom Corbett has Astro and Roger, Lucky

Starr has Bigman, Rick Brant has Scotty, Mike Mars has Johnny Bluehawk, Tom Swift (third series) has Anita and Ben, and Norby has Jeff. These friends give voice to the questions readers might be forming in their minds and thereby provide an avenue for the main protagonist to explain his action, plan, invention, or technology. Sometimes they are available to rescue or be rescued by the main protagonist. No matter what happens, there is only one main character. This does not allow the author to do much character development. The ensemble cast of characters used by recent authors of science fiction series allows authors much more freedom in, and a wider canvas for, developing characters, which serves two purposes for the child reader: to keep the series fresh for the reader, since there are a variety of personalities and greater character development, and to make the series accessible to both boys and girls, since the cast is usually composed of male and female characters.

The appearance of more female characters, females who play as important a role as the male characters, is another example of how children's science fiction series have come of age. These female characters either are part of an ensemble cast of characters or are the main characters in their own series. Considering female characters are mostly used as stock characters in most science fiction, whether intended for children, juveniles, or adults, it is not surprising to find few examples of either before 1970. The Miss Pickerell series broke ground back in 1951, but Miss Pickerell was a gray-haired woman who because of her age removed some of the imagined stigma of a "girls" series, which it might have had with a younger lead-female character. It was several years before another series appeared with a young female main character.[15]

Besides a scarcity of female main characters in pre-1970s series, science fiction series for children, like a lot of children's literature of the time, also contained a scant number of nonwhite characters. The ethnic groups represented were usually described in the accepted stereotype of the time, given minor roles, or relegated to sidekick status.[16] In *Tom Swift and His Flying Lab*, Tom Swift, Jr. and his friends meet an apparently unfriendly band of natives in a South American jungle. Chow, the cook, helped to defuse the situation:

[H]e stepped forward and haltingly spoke a jargon of guttural sounds. Slowly, smiles of understanding broke out on the faces of the Indians.

"What are you telling them?" Tom asked.

"That I fetched 'em some presents from the Lone Star State."

"Presents?"

"Sure thing. I'd never get caught in Injun country without some lil ole knick-knacks."

From his pocket he pulled several cheap bracelets, rings, brooches, and four pearl necklaces, and distributed them.

"Great way to stop a fight," he commented with a grin. (122–123)

There is no logical explanation for Chow, a Texan, to be able to speak the language of the South American natives. The impression is that grunts and sounds are all that is needed to communicate with natives. It also suggests they can be bought with a few cheap trinkets. Chow is able to avoid a fight with the natives, but the natives are represented in a stereotypical way. In *Tom Swift and His Giant Robot*, another installment of the Tom Swift, Jr. series, the Native American tribe living near Mr. Swift's nuclear laboratory is not even considered when Mr. Swift describes the location of his laboratory:

"For miles around there's no civilization, just big black boulders and crumbling, eroded pink cliffs."
   "Sounds wonderful, Dad. And no chance of harming any neighbors?"
   "That's right. The border of the nearest ranch is fifteen miles away." (52)

Later, however, we discover that "'[t]here's a tribe not many miles from the plant'" (84). Tom and his father appear concerned about ranchers but not about a tribe of Native Americans.

Finally, in 1976, a series appeared with an African American playing more than a sidekick role, but not quite equal status with the protagonist. Andre Norton and Dorothy Madlee's Star Ka'at series has a young white male protagonist, Jim, who befriends a young African American girl, Elly Mae. Each book in the series is third person, but the reader is privy to Jim's thoughts but not Elly Mae's, which seems to give Jim status as the main protagonist. Jim and Elly Mae develop a warm friendship. Jim cares and worries about Elly Mae in spite of the fact that she seems quite capable on her own.

The Tom Swift–type series entertained scores of readers. Authors could have kept writing this type of series, but that would have perhaps meant the eventual death of science fiction series for modern more sophisticated juveniles or children. It is easy to poke fun at the Tom Swift–type series, but it satisfied the interests and needs of the generation of children who read the series. It helped to impress and inspire its readers into thinking, imagining, and discovering. As time passed, the needs and interests of the reader changed. Now young adults seem to want to discover and read books that are not explicitly young adult fare. They still seem to need books that offer the coming-of-age experiences of others to help with their own journey to adulthood, but they do not want this to be a young adult book. Preadolescents no longer seem to want to read only about characters who have few self-doubts and who experience total success. They seem to need to read about other children who experience the same concerns, personal and future, and who struggle to achieve their goals. Authors of science fiction series from the past twenty years have introduced innovations into the series format to meet the needs of a new generation of readers while offering guidance for growing up, providing imaginative and thoughtful themes as well as hope for the future.

NOTES

   1. Francis J. Molson believes that "the stories after 1929 became increasingly implausible and difficult for young male readers to identify with. Thus the wedding, pre-

sumably a kind of apogee of Tom Swift's personal happiness and success, ironically marked the beginning of the decline in popularity of vintage Tom Swift" ("Tom Swift Books" 5).

2. There are many examples of popular series with female protagonists who mature throughout the series: Elsie Dinsmore begins the series as a young girl and ends the series as a grandmother; Laura Ingalls begins the series as a young girl and ends the series as a wife, the writing style changing as Laura Ingalls matures along with the supposed reader; Anne Shirley begins the series as a girl and ends the series as a wife and mother. It is interesting that female readers were willing to let their favorite females protagonists mature, but male readers were not willing to let Tom Swift do the same.

3. Readers who do not tire of this formula move on to adult pulp fiction, which offers the same things the Tom Swift series offers but wrapped in an adult package.

4. The Tom Corbett series, loosely based on Heinlein's *Space Cadet*, goes beyond what the Tom Swift-type series has to offer but does not go far enough. What sets it apart from the Tom Swift–type series is that in the first book—*Stand by For Mars!*—there is a coming of age for three of the characters. Tom Corbett, Roger Manning, and Astro are on their first real mission, which involves rescuing passengers from a derelict spaceship. They manage to save the spaceship, attempt to fly it to Mars for repairs, but lose power and clash-land on Mars and become stranded. Soon after they crash-land, they encounter the Mars version of a sandstorm, described by Astro as no small storm: "'It blows as long as a week and can pile up sand for two hundred feet. Sometimes the velocity reaches as much as a hundred and sixty miles an hour'" (175). The sandstorm imprisons the three young cadets in the wrecked space ship. Not knowing what will happen next, with their oxygen and water supplies terribly low, they must confront their fears and the prospect of death. Both Tom and Astro consider options for escape, while Roger is willing to sit back and give up: "'[W]e're stuck, Corbett, so lay off that last chance, do-or-die routine. I've been eating glory all my life. If I do have to splash in now [die], I want it to be on my own terms. And that's just to sit here and wait for it to come'" (180). All along Roger has been the difficult one of the three. He is hostile to both Tom and Astro and contemptuous of the Space Academy and Solar Guard ideals. Roger tells his story after deciding to stay in the spaceship to meet death on his terms. Astro then relates the story of his life, which was much more difficult since he grew up not knowing a mother or a father and having to survive in any way he could. Astro's dismal tale brings Roger to his senses. At this point Roger, Astro, and Tom become a cohesive team and work together against the powers of the evil for the benefit of humanity, which they do in the books that follow. However, the books that follow avoid developing the characters further, and the plots are repetitive and formulaic.

5. Perhaps this is because the perception is that today's children seem to be growing up faster and in less innocent times than when Tom Swift, Jr. invented his way through his series and need and want to move toward books and series with the coming-of-age pattern. Jack Zipes comments on studies done by Neil Postman and Marie Winn in the early 1980s: "Pointing their fingers at the mass media, drugs, sexual permissiveness, governmental indifference, and poor educational systems, Postman and Winn have argued that there is no longer a safe and carefree phase in a child's development that would allow children to make important discoveries about themselves and become truly autonomous thinkers" (367).

6. Heinlein was a wonderful storyteller. He might have been able to avoid the pitfalls with the Young Atomic Engineers series that other authors were unable to avoid in their series.

7. There does not appear to be an explanation available in print for the reason Heinlein abandoned his plan for his series.

8. Peter C. Hall describes Jerome H. Buckley's definition of a bildungsroman as containing "these principal elements: childhood, the conflict of generations, provinciality, the larger society, self-education, alienation, ordeal by love, and the search for both a vocation and a working philosophy" (153). While Buckley's discussion of the bildungsroman does not include any science fiction examples, Hall applies Buckley's principles to science fiction. Hall concludes that a science fiction bildungsroman can be approached as one would any other "as an example of how the inner resources of a youth can be marshaled to challenge an unresponsive or hostile environment and, in the end, help the emergence of an adult better equipped to survive in the universe" (158).

9. See "Heinlein's Juveniles: Growing Up in Outer Space," by C. W. Sullivan III, pp. 21, 33 (n. 3).

10. The Winston series also follows the less conventional definition of a "series." The books in the series are written by various authors, but all have similar things in common; an introduction discussing the science on which the book is based; authors who were known at the time; and entertaining and informative plots.

11. So far there are five published installments in the series: *Higher Education*, *The Billion Dollar Boy*, *Putting Up Roots*, *The Cyborg from Earth*, and *Starswarm*.

12. The article from which this quote is taken was published in 1987, but it seems to still hold true. Even Heinlein's juveniles are shelved in the adult science fiction section rather than the young adult section. There are very few science fiction series in the young adult section.

13. See "Heinlein's Juveniles: Growing Up in Outer Space," by C. W. Sullivan III, p. 33, n. 6.

14. The Young Astronauts series seems to be an updated version of the Mike Mars series. The Mike Mars series, published between 1961 and 1964, follows the adventures of Mike Mars as he attempts to be the first American in space. There is no question that the series tried to encourage the young reader to support the race for space, to encourage the young reader to study math and science, and to promote patriotism. The author thanks the United States Air Force and the National Aeronautics and Space Administration for their cooperation with each book. Similarly, the Young Astronauts series, published between 1990 and 1991, follows a group of teens as they compete for a spot on a ship bound for Mars. The group members represent various socioeconomic and racial groups and come from various countries. They will be the first to explore and colonize the planet. It is no accident that the Young Astronauts series shares the same name as the Young Astronaut Council. According to the back cover of the book, "The Young Astronaut Council is an international program designed to prepare young people for the Space Age. Founded and chaired by Jack Anderson, the Council is co-chaired by Ronald Reagan and President and Mrs. Bush and has many veteran astronauts on its Board of Directors. Its mission is to promote the study of adventure. This book is a joint venture of the The Young Astronaut Council and Zebra Books." Both the Mike Mars and the Young Astronauts series share similar missions.

15. For a more detailed discussion of female characters in juvenile science fiction series, see Chapter 4.

16. There is an African American character in The Undersea Trilogy by Frederik Pohl and Jack Williamson, and there are Native American characters in the Mike Mars and third Tom Swift series. These characters play supporting roles only, and whether the authors avoid stereotyping is debatable.

Appendix: Annotated Bibliography of Juvenile Science Fiction Series

This annotated bibliography is arranged alphabetically by author's last name and by series title. All annotations are under the series entries.

Abbott, Tony. *See* **Weird Zone.**

Abrashkin, Raymond. *See* **Danny Dunn.**

Adams, Georgie. *See* **Tubby Tin.**

A.I. Gang (1986 Series)—Bruce Coville (Jim Lawrence author of second book). Follows the exploits of a group of bright, precocious children whose parents have been invited by a noted scientist to help develop artificial intelligence. The children, after gaining access to the main computer, decide to try to achieve artificial intelligence before their parents do. Along the way, they encounter lots of adventures—a scientist who wants to blow up the island because she feels her project to utilize the sea as a source of energy is more important, a spy who tries to plant a tracking device aboard the communications robot launched into space, and the trials they face trying to unmask the evil Black Glove. This series is set on Ancoteague Island off the coast of the United States and is interesting because it is one of the first to use an ensemble cast of characters. All of the characters are of equal importance to the plot and the chapters alternate among each of the characters.

    (1) 1986—*Operation Sherlock*
    (2) 1986—*The Cutlass Clue*
    (3) 1986—*Robot Trouble*
    (4) 1986—*Forever Begins Tomorrow*

A.I. Gang (1995 Series)—Bruce Coville. The same series as above except *The Cutlass Clue* is excluded and the setting is changed to the South Sea island of Anzabora.

    (1) 1995—*Operation Sherlock*
    (2) 1995—*Robot Trouble*
    (3) 1995—*Forever Begins Tomorrow*

Anastasio, Dina. *See* **Space: Above and Beyond.**

Animorphs—K. A. Applegate. Describes the experiences of Jake, Cassie, Rachel, Marco, and Tobias, average junior high school students, as they attempt to fight a parasitic alien race (Yeerks) attempting to gain control of the human population. A dying alien, part of an effort to protect the Earth from the Yeerks, bestows on the children the ability to morph into any animal or insect whose DNA they acquire, in the hope that they will have some power to fight the Yeerks. Later, Aximili-Esgarrouth-Isthill, warrior cadet younger brother of the dying alien, shows up and joins the group. Each installment of the series is narrated by a different member of the Animorph team.

    (1) 1996—*The Invasion*
    (2) 1996—*The Visitor*
    (3) 1996—*The Encounter*
    (4) 1996—*The Message*
    (5) 1996—*The Predator*
    (6) 1997—*The Capture*
    (7) 1997—*The Stranger*
    (8) 1997—*The Alien*
    (9) 1997—*The Secret*
    (10) 1997—*The Android*
    (11) 1997—*The Forgotten*
    (12) 1997—*The Reaction*
    (13) 1997—*The Change*

Applegate, K. A. *See* **Animorphs; Megamorphs.**

Appleton, Victor. *See* **Tom Swift, Jr. (Second Series); Tom Swift (Third Series); Tom Swift (Fourth Series).**

Asimov, Isaac. *See* **Lucky Starr; Norby.**

Asimov, Janet. *See* **Norby.**

Ayyar Series—Andre Norton. Naill Renfro willingly sells himself into slavery to buy a drug for his dying mother that will ease her suffering. He is trans-

ported to the planet Janus to serve a religious agricultural community colonizing the planet. He contracts the green sickness and becomes a changeling of
the forest. He, along with others who have changed, searches for the purpose of
their change.

    (1) 1963—*Judgement on Janus*
    (2) 1966—*Victory on Janus*

Balan, Bruce. *See* **Cyberkidz.**

Beatty, Jerome, Jr. *See* **Maria Looney; Matthew Looney.**

Blaine, John. *See* **Rick Brant.**

Brinley, Bertrand Russell. *See* **Mad Scientists' Club.**

Camron, Eleanor. *See* **Mushroom Planet.**

Christopher, John. *See* **Tripods.**

Cole, Joanna. *See* **Magic School Bus.**

Commander Toad—Jane Yolen. This picture-book series is illustrated by
Bruce Degen, illustrator of the popular Magic School Bus series. Mr. Hop, Lt.
Lily, Jake Skyjumper, and Doc Peeper comprise Commander Toad's crew. The
series is written in the "I Can Read" tradition but is not broken into chapters.
Humorous illustrations match the word-play in the text. One illustration shows
the Star Wars Library, which contains editions of *Wind Sand & Frogs*, *Newt
Flystalker*, *Toad Code*, and *Moby Toad* and a biography entitled *Sir Isaac
Newt*.

    (1) 1980—*Commander Toad in Space*
    (2) 1982—*Commander Toad and the Planet of the Grapes*
    (3) 1983—*Commander Toad and the Big Black Hole*
    (4) 1985—*Commander Toad and the Dis-Asteroid*
    (5) 1986—*Commander Toad and the Intergalactic Spy*
    (6) 1987—*Commander Toad and the Space Pirates*

Coville, Bruce. *See* **A.I. Gang (1986 Series); A.I. Gang (1995 Series); My
Teacher.**

Cyberkidz—Bruce Balan. Plot lines revolve around computers and the Internet.

    (1) 1997—*In Search of SCUM*

(2) 1997—*A Picture's Worth*
(3) 1997—*The Great NASA Flu*
(4) 1997—*Blackout in the Amazon*

Danny Dunn—Jay Williams and Raymond Abrashkin. Follows the adventures of Danny, his friend Joe, and their mentor Professor Bullfinch. Irene, a strong female character, joins the team in book three of the series. Danny, Joe, and Irene are intelligent children with a strong interest in science. The direction in which their curiosity takes them, usually involving Professor Bullfinch's inventions, provides some of the impetus for the plots.

(1) 1956—*Danny Dunn and the Anti-Gravity Paint*
(2) 1957—*Danny Dunn on a Desert Island*
(3) 1958—*Danny Dunn and the Homework Machine*
(4) 1959—*Danny Dunn and the Weather Machine*
(5) 1960—*Danny Dunn on the Ocean Floor*
(6) 1961—*Danny Dunn and the Fossil Cave*
(7) 1962—*Danny Dunn and the Heat Ray*
(8) 1963—*Danny Dunn, Time Traveller*
(9) 1965—*Danny Dunn and the Automatic House*
(10) 1967—*Danny Dunn and the Voice From Space*
(11) 1969—*Danny Dunn and the Smallifying Machine*
(12) 1971—*Danny Dunn and the Swamp Monster*
(13) 1974—*Danny Dunn, Invisible Boy*
(14) 1975—*Danny Dunn, Scientific Detective*
(15) 1977—*Danny Dunn and the Universal Glue*

Danny One—Alfred Slote. Ten-year-old Jack Jameson nags his parents for a robot buddy because they live too far away for Danny to have companions his own age. His father is prevailed upon to get a Dr. Atkins robot for his son's birthday. Jack chooses Danny's appearance, age, interests, and personality. Jack and Danny One become involved in many adventures, everything from saving Danny One from robotnappers to saving Earth from a scientist bent on wiping out humanity in favor of robots.

(1) 1975—*My Robot Buddy*
(2) 1981—*C.O.L.A.R.*
(3) 1983—*Omega Station*
(4) 1985—*The Trouble on Janus*

Dickson, Gordon R. *See* **Secret Under.**

Dig Allen, Space Explorer—Joseph Greene. In the first installment of the series, Jim and Ken Barry are aboard the *S.S. Pioneer* en route to join their parents stationed at a research station on the Moon. Before reaching the Moon, an alarm sounds to alert the crew there is a stowaway aboard. Jim and Ken happen to meet the stowaway, who is Dig Allen. His father is a member of the Space Explorers and has been reported lost in space. Dig Allen refuses to believe his father is lost, eludes Space Guard Sergeant Brool, and makes his way back to the Moon as a stowaway. He is able to continue the search with Jim, Ken, and Sergeant Brool's help. Their search takes them to Mars and finally to No. 433 in the Asteroid Belt, where they discover a hollowed-out asteroid space ship. There they find what was probably an advanced civilization fallen back to primitive ways (depicted as stereotypical Native Americans) and locate Dig's father—alive. Because Jim, Ken, and Dig left Mars, without permission, with Dig's father's space ship, they all might be court-martialed, never to be allowed into space again. Because of "Code Seven," they are able to be sworn in as space explorers, which means they cannot be court-martialed and are free to explore space—which they do in further installments of the series.

(1) 1959—*The Forgotten Star*
(2) 1960—*Captives in Space*
(3) 1961—*Journey to Jupiter*
(4) 1961—*Trappers on Venus*
(5) 1962—*Robots on Saturn*
(6) 1962—*Lost City of Uranus*

Dragonfall Five—Brian Earnshaw. *Dragonfall Five* is the name of the space ship that takes Tim, brother Sanchez, Big Mother (their mother), Old Elias (their father), Jerk (their dog), and the Mims (squirrel-like creatures that are telepathic and can "speak all of the known languages of the universe" [*Empty* 6]) on adventures in space.

(1) 1972—*Dragonfall Five and the Space Cowboys*
(2) 1972—*Dragonfall Five and the Royal Beast*
(3) 1973—*Dragonfall Five and the Empty Planet*
(4) 1974—*Dragonfall Five and the Hijackers*
(5) 1975—*Dragonfall Five and the Master Mind*
(6) 1977—*Dragonfall Five and the Super Horse*
(7) 1980—*Dragonfall Five and the Haunted World*

Earnshaw, Brian. *See* **Dragonfall Five.**

Eliott, E. C. *See* **Tas.**

Enchantress—Sylvia Engdahl. In the universe, the Federation sends members of the Anthropological Services to study planets classified as Younglings, those planets not mature enough to join the Federation. Sometimes their mission is to try to rescue a less advanced Youngling planet from one more advanced wishing to colonize the other. This mission must be done without letting the Youngling planets know of the existence of the Federation and its technologies.

(1) 1970—*Enchantress from the Stars*
(2) 1971—*The Far Side of Evil*

Engdahl, Sylvia. *See* **Enchantress.**

French, Paul. *See* **Isaac Asimov; Lucky Starr.**

Greene, Joseph. *See* **Dig Allen, Space Explorer.**

Hamilton, Virginia. *See* **Justice Cycle.**

Heinlein, Robert. *See* **Heinlein's Juveniles.**

Heinlein's Juveniles—Robert A. Heinlein. Does not follow the traditional series format. Each book in the series has a different male protagonist, unlike most traditional series that follow the exploits of a particular protagonist or group of protagonist throughout. The success of this series, according to Molson, inspired the Winston to publish its Winston series (*see* Winston Series) (Molson, "Winston" 34).

(1)—*Rocket Ship Galileo*
(2)—*Space Cadet*
(3)—*Red Planet*
(4)—*Farmer in the Sky*
(5)—*Between Planets*
(6)—*The Rolling Stones*
(7)—*Starman Jones*
(8)—*The Star Beast*
(9)—*Tunnel in the Sky*
(10)—*Time for the Stars*
(11)—*Citizen of the Galaxy*
(12)—*Have Space Suit—Will Travel*

Hughes, Monica. *See* **Isis.**

Hunter, Norman. *See* **Professor Branestawm.**

Isis—Monica Hughes. Chronicles the events over three generations of a colony of humans on the planet Isis.

(1) 1980—*The Keeper of the Isis Light*
(2) 1981—*The Guardian of Isis*
(3) 1982—*The Isis Pedlar*

Johns, W. E. *See* **Space Series.**

Jupiter Novels—Charles Sheffield. Each entry in the series moves further out into the galaxy. Each focuses on a different male protagonist's coming of age. The books in the series are supposedly modeled on the juveniles of Robert A. Heinlein and Isaac Asimov.

    (1) 1996—*Higher Education* (co-author Jerry Pournelle)
    (2) 1997—*The Billion Dollar Boy*
    (3) 1997—*Putting Up Roots*

Justice Cycle—Virginia Hamilton. Follows Justice, her older twin brothers, Thomas and Levi, and her friend Dorian, as they travel into the far future. To a greater or lesser degree, all four have telepathic powers. This is the first science fiction series written with African American protagonists by an African American.

    (1) 1978—*Justice and Her Brothers*
    (2) 1980—*Dustland*
    (3) 1981—*The Gathering*

L'Engle, Madeleine. *See* **Time Trilogy.**

Lawrence, Jim. *See* **A.I. Gang (1986 series).**

Lucky Starr—Isaac Asimov. David Starr is a member of the Council of Science, as are both of his adopted uncles. He investigates the sabotage of marplubs from Mars in the first installment. He travels to Mars for his investigation, where he meets John "Bigman" Jones who becomes his partner throughout the series. Together they travel and investigate various things that could impact negatively on Earth and its colonies. Asimov used the pseudonym Paul French for *David Starr, Space Ranger* and *Lucky Starr and the Pirates of the Asteroids*.

    (1) 1952—*David Starr, Space Ranger*
    (2) 1953—*Lucky Starr and the Pirates of the Asteroids*
    (3) 1954—*Lucky Starr and the Oceans of Venus*
    (4) 1956—*Lucky Starr and the Big Sun of Mercury*
    (5) 1957—*Lucky Starr and the Moons of Jupiter*
    (6) 1958—*Lucky Starr and the Rings of Saturn*

MacGregor, Ellen. *See* **Miss Pickerell.**

Madlee, Dorothy. *See* **Star Ka'at.**

Mad Scientists' Club—Bertrand Russell Brinley. Humorous escapades of a group of boys who form a science club.

    (1) 1965—*The Mad Scientists' Club*
    (2) 1968—*The New Adventures of the Mad Scientists' Club*
    (3) 1974—*The Big Kerplop: A Mad Scientists' Club Adventure*

Magic School Bus—Joanna Cole. Miss Frizzle's class goes on several interesting field trips. The information is real, but the field trips are wonderful fantasy. PBS turned this into a TV series. This numbered list does not indicate sequence.

    (1) 1986—*The Magic School Bus at the Waterworks*
    (2) 1987—*The Magic School Bus Inside the Earth*
    (3) 1989—*The Magic School Bus Inside the Human Body*
    (4) 1990—*The Magic School Bus Lost in the Solar System*
    (5) 1992—*The Magic School Bus on the Ocean Floor*
    (6) 1994—*The Magic School Bus in the Time of the Dinosaurs*
    (7) 1994—*The Magic School Bus Inside Ralphie: A Book About Germs* (John May)
    (8) 1995—*The Magic School Bus Plants Seeds: A Book About How Living Things Grow* (Patricia Relf)
    (9) 1995—*The Magic School Bus in the Haunted Museum: A Book About Sound* (Linda Beech)
    (10) 1995—*The Magic School Bus Gets Baked in a Cake: A Book About Kitchen Chemistry* (Linda Beech)
    (11) 1995—*The Magic School Bus Inside a Hurricane*
    (12) 1995—*The Magic School Bus Hops Home: A Book About Animal Habitats* (Patricia Relf)
    (13) 1995—*The Magic School Bus Gets Eaten: A Book About Food Chains* (Patricia Relf)
    (14) 1996—*The Magic School Bus Gets Ants in Its Pants: A Book About Ants* (Linda Beech)
    (15) 1996—*The Magic School Bus Gets All Dried Up: A Book About Deserts* (Suzanne Weyn)
    (16) 1996—*The Magic School Bus Blows Its Top: A Book About Volcanoes* (Gail Herman)
    (17) 1996—*The Magic School Bus Out of This World*
    (18) 1996—*The Magic School Bus Going Batty: A Book About Bats* (Ronnie Krauss)
    (19) 1996—*The Magic School Bus Inside a Beehive*
    (20) 1997—*The Magic School Bus Goes Upstream: A Book About Salmon on Migration*
    (21) 1997—*The Magic School Bus Spins a Web: A Book About Spiders* (Tracey West)
    (22) 1997—*The Magic School Bus and the Electric Field Trip*

(23) 1997—*The Magic School Bus Makes a Rainbow: A Book About Color* (George Bloom)

Maria Looney—Jerome Beatty, Jr. Maria is Matthew Looney's younger but very capable sister. She has some adventures of her own. Humorous series with wonderful illustrations by Gahan Wilson.

(1) 1977—*Maria Looney and the Red Planet*
(2) 1978—*Maria Looney and the Cosmic Circus*
(3) 1979—*Maria Looney and the Remarkable Robot*

Matthew Looney—Jerome Beatty, Jr. Matthew Looney travels to Earth in the first installment and manages to prove there is life on Earth. In both this series and the Maria Looney series, there are inconsistencies in the science described. Illustrated by Gahan Wilson.

(1) 1961—*Matthew Looney's Voyage to the Earth*
(2) 1965—*Matthew Looney's Invasion of the Earth*
(3) 1969—*Matthew Looney in the Outback*
(4) 1972—*Matthew Looney and the Space Pirates*

McEvoy, Seth. *See* **Not Quite Human.**

Megamorphs—K. A. Applegate. Follows the original Animorphs scenario, but are longer. The second Megamorphs is Ax's brother's story.

(1) 1997—*The Andalite's Gift*
(2) 1997—*The Andalite Chronicles*

Mike Mars—Donald Wollheim. Near future science fiction series about Mike Mars's attempt to be the first American in space. It anticipated the NASA (National Aeronautics and Space Administration) space flight programs.

(1) 1961—*Mike Mars, Astronaut*
(2) 1961—*Mike Mars Flies the X-15*
(3) 1961—*Mike Mars at Cape Canaveral* (changed to *Cape Kennedy*)
(4) 1961—*Mike Mars in Orbit*
(5) 1962—*Mike Mars Flies the Dyna-Soar*
(6) 1962—*Mike Mars, South Pole Spaceman*
(7) 1963—*Mike Mars and the Mystery Satellite*
(8) 1964—*Mike Mars Around the Moon*

Miss Pickerell—Ellen MacGregor. Miss Pickerell is one of the first female protagonists in science fiction series after 1945. She is old but eccentric enough for children to enjoy.

    (1) 1951—*Miss Pickerell Goes to Mars*
    (2) 1953—*Miss Pickerell and the Geiger Counter*
    (3) 1953—*Miss Pickerell Goes Undersea*
    (4) 1954—*Miss Pickerell Goes to the Arctic*

Miss Pickerell (Pantell)—Ellen MacGregor and Dora Pantell. Dora Pantell continued the series after Ellen MacGregor died.

    (1) 1965—*Miss Pickerell on the Moon*
    (2) 1966—*Miss Pickerell Goes on a Dig*
    (3) 1968—*Miss Pickerell Harvests the Sea*
    (4) 1971—*Miss Pickerell and the Weather Satellite*
    (5) 1974—*Miss Pickerell Meets Mr. H.U.M.*
    (6) 1976—*Miss Pickerell Takes the Bull by the Horns*
    (7) 1977—*Miss Pickerell to the Earthquake Rescue*
    (8) 1978—*Miss Pickerell and the Supertanker*
    (9) 1980—*Miss Pickerell Tackles the Energy Crisis*
    (10) 1982—*Miss Pickerell on the Trail*
    (11) 1983—*Miss Pickerell and the Blue Whales*
    (12) 1984—*Miss Pickerell and the War of the Computers*
    (13) 1986—*Miss Pickerell and the Lost World*

Mogridge, Stephen. *See* **Peter's Adventures.**

Mushroom Planet—Eleanor Cameron. David and Chuck answer an ad placed in the newspaper by Mr. Bass for two boys who would build a space-ship,—"An adventure and a chance to do a good deed await the boys who build the spaceship" (3). This takes the boys on an adventure to Basidium, where they help its inhabitants. In later installments they return to Basidium and continue to help the Basidiumites as well as their descendants living on Earth.

    (1) 1954—*The Wonderful Flight to the Mushroom Planet*
    (2) 1956—*Stowaway to the Mushroom Planet*
    (3) 1958—*Mr. Bass's Planetoid*
    (4) 1960—*A Mystery for Mr. Bass*
    (5) 1967—*Time and Mr. Bass*

My Teacher—Bruce Coville. The Interplanetary Council is worried about the possibility of humans moving out beyond their universe. They assign two aliens, Kreeblim and Broxholm, to observe earthlings. They disguise themselves as elementary school teachers and arouse the suspicions of three children, Susan, Duncan, and Peter. Once the children discover the true identity of Kreeblim and Broxholm, they are recruited to defend Earth from being destroyed or quarantined. The situation looks bleak until one of Peter's alien mentors admits to meddling in Earth's affairs, causing damage to humans.

Peter uses this to persuade the Council they owe humans an opportunity to become better through sending teachers, "'because teachers and children can change the world'" (*My Teacher Flunked* 159).

(1) 1989—*My Teacher Is an Alien*
(2) 1991—*My Teacher Fried My Brains*
(3) 1991—*My Teacher Glows in the Dark*
(4) 1992—*My Teacher Flunked the Planet*

Norby—Isaac and Janet Asimov. Jeff searches for a "teaching robot" to help tutor him so he can win a scholarship to help pay for his education at the Space Academy. He goes to a shop with used robots and discovers Norby. Norby is a very special robot. He was originally built by aliens but had to be rebuilt after he is discovered on board their damaged ship. Because he has personality and seems very humanlike, Jeff allows him some self-determination. Norby's ability to move through space and time, although he is not always able to control where they end up or when, takes them on all kinds of adventures. Their adventures usually include Jeff's older brother Fargo, Fargo's girlfriend Albany, and Space Academy Commander Yobo.

(1) 1983—*Norby, the Mixed-Up Robot*
(2) 1984—*Norby's Other Secret*
(3) 1985—*Norby and the Lost Princess*
(4) 1985—*Norby and the Invaders*
(5) 1986—*Norby and the Queen's Necklace*
(6) 1987—*Norby Finds a Villain*
(7) 1989—*Norby Down to Earth*
(8) 1989—*Norby and Yobo's Great Adventure*
(9) 1990—*Norby and the Oldest Dragon*
(10) 1991—*Norby and the Court Jester*

North, Rick. *See* **Young Astronauts.**

Norton, Andre. *See* **Ayyar Series; Star Books; Star Ka'at.**

Not Quite Human—Seth McEvoy. Dr. Carson builds an android to "show the world that androids can perform many tasks as well as human beings, and can offer a valuable service to society" (*Batteries* 2). He moves to a new town with his daughter Becky and Chip, the android, and takes a job as a junior high school science teacher. Chip seems like the kind of eighth grader almost any teacher would want in class, because as an android he does exactly as he is told, but because he takes everything literally, he is the kind of student teachers often dread. Chip's taking things literally is the source of much humor in the series.

(1) 1985—*Batteries Not Included*

  (2) 1985—*All Geared Up*
  (3) 1985—*A Bug in the System*
  (4) 1986—*Reckless Robot*
  (5) 1986—*Terror at Play*
  (6) 1986—*Killer Robot*

Pantell, Dora. *See* **Miss Pickerell (Pantell).**

Pearl, Jack. *See* **Space Eagle.**

Peter's Adventures—Stephen Mogridge. Follows the adventures of Peter.

  (1) 1954—*Peter and the Flying Saucers*
  (2) 1955—*Peter and the Atomic Valley*
  (3) 1956—*Peter and the Moon Bomb*
  (4) 1957—*Peter and the Flying Submarine*
  (5) 1958—*Peter's Denmark Adventure*

Pohl, Frederik. *See* **Undersea Trilogy.**

Pournelle, Jerry. *See* **Jupiter Novels.**

Professor Branestawm—Norman Hunter. Professor Branestawm has goofy adventures as a result of his ridiculous inventions. Things usually go terribly wrong—but the Professor hardly notices—and always manage to right themselves by the end of the adventure. All of this usually results in the Professor meeting and making new friends. British series.

  (1) 1933—*The Incredible Adventures of Professor Branestawm*
  (2) 1937—*Professor Branestawm's Treasure Hunt*
  (3) 1939—*Stories of Professor Branestawm*
  (4) 1970—*Peculiar Triumph of Professor Branestawm*
  (5) 1972—*Professor Branestawm up the Pole*
  (6) 1974—*Professor Branestawm's Great Revolution*
  (7) 1977—*Professor Branestawm 'Round the Bend*
  (8) 1979—*Professor Branestawm's Perilous Pudding*
  (9) 1980—*The Best of Branestawm*
  (10) 1981—*Professor Branestawm and the Wild Letters*
  (11) 1982—*Professor Branestawm's Pocket Motor Car*
  (12) 1982—*Professor Branestawm's Mouse War*
  (13) 1983—*Professor Branestawm's Crunchy Crockery*
  (14) 1983—*Professor Branestawm's Hair-Raising Idea*

Rick Brant—John Blaine. This series seems very much patterned after the Tom Swift series. Rick does not appear to be the type of inventive genius Tom

Swift is, but he is able to solve the mysteries he and his ex-marine friend Scotty encounter involving science and technology.

    (1) 1947—*The Rocket's Shadow*
    (2) 1947—*The Lost City*
    (3) 1947—*Sea Gold*
    (4) 1947—*One Hundred Fathoms Under*
    (5) 1948—*The Whispering Box Mystery*
    (6) 1949—*The Phantom Shark*
    (7) 1950—*Smuggler's Reef*
    (8) 1951—*Caves of Fear*
    (9) 1952—*Stairway to Danger*
  (10) 1954—*The Golden Skull*
  (11) 1956—*The Wailing Octopus*
  (12) 1957—*The Electronic Mind Reader*
  (13) 1958—*The Scarlet Lake Mystery*
  (14) 1958—*The Pirates of Shan*
  (15) 1960—*The Blue Ghost Mystery*
  (16) 1961—*The Egyptian Cat Mystery*
  (17) 1962—*The Flaming Mountain*
  (18) 1963—*The Flying Stingaree*
  (19) 1964—*The Ruby Ray Mystery*
  (20) 1965—*The Veiled Raiders*
  (21) 1966—*Rocket Jumper*
  (22) 1967—*Deadly Dutchman*
  (23) 1968—*Danger Below*

Robot & Rebecca—Jane Yolen. It is the year 2121 and Rebecca is quite happy when she receives a robot for her birthday. Since she wants to be a detective like Sherlock Holmes, she decides he will be her "Dr. Watson," and together they search for mysteries to solve.

    (1) 1980—*The Robot and Rebecca*
    (2) 1981—*The Robot and Rebecca and the Missing Owser*

Rockwell, Carey. *See* **Tom Corbett Space Cadett.**

Schealer, John. *See* **Zip-Zip.**

Secret Under—Gordon R. Dickson. Twelve-year-old Robby lives with his parents at the Point Loma Research Station, where his father is a marine biologist working for "the International Department of Fisheries—Salt Water Research Division" (*Sea* 3). The year is 2013, but women still seem to find it difficult to combine a career with family. Robby's "mother was a marine biologist, too, but she had given up active work in the field when she had married his father. Times were not the same as they had been back in the twentieth century when a marine biologist was anyone who cared to study the plants and animals of the seas and Oceans. The was the year 2013, and all the sciences had moved so fast and become so complicated that it was just not possible—as Robby's mother said with a sigh—to do honest research and take care of a son and a husband at the same time. One or the other of the jobs had to go. . . . [She] concentrated on seeing that Robby and his father got their meals on time and sleep enough to keep them going" (*Secret Under the Sea* 2-3).

    (1) 1960—*Secret Under the Sea*
    (2) 1963—*Secret Under Antarctica*
    (3) 1964—*Secret Under the Caribbean*

Service, Pamela. *See* **Stinker.**

Sheffield, Charles. *See* **Jupiter Novels.**

Slobodkin, Louis. *See* **Space Ship.**

Slote, Alfred. *See* **Danny One.**

Space: Above and Beyond—Various Authors. A rather bleak picture of the future is presented in this series for the middle reader. Androids have joined forces with aliens to try to destroy humans on Earth and its colonies in space. Based on a television series of the same title.

    (1) 1996—*The Aliens Approach* (Easton Royce)
    (2) 1996—*Dark Side of the Sun* (Dina Anastasio)
    (3) 1996—*Mutiny* (Easton Royce)
    (4) 1996—*The Enemy* (Dina Anastasio)
    (5) 1997—*Demolition Winter* (Peter Telep)

Space Cat—Ruthven Todd. About the adventures of a cat and his astronaut owner. Together they travel to the Moon, Mars, and Venus.

    (1) 1952—*Space Cat*
    (2) 1955—*Space Cat Visits Venus*
    (3) 1957—*Space Cat Meets Mars*
    (4) 1958—*Space Cat and the Kittens*

Space Eagle—Jack Pearl. Protagonist Paul Girard is the head of the Girard Industrial Empire, is described as a "millionaire, whiz kid, playboy" (*Operation Doomsday* 11), and works with the United States Air Force. There is even a "Space Eagle Pledge to America."

    (1) 1967—*Operation Doomsday*
    (2) 1970—*Operation Star Voyage*

Space Series—W. E. Johns. Group Captain "Tiger" Clinton and his son Rex on a deer-stalking holiday in the Scottish Highlands happen upon Professor Lucius Brane's castle. They are just the ones he has been looking for to pilot his space ship. Their many adventures center around the search for a perfect planet that humans may colonize. British series.

    (1) 1954—*Kings of Space*
    (2) 1955—*Return to Mars*
    (3) 1956—*Now to the Stars*
    (4) 1957—*To Outer Space*
    (5) 1958—*The Edge of Beyond*
    (6) 1959—*The Death Rays of Ardilla*
    (7) 1960—*To Worlds Unknown*
    (8) 1961—*The Quest for the Perfect Planet*
    (9) 1962—*Worlds of Wonder*

Space Ship—Louis Slobodkin. While visiting his grandmother, Eddie meets "Marty," an alien from the planet Martinea who crash landed under a special apple tree in the orchard. Eddie and "Marty" must learn how to communicate with one another and ways to trust one another. They become friends in the first book and renew their friendship in the books following through their various adventures.

    (1) 1952—*The Space Ship Under the Apple Tree*
    (2) 1958—*The Space Ship Returns to the Apple Tree*
    (3) 1962—*The Three-Seated Space Ship*
    (4) 1968—*Round Trip Space Ship*

Star Books—Andre Norton. Francis J. Molson groups these together because he contends, "There are also Norton novels which, although not linked by reappearing characters, are related in subject matter or approach because of similarity in title. There are, for example, the Star books—" ("Andre" 274). *Star Born* is a sequel to *The Stars Are Ours!*

    (1) 1953—*Star Man's Son 2250 A.D.*
    (2) 1953—*Star Rangers*
    (3) 1954—*The Stars Are Ours!*
    (4) 1955—*Star Guard*
    (5) 1957—*Star Born*
    (6) 1958—*Star Gate*

Star Ka'at—Andre Norton and Dorothy Madlee. Jim, a young white boy, and Elly Mae, a young black girl, are adopted by two catlike aliens, Mer and Tiro. Mer and Tiro are on Earth to rescue any kin left from an earlier visitation, because it is believed Earth is headed toward destruction. Jim and Elly Mae end up on the Star Ka'at space ship and travel to the Star Ka'at planet. Interesting characters. Jim is the protagonist, but Elly Mae is usually the one who answers Jim's questions and cautions him about danger.

    (1) 1976—*Star Ka'at*
    (2) 1978—*Star Ka'at World*
    (3) 1979—*Star Ka'ats and Plant People*
    (4) 1981—*Star Ka'ats and the Winged Warriors*

Star Trek: Deep Space Nine—**Various Authors.** Based on the TV series but focuses on the adventures of Jake, son of the station commander, and Nog, nephew of the owner of a casino-type establishment.

    (1) 1994—*The Star Ghost* (Brad Strickland)
    (2) 1994—*Stowaways* (Brad Strickland)
    (3) 1994—*Prisoners of Peace* (John Peel)
    (4) 1994—*The Pet* (Mel Gilden and Ted Pedersen)
    (5) 1995—*Arcade* (Diana G. Gallagher)
    (6) 1995—*Field Trip* (John Peel)
    (7) 1996—*Gypsy World* (Ted Pedersen)
    (8) 1996—*Highest Score* (Kem Antilles)
    (9) 1997—*Cardassian Imps* (Mel Gilden)
    (10) 1997—*Space Camp* (Ted Pedersen)
    (11) 1997—*Day of Honor: Honor Bound* (Diana G. Gallagher)

Star Trek: **Starfleet Academy—Various Authors.** Based on the characters of the original *Star Trek* TV series. This describes the adventures of the TV characters while they were mere cadets, ensigns, and interns.

    (1) 1996—*Crisis on Vulcan* (Brad Strickland and Barbara Strickland)
    (2) 1996—*Aftershock* (John Vornholt)
    (3) 1996—*Cadet Kirk* (Todd C. Hamilton and Diane Carey)

Star Trek: The Next Generation: **Starfleet Academy—Various Authors.** Follows the adventures of the *Star Trek: The Next Generation* characters as they assume their places at Starfleet Academy.

    (1) 1993—*Worf's First Adventure* (Peter David)
    (2) 1993—*Line of Fire* (Peter David)
    (3) 1993—*Survival* (Peter David)
    (4) 1994—*Capture the Flag* (John Vornholt)

(5) 1994—*Atlantis Station* (Todd Cameron Hamilton)

(6) 1995—*Mystery of the Missing Crew* (Michael Jan Friedman)

(7) 1995—*Secret of the Lizard People* (Michael Jan Friedman)

(8) 1995—*Starfall* (Brad Strickland)

(9) 1995—*Nova Command* (Brad and Barbara Strickland)

(10) 1996—*Loyalties* (Patricia Barnes-Svarney)

(11) 1996—*Crossfire* (John Vornholt)

(12) 1997—*Breakaway* (Bobbi J. G. Weiss and David Cody Weiss)

(13) 1997—*The Haunted Spaceship* (Brad Ferguson)

(14) 1998—*Deceptions* (David Cody Weiss)

Star Trek: Voyager: **Starfleet Academy—Various Authors.** Follows the adventures of the *Star Trek: Voyager* crew as they make their way through Starfleet Academy.

(1) 1997—*Lifeline* (Bobbi J. G. Weiss)

(2) 1997—*The Chance Factor* (Diana G. Gallagher)

(3) 1997—*Quarantine* (Patricia Barnes-Svarney)

Stannard, Russell. *See* **Uncle Albert.**

Stinker—Pamela Service. Karen and Jonathan are befriended by an alien who takes the form of a skunk while on Earth.

(1) 1988—*Stinker from Space*

(2) 1993—*Stinker's Return*

Tas—E. C. Eliott. Australian version of space adventures.

(1) 1955—*Tas and the Space Machine*

(2) 1955—*Tas and the Postal Rocket*

Time Trilogy—Madeleine L'Engle.
Continuing adventures of Meg, Charles Wallace, Calvin, and the twins. The battle between good and evil continues.

(1) 1962—*A Wrinkle in Time*

(2) 1973—*A Wind in the Door*

(3) 1978—*A Swiftly Tilting Planet*

Todd, Ruthven. *See* **Space Cat.**

Tom Corbett Space Cadet—Carey Rockwell. Loosely based on *Space Cadet* by Robert A. Heinlein. Follows the adventures of Tom, Astro, and Roger.

    (1) 1952—*Stand by for Mars*
    (2) 1953—*Danger in Deep Space*
    (3) 1953—*On the Trail of the Space Pirates*
    (4) 1953—*The Space Pioneers*
    (5) 1954—*The Revolt on Venus*
    (6) 1954—*Treachery in Outer Space*
    (7) 1955—*Sabotage in Space*
    (8) 1956—*The Robot Rocket*

Tom Swift, Jr. (Second Series)—Victor Appleton. Chronicles the adventures of the son of the original Tom Swift. Aliens send a coded note seeking a meeting with Tom Jr. and his father for advice on passing through Earth's atmosphere. This alien interaction is a thread that follows throughout the series.

    (1) 1954—*Tom Swift and His Flying Lab*
    (2) 1954—*Tom Swift and His Jetmarine*
    (3) 1954—*Tom Swift and His Rocket Ship*
    (4) 1954—*Tom Swift and His Giant Robot*
    (5) 1954—*Tom Swift and His Atomic Earth Blaster*
    (6) 1955—*Tom Swift and His Outpost in Space*
    (7) 1956—*Tom Swift and His Diving Seacopter*
    (8) 1956—*Tom Swift in the Caves of Nuclear Fire*
    (9) 1956—*Tom Swift on the Phantom Satellite*
  (10) 1957—*Tom Swift and His Ultrasonic Cycloplane*
  (11) 1958—*Tom Swift and His Deep-Sea Hydrodome*
  (12) 1958—*Tom Swift in the Race to the Moon*
  (13) 1958—*Tom Swift and His Space Solartron*
  (14) 1959—*Tom Swift and His Electronic Retroscope*
  (15) 1960—*Tom Swift and His Spectromarine Selector*
  (16) 1960—*Tom Swift and the Cosmic Astronauts*
  (17) 1961—*Tom Swift and the Visitor from Planet X*
  (18) 1961—*Tom Swift and the Electronic Hydrolung*
  (19) 1962—*Tom Swift and His Triphibian Atomicar*
  (20) 1962—*Tom Swift and His Megascope Space Prober*
  (21) 1963—*Tom Swift and the Asteroid Pirates*
  (22) 1963—*Tom Swift and His Repalatron Skyway*
  (23) 1964—*Tom Swift and His Aquatomic Tracker*
  (24) 1964—*Tom Swift and His 3-D Telejector*
  (25) 1965—*Tom Swift and His Polar-Ray Dynasphere*
  (26) 1965—*Tom Swift and His Sonic Boom Trap*
  (27) 1966—*Tom Swift and His Subocean Geotron*
  (28) 1966—*Tom Swift and the Mystery Comet*
  (29) 1967—*Tom Swift and the Captive Planetoid*
  (30) 1968—*Tom Swift and His G-Force Inverter*
  (31) 1969—*Tom Swift and His Dyna-4 Capsule*
  (32) 1970—*Tom Swift and His Cosmotron Express*

(33) 1971—*Tom Swift and the Galaxy Ghosts*

Tom Swift (Third Series)—Victor Appleton. Most interesting of the Tom Swift series. A young woman and a Native American join Tom on his adventures in space.

    (1) 1981—*The City in the Stars*
    (2) 1981—*Terror on the Moons of Jupiter*
    (3) 1981—*The Alien Probe*
    (4) 1981—*The War in Outer Space*
    (5) 1981—*Astral Fortress*
    (6) 1981—*The Rescue Mission*
    (7) 1982—*Ark Two*
    (8) 1983—*Crater of Mystery*
    (9) 1983—*Gateway to Doom*
    (10) 1983—*The Invisible Force*
    (11) 1984—*Planet of Nightmares*

Tom Swift (Fourth Series)—Victor Appleton. Further updating the Tom Swift persona.

    (1) 1991—*The Black Dragon*
    (2) 1991—*The Negative Zone*
    (3) 1991—*Cyborg Kickboxer*
    (4) 1991—*The DNA Disaster*
    (5) 1991—*Monster Machine*
    (6) 1991—*Aquatech Warriors*
    (7) 1992—*Moonstalker*
    (8) 1992—*The Microbots*
    (9) 1992—*Fire Biker*
    (10) 1992—*Mind Games*
    (11) 1992—*Mutant Beach*
    (12) 1993—*Death Quake*
    (13) 1993—*Quantum Force*

Tripods—John Christopher. Series with strong themes on self-determination, free will, and anticolonialism.

    (1) 1967—*The White Mountains*
    (2) 1967—*The City of Gold and Lead*
    (3) 1968—*The Pool of Fire*
    (4) 1988—*When the Tripods Came* (Prequel)

Tubby Tin—Georgie Adams. British picture-book series about Tubby Tin and his creator Professor Stargazen. "If anyone can, Tubby Tin can!" is a phrase repeated throughout the books. Brightly colored illustrations.

    (1) 1982—*Tubby Tin and the Footies*
    (2) 1982—*Tubby Tin and the Munching Moon*
    (3) 1982—*Tubby Tin and the No Such Things*
    (4) 1982—*Tubby Tin and the Runaway Rainbow*

Uncle Albert—Russell Stannard. Attempts to introduce the reader to physics through science fiction adventures of Uncle Albert (Einstein) and his niece.

    (1) 1989—*The Time and Space of Uncle Albert*
    (2) 1991—*Black Holes and Uncle Albert*
    (3) 1994—*Uncle Albert and the Quantum Quest*
    (4) 1997—*More Letters to Uncle Albert*

Undersea Trilogy—Frederik Pohl and Jack Williamson. Jim Eden enters the Sub-Sea Academy hoping to join the Sub-Sea Fleet. This series tries to interest readers in ocean exploration, as opposed to space exploration. There are a number of similarities between the two: Explorers must wear special paraphernalia and use special vessels to reach the ocean bottom. The ocean, like space, is a mostly uncharted, hostile environment. Jim experiences many adventures as he makes his way through the Academy.

    (1) 1954—*Undersea Quest*
    (2) 1956—*Undersea Fleet*
    (3) 1958—*Undersea City*

Weird Zone—Tony Abbott. Humorously describes the strange happenings in a fictional town. Each installment includes a map of the town where you can locate the Baits Motel, WYRD radio station, and Usher's House of Pancakes. Each installment is narrated by a different student at W. Reid Elementary.

    (1) 1996—*Zombie Surf Commandos from Mars!*
    (2) 1996—*The Incredible Shrinking Kid!*
    (3) 1996—*The Beast from Beneath the Cafeteria!*
    (4) 1996—*Attack of the Alien Mole Invaders!*
    (5) 1997—*The Brain That Wouldn't Obey*
    (6) 1997—*Gigantopus from Planet X!*
    (7) 1997—*Cosmic Boy Versus Mezmo Head*

Williams, Jay, and Raymond Abrashkin. *See* **Danny Dunn.**

Williamson, Jack. *See* **Undersea Trilogy.**

Winston Series—Various Authors. Each entry in the series was to include an introduction to explain the technology or science on which the story is based, to include a glossary defining scientific or technologic terminology, and to provide novels that instruct and entertain (Molson "Winston" 37).

(1) 1952—*Earthbound* (Milton Lesser)
(2) 1952—*Find the Feathered Serpent* (Evan Hunter)
(3) 1952—*Marooned on Mars* (Lester Del Rey)
(4) 1952—*Son of the Stars* (Raymond Jones)
(5) 1952—*Five Against Venus* (Philip Latham)
(6) 1952—*Sons of the Ocean Deeps* (Bryce Walton)
(7) 1952—*Mists of Dawn* (Chad Oliver)
(8) 1952—*Rocket Jockey* (Philip St. John)
(9) 1952—*Islands in the Sky* (Arthur Clarke)
(10) 1952—*Vault of the Ages* (Poul Anderson)
(11) 1953—*Battle on Mercury* (Erik Van Lhin)
(12) 1953—*Vandals of the Void* (Jack Vance)
(13) 1953—*The Mysterious Planet* (Kenneth Wright)
(14) 1953—*Mystery of the Third Mine* (Robert W. Lowndes)
(15) 1953—*Rocket to Luna* (Richard Marsten)
(16) 1953—*Danger: Dinosaurs!* (Richard Marsten)
(17) 1953—*Attack from Atlantis* (Lester Del Rey)
(18) 1953—*Planet of Light* (Raymond Jones)
(19) 1953—*The Star Seekers* (Milton Lesser)
(20) 1953—*Missing Men of Saturn* (Philip Latham)
(21) 1954—*The Year After Tomorrow* (Lester Del Rey)
(22) 1954—*The Secret of Saturn's Rings* (Donald Wollheim)
(23) 1954—*Rockets to Nowhere* (Philip St. John)
(24) 1954—*Trouble on Titan* (Alan Nourse)
(25) 1954—*Step to the Stars* (Lester Del Rey)
(26) 1954—*The World at Bay* (Paul Capon)
(27) 1955—*The Ant Men* (Eric North)
(28) 1955—*The Secret of the Martian Moons* (Donald Wollheim)
(29) 1956—*Mission to the Moon* (Lester Del Rey)
(30) 1956—*The Lost Planet* (Paul V. Dallas)

Wollheim, Donald. *See* **Mike Mars.**

Yolen, Jane. *See* **Commander Toad; Robot & Rebecca.**

Young Astronauts—Rick North. This series is very similar to the Mike Mars series. It can be considered near future science fiction. Its purpose is to interest young readers in space exploration, Mars colonization specifically. There is an ensemble cast of characters representing different ethnic and socioeconomic groups. Unfortunately, the characters are difficult to differentiate.

   (1) 1990—*The Young Astronauts*
   (2) 1990—*Ready for Blastoff!*
   (3) 1990—*Space Blazers*
   (4) 1991—*Destination: Mars*
   (5) 1991—*Space Pioneers*
   (6) 1991—*Citizens of Mars*

Zip-Zip—John Schealer. According to Judith and Kenyon Rosenberg, this series "is an entertaining, humorous science fiction series for the 8 to 10 age group. Afficionadoes might be offended at the levity" (123).

   (1) 1956—*Zip-Zip and His Flying Saucer*
   (2) 1958—*Zip-Zip Goes to Venus*
   (3) 1961—*Zip-Zip and the Red Planet*

Bibliography

PRIMARY SOURCES

Abbott, Tony. *Attack of the Alien Mole Invaders!* Weird Zone 4. New York: Scholastic, 1996.
———. *The Beast from Beneath the Cafeteria!* Weird Zone 3. New York: Scholastic, 1996.
———. *The Brain That Wouldn't Obey.* Weird Zone 5. New York: Scholastic, 1997.
———. *Cosmic Boy Versus Mezmo Head.* Weird Zone 7. New York: Scholastic, 1997.
———. *Gigantopus from Planet X!* Weird Zone 6. New York: Scholastic, 1997.
———. *The Incredible Shrinking Kid!* Weird Zone 2. New York: Scholastic, 1996.
———. *Zombie Surf Commandos from Mars!* Weird Zone 1. New York: Scholastic, 1996.
Adams, Georgie. *Tubby Tin and the Footies.* London: Thurman, 1982.
———. *Tubby Tin and the Munching Moon.* London: Thurman, 1982.
———. *Tubby Tin and the No Such Things.* London: Thurman, 1982.
———. *Tubby Tin and the Runaway Rainbow.* London: Thurman, 1982.
Anastasio, Dina. *Dark Side of the Sun.* New York: HarperTrophy, 1996.
———. *The Enemy.* New York: HarperTrophy, 1996.
Anderson, Poul. *Vault of the Ages.* Philadelphia: Winston, 1952.
Antilles, Kem. *Highest Score. Star Trek: Deep Space Nine* 8. New York: Pocket, 1996.
Applegate, K. A. *The Alien.* Animorphs 8. New York: Scholastic, 1997.
———. *The Andalite Chronicles.* Megamorphs 2. New York: Scholastic, 1997.
———. *The Andalite's Gift.* Megamorphs 1. New York: Scholastic, 1997.
———. *The Android.* Animorphs 10. New York: Scholastic, 1997.
———. *The Capture.* Animorphs 6. New York: Scholastic, 1997.
———. *The Change.* Animorphs 13. New York: Scholastic, 1997.
———. *The Encounter.* Animorphs 3. New York: Scholastic, 1996.
———. *The Forgotten.* Animorphs 11. New York: Scholastic, 1997.
———. *The Invasion.* Animorphs 1. New York: Scholastic, 1996.
———. *The Message.* Animorphs 4. New York: Scholastic, 1996.

————. *The Predator*. Animorphs 5. New York: Scholastic, 1996.

————. *The Reaction*. Animorphs 12. New York: Scholastic, 1997.

————. *The Secret*. Animorphs 9. New York: Scholastic, 1997.

————. *The Stranger*. Animorphs 7. New York: Scholastic, 1997.

————. *The Visitor*. Animorphs 2. New York: Scholastic, 1996.

Tom Swift

Appleton, Victor

Original Series

————. *Tom Swift in the City of Gold*. New York: Grosset & Dunlap, 1912.

Third Series

————. *The Alien Probe* (3). New York: Simon & Schuster, 1981.

————. *Ark Two* (7). New York: Simon & Schuster, 1982.

————. *Astral Fortress* (5). New York: Simon & Schuster, 1981.

————. *The City in the Stars* (1). New York: Simon & Schuster, 1981.

————. *Crater of Mystery* (8). New York: Simon & Schuster, 1983.

————. *Gateway to Doom* (9). New York: Simon & Schuster, 1983.

————. *The Invisible Force* (10). New York: Simon & Schuster, 1983.

————. *Planet of Nightmares* (11). New York: Simon & Schuster, 1984.

————. *Rescue Mission* (6). New York: Simon & Schuster, 1981.

————. *Terror on the Moons of Jupiter* (2). New York: Simon & Schuster, 1981.

————. *The War in Outer Space* (4). New York: Simon & Schuster, 1981.

Fourth Series

————. *Aquatech Warriors* (6). New York: Simon & Schuster, 1991.

————. *The Black Dragon* (1). New York: Simon & Schuster, 1991.

————. *Cyborg Kickboxer* (3). New York: Simon & Schuster, 1991.

————. *Death Quake* (12). New York: Simon & Schuster, 1993.

————. *The DNA Disaster* (4). New York: Simon & Schuster, 1991.

————. *Fire Biker* (9). New York: Simon & Schuster, 1992.

————. *The Microbots* (8). New York: Simon & Schuster, 1992.

————. *Mind Games* (10). New York: Simon & Schuster, 1992.

————. *Monster Machine* (5). New York: Simon & Schuster, 1991.

————. *Moonstalker* (7). New York: Simon & Schuster, 1992.

————. *Mutant Beach* (11). New York: Simon & Schuster, 1992.

————. *The Negative Zone* (2). New York: Simon & Schuster, 1991.

————. *Quantum Force* (13). New York: Simon & Schuster, 1993.

Tom Swift, Jr.

Second Series

————. *Tom Swift and His Aquatomic Tracker* (23). New York: Grosset & Dunlap, 1964.

————. *Tom Swift and His Atomic Earth Blaster* (5). New York: Grosset & Dunlap, 1954.

————. *Tom Swift and His Cosmotron Express* (32). New York: Grosset & Dunlap, 1970.

———. *Tom Swift and His Deep-Sea Hydrodome* (11). New York: Grosset & Dunlap, 1958.

———. *Tom Swift and His Diving Seacopter* (7). New York: Grosset & Dunlap, 1956.

———. *Tom Swift and His Dyna-4 Capsule* (31). New York: Grosset & Dunlap, 1969.

———. *Tom Swift and His Electronic Retroscope* (14). New York: Grosset & Dunlap, 1959.

———. *Tom Swift and His Flying Lab* (1). New York: Grosset & Dunlap, 1954.

———. *Tom Swift and His G-Force Inverter* (30). New York: Grosset & Dunlap, 1968.

———. *Tom Swift and His Giant Robot* (4). New York: Grosset & Dunlap, 1954.

———. *Tom Swift and His Jetmarine* (2). New York: Grosset & Dunlap, 1954.

———. *Tom Swift and His Megascope Space Prober* (20). New York: Grosset & Dunlap, 1962.

———. *Tom Swift and His Outpost in Space* (6). New York: Grosset & Dunlap, 1955.

———. *Tom Swift and His Polar-Ray Dynasphere* (25). New York: Grosset & Dunlap, 1965.

———. *Tom Swift and His Repalatron Skyway* (22). New York: Grosset & Dunlap, 1963.

———. *Tom Swift and His Rocket Ship* (3). New York: Grosset & Dunlap, 1954.

———. *Tom Swift and His Sonic Boom Trap* (26). New York: Grosset & Dunlap, 1965.

———. *Tom Swift and His Space Solartron* (13). New York: Grosset & Dunlap, 1958.

———. *Tom Swift and His Spectromarine Selector* (15). New York: Grosset & Dunlap, 1960.

———. *Tom Swift and His Subocean Geotron* (27). New York: Grosset & Dunlap, 1966.

———. *Tom Swift and His 3-D Telejector* (24). New York: Grosset & Dunlap, 1964.

———. *Tom Swift and His Triphibian Atomicar* (19). New York: Grosset & Dunlap, 1962.

———. *Tom Swift and His Ultrasonic Cycloplane* (10). New York: Grosset & Dunlap, 1957.

———. *Tom Swift and the Asteroid Pirates* (21). New York: Grosset & Dunlap, 1963.

———. *Tom Swift and the Captive Planetoid* (29). New York: Grosset & Dunlap, 1967.

———. *Tom Swift and the Cosmic Astronauts* (16). New York: Grosset & Dunlap, 1960.

———. *Tom Swift and the Electronic Hydrolung* (18). New York: Grosset & Dunlap, 1961.

———. *Tom Swift and the Galaxy Ghosts* (33). New York: Grosset & Dunlap, 1971.

———. *Tom Swift and the Mystery Comet* (28). New York: Grosset & Dunlap, 1966.

———. *Tom Swift and the Visitor from Planet X* (17). New York: Grosset & Dunlap, 1961.

———. *Tom Swift in the Caves of Nuclear Fire* (8). New York: Grosset & Dunlap, 1956.

———. *Tom Swift in the Race to the Moon* (12). New York: Grosset & Dunlap, 1958.

———. *Tom Swift on the Phantom Satellite* (9). New York: Grosset & Dunlap, 1956.

Asimov, Isaac (as Paul French). *David Starr, Space Ranger*. New York: Doubleday, 1952.

———. *Lucky Starr and the Big Sun of Mercury*. New York: Doubleday, 1956.

——. *Lucky Starr and the Moons of Jupiter*. New York: Doubleday, 1957.

——. *Lucky Starr and the Oceans of Venus*. New York: Doubleday, 1954.

——. *Lucky Starr and the Pirates of the Asteroids*. New York: Doubleday, 1953.

——. *Lucky Starr and the Rings of Saturn*. New York: Doubleday, 1958.

Asimov, Isaac, and Janet Asimov. *Norby, the Mixed-Up Robot*. New York: Walker, 1983.

——. *Norby and the Court Jester*. New York: Walker, 1991.

——. *Norby and the Invaders*. New York: Walker, 1985.

——. *Norby and the Lost Princess*. New York: Walker, 1985.

——. *Norby and the Oldest Dragon*. New York: Walker, 1990.

——. *Norby and the Queen's Necklace*. New York: Walker, 1986.

——. *Norby and Yobo's Great Adventure*. New York: Walker, 1989.

——. *Norby Down to Earth*. New York: Walker, 1989.

——. *Norby Finds a Villain*. New York: Walker, 1987.

——. *Norby's Other Secret*. New York: Walker, 1984.

Balan, Bruce. *Blackout in the Amazon*. Cyber.kdz 4. New York: Avon, 1997.

——. *The Great NASA Flu*. Cyber.kdz 3. New York: Avon, 1997.

——. *In Search of SCUM*. Cyber.kdz 1. New York: Avon, 1997.

——. *A Picture's Worth*. Cyber.kdz 2. New York: Avon, 1997.

Barnes-Svarney, Patricia. *Loyalties*. *Star Trek: The Next Generation*: Starfleet Academy 10. New York: Pocket, 1996.

——. *Quarantine*. *Star Trek: Voyager*: Starfleet Academy 3. New York: Pocket, 1997.

Beatty, Jerome, Jr. *Maria Looney and the Cosmic Circus*. New York: Avon, 1978.

——. *Maria Looney and the Remarkable Robot*. New York: Avon, 1979.

——. *Maria Looney and the Red Planet*. New York: Avon, 1977.

——. *Matthew Looney and the Space Pirates*. 1972. New York: Avon, 1974.

——. *Matthew Looney in the Outback*. 1969. New York: Avon, 1973.

——. *Matthew Looney's Invasion of the Earth*. 1965. New York: Avon, 1972.

——. *Matthew Looney's Voyage to the Earth*. 1961. New York: Avon, 1972.

Beech, Linda. *The Magic School Bus Gets Ants in Its Pants: A Book About Ants*. New York: Scholastic, 1996.

——. *The Magic School Bus Gets Baked in a Cake: A Book About Kitchen Chemistry*. New York: Scholastic, 1995.

——. *The Magic School Bus in the Haunted Museum: A Book About Sound*. New York: Scholastic, 1995.

Blaine, John. *The Blue Ghost Mystery*. Rick Brant Scientific Adventure 15. New York: Grosset & Dunlap, 1960.

——. *Caves of Fear*. Rick Brant 8. New York: Grosset & Dunlap, 1951.

——. *Danger Below*. Rick Brant 23. New York: Grosset & Dunlap, 1968.

——. *Deadly Dutchman*. Rick Brant 22. New York: Grosset & Dunlap, 1967.

——. *The Egyptian Cat Mystery*. Rick Brant 16. New York: Grosset & Dunlap, 1961.

——. *The Electronic Mind Reader*. Rick Brant 12. New York: Grosset & Dunlap, 1957.

——. *The Flaming Mountain*. Rick Brant 17. New York: Grosset & Dunlap, 1962.

——. *The Flying Stingaree*. Rick Brant 18. New York: Grosset & Dunlap, 1963.

——. *The Golden Skull*. Rick Brant 10. New York: Grosset & Dunlap, 1954.

——. *The Lost City*. Rick Brant 2. New York: Grosset & Dunlap, 1947.

———. *One Hundred Fathoms Under*. Rick Brant 4. New York: Grosset & Dunlap, 1947.

———. *The Phantom Shark*. Rick Brant 6. New York: Grosset & Dunlap, 1949.

———. *The Pirates of Shan*. Rick Brant 14. New York: Grosset & Dunlap, 1958.

———. *Rocket Jumper*. Rick Brant 21. New York: Grosset & Dunlap, 1966.

———. *The Rocket's Shadow*. Rick Brant 1. New York: Grosset & Dunlap, 1947.

———. *The Ruby Ray Mystery*. Rick Brant 19. New York: Grosset & Dunlap, 1964.

———. *The Scarlet Lake Mystery*. Rick Brant 13. New York: Grosset & Dunlap, 1958.

———. *Sea Gold*. Rick Brant 3. New York: Grosset & Dunlap, 1947.

———. *Smuggler's Reef*. Rick Brant 7. New York: Grosset & Dunlap, 1950.

———. *Stairway to Danger*. Rick Brant 9. New York: Grosset & Dunlap, 1952.

———. *The Veiled Raiders*. Rick Brant 20. New York: Grosset & Dunlap, 1965.

———. *The Wailing Octopus*. Rick Brant 11. New York: Grosset & Dunlap, 1956.

———. *The Whispering Box Mystery*. Rick Brant 5. New York: Grosset & Dunlap, 1948.

Bloom, George. *The Magic School Bus Makes a Rainbow: A Book About Color*. New York: Scholastic, 1997.

Brinley, Bertrand Russell. *The Big Kerplop: A Mad Scientists' Club Adventure*. Philadelphia: Macrae Smith, 1974.

———. *The Mad Scientists' Club*. Philadelphia: Macrae Smith, 1965.

———. *The New Adventures of the Mad Scientists' Club*. Philadelphia: Macrae Smith, 1968.

Cameron, Eleanor. *Mr. Bass's Planetoid*. Boston: Little, Brown, 1958.

———. *A Mystery for Mr. Bass*. Boston: Little, Brown, 1960.

———. *Stowaway to the Mushroom Planet*. Boston: Little, Brown, 1956.

———. *Time and Mr. Bass*. Boston: Little, Brown, 1967.

———. *The Wonderful Flight to the Mushroom Planet*. 1954. New York: Scholastic, 1966.

Capon, Paul. *The World at Bay*. Philadelphia: Winston, 1954.

Christopher, John. *The City of Gold and Lead*. 1967. New York: Collier, 1988.

———. *The Pool of Fire*. 1968. New York: Collier, 1988.

———. *When the Tripods Came*. New York: Dutton, 1988.

———. *The White Mountains*. 1967. New York: Collier, 1988.

Clarke, Arthur. *Islands in the Sky*. Philadelphia: Winston, 1952.

Cole, Joanna. *The Magic School Bus and the Electric Field Trip*. New York: Scholastic, 1997.

———. *The Magic School Bus at the Waterworks*. New York: Scholastic, 1986.

———. *The Magic School Bus Goes Upstream: A Book About Salmon on Migration*. New York: Scholastic, 1997.

———. *The Magic School Bus in the Time of the Dinosaurs*. New York: Scholastic, 1994.

———. *The Magic School Bus Inside a Beehive*. New York: Scholastic, 1996.

———. *The Magic School Bus Inside a Hurricane*. New York: Scholastic, 1995.

———. *The Magic School Bus Inside the Earth*. New York: Scholastic, 1987.

———. *The Magic School Bus Inside the Human Body*. New York: Scholastic, 1989.

———. *The Magic School Bus Lost in the Solar System*. New York: Scholastic, 1990.

———. *The Magic School Bus on the Ocean Floor*. New York: Scholastic, 1992.

———. *The Magic School Bus Out of This World*. New York: Scholastic, 1996.

Coville, Bruce. *Forever Begins Tomorrow*. 1986. New York: Pocket, 1995.

———. *My Teacher Flunked the Planet*. New York: Pocket, 1992.

———. *My Teacher Fried My Brains*. New York: Pocket, 1991.

———. *My Teacher Glows in the Dark*. New York: Pocket, 1991.

———. *My Teacher Is an Alien*. New York: Pocket, 1989.

———. *Operation Sherlock*. 1986. New York: Pocket, 1995.

———. *Robot Trouble*. 1986. New York: Pocket, 1995.

Dallas, Paul V. *The Lost Planet*. Philadelphia: Winston, 1956.

David, Peter. *Line of Fire*. *Star Trek: The Next Generation*: Starfleet Academy 2. New York: Pocket, 1993.

———. *Survival*. *Star Trek: The Next Generation*: Starfleet Academy 3. New York: Pocket, 1993.

———. *Worf's First Adventure*. *Star Trek: The Next Generation*: Starfleet Academy 1. New York: Pocket, 1993.

Del Rey, Lester. *Attack from Atlantis*. Philadelphia: Winston, 1953.

———. *Mission to the Moon*. Philadelphia: Winston, 1956.

———. *Moon of Mutiny*. 1961. New York: Signet, 1969.

———. *Step to the Stars*. Philadelphia: Winston, 1954.

———. *The Year After Tomorrow*. Philadelphia: Winston, 1954.

Dickson, Gordon R. *Secret Under Antarctica*. New York: Holt, Rinehart & Winston, 1963.

———. *Secret Under the Caribbean*. New York: Holt, Rinehart & Winston, 1964.

———. *Secret Under the Sea*. New York: Holt, Rinehart & Winston, 1960.

Earnshaw, Brian. *Dragonfall Five and the Empty Planet*. New York: Lothrop, 1973.

———. *Dragonfall Five and the Haunted World*. New York: Methuen, 1980.

———. *Dragonfall Five and the Hijackers*. New York: Methuen, 1974.

———. *Dragonfall Five and the Master Mind*. New York: Methuen, 1975.

———. *Dragonfall Five and the Royal Beast*. New York: Lothrop, 1972.

———. *Dragonfall Five and the Space Cowboys*. New York: Methuen, 1972.

———. *Dragonfall Five and the Super Horse*. New York: Methuen, 1977.

Eliott, E. C. *Tas and the Postal Rocket*. London: Nelson, 1955.

———. *Tas and the Space Machine*. London: Nelson, 1955.

Engdahl, Sylvia. *Enchantress from the Stars*. 1970. New York: Aladdin, 1989.

———. *Far Side of Evil*. 1971. New York: Collier, 1989.

Ferguson, Brad. *The Haunted Spaceship*. *Star Trek: The Next Generation*: Starfleet Academy 13. New York: Pocket, 1997.

Friedman, Michael Jan. *Mystery of the Missing Crew*. *Star Trek: The Next Generation*: Starfleet Academy 6. New York: Pocket, 1995.

———. *Secret of the Lizard People*. *Star Trek: The Next Generation*: Starfleet Academy 7. New York: Pocket, 1995.

Gallagher, Diana G. *Arcade*. *Star Trek: Deep Space Nine* 5. New York: Pocket, 1995.

———. *The Chance Factor*. *Star Trek: Voyager*: Starfleet Academy 2. New York: Pocket, 1997.

———. *Day of Honor: Honor Bound*. *Star Trek: Deep Space Nine* 11. New York: Pocket, 1997.

Gilden, Mel. *Cardassian Imps*. *Star Trek: Deep Space Nine* 9. New York: Pocket, 1997.

Gilden, Mel, and Ted Pedersen. *The Pet*. *Star Trek: Deep Space Nine* 4. New York: Pocket, 1994.

Greene, Joseph. *Captives in Space*. Dig Allen Space Explorer 2. New York: Golden, 1960.

———. *The Forgotten Star*. Dig Allen Space Explorer 1. New York: Golden, 1959.

———. *Journey to Jupiter*. Dig Allen Space Explorer 3. New York: Golden, 1961.

———. *Lost City of Uranus*. Dig Allen Space Explorer 6. New York: Golden, 1962.

———. *Robots on Saturn*. Dig Allen Space Explorer 5. New York: Golden, 1961.

———. *Trappers on Venus*. Dig Allen Space Explorer 4. New York: Golden, 1961.

Hamilton, Todd C. *Atlantis Station*. *Star Trek: The Next Generation*: Starfleet Academy 3. New York: Pocket, 1996.

Hamilton, Virginia. *Dustland*. New York: Harcourt, 1980.

———. *The Gathering*. New York: Harcourt, 1981.

———. *Justice and Her Brothers*. New York: Harcourt, 1978.

Heinlein, Robert A. *Between Planets*. New York: Ace-Charter, 1951.

———. *Citizen of the Galaxy*. 1957. New York: Scribner's, 1985.

———. *Farmer in the Sky*. 1950. New York: Ballantine, 1975.

———. *Have Space Suit—Will Travel*. New York: Scribner's, 1958.

———. *Red Planet*. New York: Scribner's 1949.

———. *Rocket Ship Galileo*. New York: Scribner's 1947.

———. *The Rolling Stones*. 1952. New York: Del Rey-Ballantine, 1978.

———. *Space Cadet*. New York: Ace-Charter, 1948.

———. *The Star Beast*. 1954. New York: Del Rey-Ballantine, 1978.

———. *Starman Jones*. 1953. New York: Del Rey-Ballantine, 1978.

———. *Time for the Stars*. New York: Scribner's 1956.

———. *Tunnel in the Sky*. New York: Ace-Charter, 1955.

Herman, Gail. *The Magic School Bus Blows Its Top: A Book About Volcanoes*. New York: Scholastic, 1996.

Hughes, Monica. *The Guardian of Isis*. New York: Atheneum, 1981.

———. *The Isis Pedlar*. New York: Atheneum, 1982.

———. *The Keeper of the Isis Light*. New York: Atheneum, 1980.

Hunter, Evan. *Find the Feathered Serpent*. Philadelphia: Winston, 1952.

Hunter, Norman. *The Best of Branestawm*. London: Bodley Head, 1980.

———. *The Incredible Adventures of Professor Branestawm*. 1933. Harmondsworth, England: Puffin, 1946.

———. *The Peculiar Triumph of Professor Branestawm*. 1970. Harmondsworth, England: Penguin, 1972.

———. *Professor Branestawm and the Wild Letters*. London: Bodley Head, 1981.

———. *Professor Branestawm 'Round the Bend*. Harmondsworth, England: Penguin, 1980.

———. *Professor Branestawm Up the Pole*. Harmondsworth, England: Puffin, 1975.

———. *Professor Branestawm's Crunchy Crockery*. London: Bodley Head, 1983.

———. *Professor Branestawm's Great Revolution*. Harmondsworth, England: Puffin, 1977.

———. *Professor Branestawm's Hair-Raising Idea*. London: Bodley Head, 1983.

———. *Professor Branestawm's Mouse at War*. London: Bodley Head, 1982.

———. *Professor Branestawm's Perilous Pudding*. London: Bodley Head, 1979.

———. *Professor Branestawm's Pocket Motor Car*. 1982. Harmondsworth, England: Puffin, 1985.

———. *Professor Branestawm's Treasure Hunt*. 1937. Baltimore: Penguin, 1972.

Johns, W. E. *The Death Rays of Ardilla*. London: Hodder and Stoughton, 1958.

————. *The Edge of Beyond*. London: Hodder and Stoughton, 1958.

————. *Kings of Space*. London: Hodder and Stoughton, 1954.

————. *Now to the Stars*. London: Hodder and Stoughton, 1956.

————. *The Quest for the Perfect Planet*. London: Children's, 1961.

————. *Return to Mars*. 1955. London: May Fair, 1970.

————. *Worlds of Wonder*. London: Children's, 1962.

————. *To Outer Space*. London: Hodder and Stoughton, 1957.

————. *To Worlds Unknown*. London: Hodder and Stoughton, 1960.

Jones, Raymond. *Planet of Light*. Philadelphia: Winston, 1953.

————. *Son of the Stars*. Philadelphia: Winston, 1952.

Krauss, Ronnie. *The Magic School Bus Going Batty: A Book About Bats*. New York: Scholastic, 1996.

Latham, Philip. *Five Against Venus*. Philadelphia: Winston, 1952.

————. *Missing Men of Saturn*. Philadelphia: Winston, 1953.

Lawrence, Jim. *The Cutlass Clue*. New York: New American Library, 1986.

L'Engle, Madeleine. *A Swiftly Tilting Planet*. 1978. New York: Dell, 1979.

————. *A Wind in the Door*. 1973. New York: Dell, 1983.

————. *A Wrinkle in Time*. New York: Farrar, Straus and Giroux, 1962.

Lesser, Milton. *Earthbound*. Philadelphia: Winston, 1952.

————. *The Star Seekers*. Philadelphia: Winston, 1953.

Lowndes, Robert W. *Mystery of the Third Mine*. Philadelphia: Winston, 1953.

MacGregor, Ellen. *Miss Pickerell and the Geiger Counter*. New York: McGraw-Hill, 1953.

————. *Miss Pickerell Goes to Mars*. New York: McGraw-Hill, 1951.

————. *Miss Pickerell Goes to the Arctic*. New York: McGraw-Hill, 1954.

————. *Miss Pickerell Goes Undersea*. New York: McGraw-Hill, 1953.

MacGregor, Ellen, and Dora Pantell. *Miss Pickerell and the Blue Whales*. New York: McGraw-Hill, 1983.

————. *Miss Pickerell and the Lost World*. New York: Watts, 1986.

————. *Miss Pickerell and the Supertanker*. New York: McGraw-Hill, 1978.

————. *Miss Pickerell and the War of the Computers*. New York: Watts, 1984.

————. *Miss Pickerell and the Weather Satellite*. New York: McGraw-Hill, 1971.

————. *Miss Pickerell Goes on a Dig*. New York: McGraw-Hill, 1966.

————. *Miss Pickerell Harvests the Sea*. New York: McGraw-Hill, 1968.

————. *Miss Pickerell Meets Mr. H.U.M.*. New York: McGraw-Hill, 1974.

————. *Miss Pickerell on the Moon*. New York: McGraw-Hill, 1965.

————. *Miss Pickerell on the Trail*. New York: McGraw-Hill, 1981.

————. *Miss Pickerell Tackles the Energy Crisis*. New York: McGraw-Hill, 1980.

————. *Miss Pickerell Takes the Bull by the Horns*. New York: McGraw-Hill, 1976.

————. *Miss Pickerell to the Earthquake Rescue*. New York: McGraw-Hill, 1977.

Marsten, Richard. *Danger: Dinosaurs!* Philadelphia: Winston, 1953.

————. *Rocket to Luna*. Philadelphia: Winston, 1953.

May, John. *The Magic School Bus Inside Ralphie: A Book About Germs*. New York: Scholastic, 1994.

McEvoy, Seth. *All Geared Up*. Not Quite Human 2. New York: Simon & Schuster, 1985.

————. *Batteries Not Included*. Not Quite Human 1. New York: Simon & Schuster, 1985.

————. *A Bug in the System*. Not Quite Human 3. New York: Simon & Schuster,

1985.

———. *Killer Robot*. Not Quite Human 6. New York: Simon & Schuster, 1986.

———. *Reckless Robot*. Not Quite Human 4. New York: Simon & Schuster, 1986.

———. *Terror at Play*. Not Quite Human 5. New York: Simon & Schuster, 1986.

Mogridge, Stephen. *Peter and the Atomic Valley*. London: Hutchinson, 1955.

———. *Peter and the Flying Saucers*. London: Hutchinson, 1954.

———. *Peter and the Flying Submarine*. London: Hutchinson, 1957.

———. *Peter and the Moon Bomb*. London: Hutchinson, 1956.

———. *Peter's Denmark Adventure*. London: Hutchinson, 1958.

North, Eric. *The Ant Men*. Philadelphia: Winston, 1955.

North, Rick. *Citizens of Mars*. Young Astronauts 6. New York: Kensington, 1991.

———. *Destination Mars*. Young Astronauts 4. New York: Kensington, 1991.

———. *Ready for Blastoff!* Young Astronauts 2. New York: Kensignton, 1990.

———. *Space Blazers*. Young Astronauts 3. New York: Kensington, 1990.

———. *Space Pioneers*. Young Astronauts 5. New York: Kensington, 1991.

———. *The Young Astronauts*. Young Astronauts 1. New York: Kensington, 1990.

Norton, Andre. *Star Born*. New York: Ace, 1957.

———. *Star Gate*. New York: Ace, 1958.

———. *Star Guard*. New York: Ace, 1955.

———. *Star Man's Son, 2250 A.D.* 1953. Boston: Gregg, 1980.

———. *Star Rangers*. 1983. New York: Ballantine, 1985.

———. *The Stars Are Ours!* New York: Ace, 1954.

Norton, Andre, and Dorothy Madlee. *Star Ka'at*. New York: Walker, 1976.

———. *Star Ka'ats and Plant People*. New York: Walker, 1979.

———. *Star Ka'ats and the Winged Warriors*. New York: Walker, 1981.

———. *Star Ka'at World*. New York: Walker, 1978.

Nourse, Alan. *Trouble on Titan*. Philadelphia: Winston, 1954.

Oliver, Chad. *Mists of Dawn*. Philadelphia: Winston, 1952.

Pearl, Jack. *Operation Doomsday*. Racine, WI: Western, 1967.

———. *Operation Star Voyage*. Racine, WI: Western, 1970.

Pedersen, Ted. *Gypsy World*. *Star Trek: Deep Space Nine* 7. New York: Pocket, 1996.

———. *Space Camp*. *Star Trek: Deep Space Nine* 10. New York: Pocket, 1997.

Peel, John. *Field Trip*. *Star Trek: Deep Space Nine* 6. New York: Pocket, 1995.

———. *Prisoners of Peace*. *Star Trek: Deep Space Nine* 3. New York: Pocket, 1994.

Pohl, Frederik, and Jack Williamson. *Undersea City*. 1958. New York: Baen, 1986.

———. *Undersea Fleet*. 1956. New York: Baen, 1984.

———. *Undersea Quest*. 1954. New York: Baen, 1982.

Relf, Patricia. *The Magic School Bus Gets Eaten: A Book About Food Chains*. New York: Scholastic, 1996.

———. *The Magic School Bus Hops Home: A Book About Animal Habitats*. New York: Scholastic, 1995.

———. *The Magic School Bus Plants Seeds: A Book About How Living Things Grow*. New York: Scholastic, 1995.

Rockwell, Carey. *Danger in Deep Space*. Tom Corbett Space Cadet 2. New York: Grosset & Dunlap, 1953.

———. *On the Trail of the Space Pirates*. Tom Corbett Space Cadet 3. New York: Grosset & Dunlap, 1953.

———. *The Revolt on Venus*. Tom Corbett Space Cadet 5. New York: Grosset & Dunlap, 1954.

—————. *The Robot Rocket*. Tom Corbett Space Cadet 8. New York: Grosset & Dunlap, 1956.

—————. *Sabotage in Space*. Tom Corbett Space Cadet 7. New York: Grosset & Dunlap, 1955.

—————. *The Space Pioneers*. Tom Corbett Space Cadet 4. New York: Grosset & Dunlap, 1953.

—————. *Stand by for Mars*. Tom Corbett Space Cadet 1. New York: Grosset & Dunlap, 1952.

—————. *Treachery in Outer Space*. Tom Corbett Space Cadet 7. New York: Grosset & Dunlap, 1954.

Royce, Easton. *The Aliens*. New York: HarperTrophy, 1996.

—————. *Mutiny*. New York: HarperTrophy, 1996.

Schealer, John. *Zip-Zip and His Flying Saucer*. New York: Dutton, 1956.

—————. *Zip-Zip and the Red Planet*. New York: Dutton, 1961.

—————. *Zip-Zip Goes to Venus*. New York: Dutton, 1958.

Service, Pamela. *Stinker From Space*. New York: Fawcett, 1988.

—————. *Stinker's Return*. New York: Scribner, 1993.

Sheffield, Charles. *Billion Dollar Boy*. New York: Tor, 1997.

—————. *Putting Up Roots*. New York: Tor, 1997.

Sheffield, Charles, and Jerry Pournelle. *Higher Education*. New York: Tor, 1996.

Slobodkin, Louis. *Round Trip Space Ship*. New York: Macmillan, 1968.

—————. *The Space Ship Returns to the Apple Tree*. 1958. New York: Aladdin, 1994.

—————. *The Space Ship Under the Apple Tree*. 1952. New York: Collier, 1971.

—————. *The Three-Seated Space Ship*. New York: Macmillan, 1962.

Slote, Alfred. *C.O.L.A.R.* New York: Lippincott, 1981.

—————. *My Robot Buddy*. 1975. New York: Avon, 1978.

—————. *Omega Station*. New York: Lippincott, 1983.

—————. *The Trouble on Janus*. New York: Lippincott, 1985.

St. John, Philip. *Rocket Jockey*. Philadelphia: Winston, 1952.

—————. *Rockets to Nowhere*. Philadelphia: Winston, 1954.

Stannard, Russell. *Black Holes and Uncle Albert*. London: Faber, 1991.

—————. *More Letters to Uncle Albert*. London: Faber, 1997.

—————. *The Time and Space of Uncle Albert*. London: Faber, 1989.

—————. *Uncle Albert and the Quantum Quest*. London: Faber, 1989.

Strickland, Brad. *The Star Ghost*. *Star Trek: Deep Space Nine* 1. New York: Pocket, 1994.

—————. *Starfall*. *Star Trek: The Next Generation*: Starfleet Academy 8. New York: Pocket, 1995.

—————. *Stowaways*. *Star Trek: Deep Space Nine* 2. New York: Pocket, 1994.

Strickland, Brad, and Barbara Strickland. *Crisis on Vulcan*. *Star Trek*: Starfleet Academy 1. New York: Pocket, 1996.

—————. *Nova Command*. *Star Trek: The Next Generation* 9. New York: Pocket, 1995.

Telep, Peter. *Demolition Winter*. New York: HarperTrophy, 1997.

Todd, Ruthven. *Space Cat*. New York: Scribner's, 1952.

—————. *Space Cat and the Kittens*. New York: Scribner's, 1958.

—————. *Space Cat Meets Mars*. New York: Scribner's, 1957.

—————. *Space Cat Visits Venus*. New York: Scribner's, 1955.

Van Lhin, Erik. *Battle on Mercury*. Philadelphia: Winston, 1953.

Vance, Jack. *Vandals of the Void*. Philadelphia: Winston, 1953.

Vornholt, John. *Aftershock*. *Star Trek*: Starfleet Academy 2. New York: Pocket, 1996.

———. *Capture the Flag*. *Star Trek: The Next Generation*: Starfleet Academy 4. New York: Pocket, 1994.

———. *Crossfire*. *Star Trek: The Next Generation*: Starfleet Academy 11. New York: Pocket, 1996.

Walton, Bryce. *Sons of the Ocean Deeps*. Philadelphia: Winston, 1952.

Weiss, Bobbi J. G. *Lifeline*. *Star Trek: Voyager*: Starfleet Academy 1. New York: Pocket, 1997.

Weiss, Bobbi J. G., and David Cody Weiss. *Breakaway*. *Star Trek: The Next Generation*: Starfleet Academy 12. New York: Pocket, 1997.

Weiss, David Cody. *Deceptions*. *Star Trek: The Next Generation*: Starfleet Academy 14. New York: Pocket, 1998.

West, Tracey. *The Magic School Bus Spins a Web: A Book About Spiders*. New York: Scholastic, 1997.

Weyn, Suzanne. *The Magic School Bus Gets All Dried Up: A Book About Deserts*. New York: Scholastic, 1996.

Williams, Jay, and Raymond Abrashkin. *Danny Dunn, Invisible Boy*. New York: Simon & Schuster, 1975.

———. *Danny Dunn, Scientific Detective*. New York: Simon & Schuster, 1977.

———. *Danny Dunn, Time Traveller*. New York: McGraw-Hill, 1963.

———. *Danny Dunn and the Anti-Gravity Paint*. 1956. New York: McGraw-Hill, 1957.

———. *Danny Dunn and the Automatic House*. New York: McGraw-Hill, 1965.

———. *Danny Dunn and the Fossil Cave*. New York: McGraw-Hill, 1961.

———. *Danny Dunn and the Heat Ray*. New York: McGraw-Hill, 1962.

———. *Danny Dunn and the Homework Machine*. 1958. New York: Simon & Schuster, 1979.

———. *Danny Dunn and the Smallifying Machine*. 1969. New York: Simon & Schuster, 1971.

———. *Danny Dunn and the Swamp Monster*. New York: McGraw-Hill, 1971.

———. *Danny Dunn and the Universal Glue*. 1977. New York: Simon & Schuster, 1979.

———. *Danny Dunn and the Voice from Space*. New York: McGraw-Hill, 1967.

———. *Danny Dunn and the Weather Machine*. New York: McGraw-Hill, 1959.

———. *Danny Dunn on a Desert Island*. New York: McGraw-Hill, 1957.

———. *Danny Dunn on the Ocean Floor*. 1960. New York: McGraw-Hill, 1967.

Wollheim, Donald. *Mike Mars and the Mystery Satellite*. 1963. New York: Paperback Library, 1966.

———. *Mike Mars Around the Moon*. 1964. New York: Paperback Library, 1966.

———. *Mike Mars Astronaut*. 1961. New York: Paperback Library, 1966.

———. *Mike Mars at Cape Kennedy*. 1961. New York: Paperback Library, 1966.

———. *Mike Mars Flies the Dyna-Soar*. 1962. New York: Paperback Library, 1966.

———. *Mike Mars Flies the X-15*. 1961. New York: Paperback Library, 1966.

———. *Mike Mars in Orbit*. Garden City, NY: Doubleday, 1961.

———. *Mike Mars South Pole Spaceman*. 1962. New York: Paperback Library, 1966.

———. *The Secret of Saturn's Rings*. Philadelphia: Winston, 1954.

———. *The Secret of the Martian Moons*. Philadelphia: Winston, 1955.

Wright, Kenneth. *The Mysterious Planet*. Philadelphia: Winston, 1953.

Yolen, Jane. *Commander Toad and the Big Black Hole*. New York: Coward-McCann, 1983.
————. *Commander Toad and the Dis-Asteroid*. 1985. New York: Putnam, 1996.
————. *Commander Toad and the Intergalactic Spy*. 1986. New York: Putnam, 1997.
————. *Commander Toad in Space*. 1980. New York: Putnam, 1996.
————. *The Robot and Rebecca*. New York: Knopf, 1980.
————. *The Robot and Rebecca and the Missing Owser*. New York: Knopf, 1981.

SECONDARY SOURCES

Aldiss, Brian W. *The Detached Retina*. Syracuse, NY: Syracuse UP, 1995.
————. *Trillion Year Spree*. Assisted by David Wingrove. New York: Atheneum, 1986.
Amis, Kingsley. *New Maps of Hell: A Survey of Science Fiction*. New York: Harcourt, 1960.
Antczak, Janice. *Science Fiction: The Mythos of a New Romance*. New York: Neal-Schuman, 1985.
Ariès, Philippe. *Centuries of Childhood: A Social History of Family Life*. Trans. Robert Baldick. New York: Vintage, 1962.
Attebery, Brian. *The Fantasy Tradition in American Literature*. Bloomington: Indiana UP, 1980.
Bailey, K. V. "Masters, Slaves, and Rebels: Dystopia as Defined and Defied by John Christopher." *Science Fiction for Young Readers*. Ed. C. W. Sullivan III. Westport, CT: Greenwood, 1993. 97–112.
Barr, Marleen. "Science Fiction and the Fact of Women's Repressed Creativity: Anne McCaffrey Portrays a Female Artist." *Extrapolation* 23 (1982): 70–76.
Barrow, Craig. "Aliens." *New Encyclopedia of Science Fiction*. Ed. James Gunn. New York: Viking, 1988. 9–11.
Bassnett, Susan. "Remaking the Old World: Ursula LeGuin and the American Tradition." *Where No Man Has Gone Before: Women and Science Fiction*. Ed. Lucie Armitt. London: Routledge, 1991. 50–66.
Benford, Gregory. "Is There a Technological Fix for the Human Condition?" *Hard Science Fiction*. Ed. George S. Slusser and Eric S. Rabkin. Carbondale: Southern Illinois UP, 1986. 82–98.
Bettelheim, Bruno. *The Uses of Enchantment*. New York: Vintage, 1989.
Billman, Carol. *The Secret of the Stratemeyer Syndicate: Nancy Drew, the Hardy Boys, and the Million Dollar Fiction Factory*. New York: Ungar, 1986.
Bleiler, E. F. "From the Newark Steam Man to Tom Swift." *Extrapolation* 30 (1989): 10–16.
Bottigheimer, Ruth. "The Child Reader of Children's Bibles, 1656-1753." *Infant Tongues: The Voice of the Child in Literature*. Ed. Elizabeth Goodenough, Mark A. Heberle, and Naomi Sokoloff. Detroit: Wayne State UP, 1994. 44–56.
Brin, David. "Running Out of Speculative Niches: A Crisis for Hard SF?" *Hard Science Fiction*. Ed. George E. Slusser and Eric S. Rabkin. Carbondale, IL: Southern Illinois UP, 1986. 8–13.
Buckley, Jerome Hamilton. "Introduction: The Space Between." *Season of Youth: The Bildungsroman from Dickens to Golding*. Cambridge, MA: Harvard UP, 1974. 1–27.

Cameron, Eleanor. "Fantasy, SF and the Mushroom Planet Books." *Children's Literature Association Quarterly* 7 (1981): 1, 5–9.

———. *The Green and Burning Tree: On the Writing and Enjoyment of Children's Books*. Boston: Little,Brown, 1962.

———. *The Seed and the Vision*. New York: Dutton, 1993.

Carter, Paul A. "The Bright Illusion: The Feminine Mystique in Science Fiction." *The Creation of Tomorrow: Fifty Years of Magazine Science Fiction*. New York: Columbia UP, 1977. 171–200.

———. "From the Golden Age to the Atomic Age: 1940–1963." *Anatomy of Wonder 4: A Critical Guide to Science Fiction*. Ed. Neil Barron. New Providence, NJ: Bowker, 1995. 115–221.

Clareson, Thomas D. *Many Futures, Many Worlds: Theme and Form in Science Fiction*. Kent, OH: Kent State UP, 1977.

———. *Some Kind of Paradise: The Emergence of American Science Fiction*. Westport, CT: Greenwood, 1985.

Davies, Philip John. "Science Fiction and Conflict." *Science Fiction, Social Conflict and War*. Ed. Philip John Davies. Manchester, England: Manchester UP, 1990. 1–7.

Deane, Paul. *Mirrors of American Culture: Children's Fiction Series in the Twentieth Century*. Metuchen, NJ: Scarecrow, 1991.

De Camp, L. Sprague. "Humor in Science Fiction." *Of Worlds Beyond: The Science of Science Fiction Writing*. Ed. Lloyd Arthur Eshbach. Chicago: Advent, 1964. 67–76.

Dizer, John. *Tom Swift and Company: "Boys' Books" by Stratemeyer and Others*. Jefferson, NC: McFarland, 1982.

Doane, Janice, and Devon Hodges. *Nostalgia and Sexual Difference: The Resistance to Contemporary Feminism*. New York: Methuen, 1987.

Earnshaw, Brian. "Planets of Awful Dread." *Children's Literature in Education* 14 (1983): 237–242.

Easthope, Antony. "The Personal and the Political." *Science Fiction, Social Conflict and War*. Ed. Philip John Davies. Manchester, England: Manchester UP, 1990. 50–67.

Eggeling, John, and Peter Nicholls. "Juvenile Series*." The Encyclopedia of Science Fiction*. Ed. John Clute and Peter Nicholls. New York: St. Martin's, 1995. 653–54.

Egoff, Sheila. "Science Fiction." *Only Connect: Readings on Children's Literature*. Ed. Sheila Egoff, G. T. Stubbs, and L. F. Ashley. Toronto: Oxford UP, 1969.

———. *Worlds Within: Children's Fantasy from the Middle Ages to Today*. Chicago: ALA, 1988.

Ernst, Shirley B. "Gender Issues in Books for Children and Young Adults." *Battling Dragons: Issues and Controversy in Children's Literature*. Ed. Susan Lehr. Portsmouth, NH: Heinemann, 1995. 66–78.

Esmonde, Margaret P. "Children's Science Fiction." *Signposts to Criticism of Children's Literature*. Ed. Robert Bator. Chicago: ALA, 1983. 284–287.

———. "From Little Buddy to Big Brother: The Icon of the Robot in Children's Science Fiction." *The Mechanical God: Machines in Science Fiction*. Ed. Thomas P. Dunn and Richard D. Erlich. Westport, CT: Greenwood, 1982. 85-98.

Fabun, Don. "Science Fiction in Motion Pictures, Radio, and Television." *Modern*

Science Fiction: Its Meaning and Its Future. Ed. Reginald Bretnor. Chicago: Advent, 1979. 43–70.

Foote, Bud. *The Connecticut Yankee in the Twentieth Century: Travel to the Past in Science Fiction.* New York: Greenwood, 1991.

Forward, Robert L. "When Science Writes the Fiction." *Hard Science Fiction.* Ed. George E. Slusser and Eric S. Rabkin. Carbondale, IL: Southern Illinois UP, 1986. 1–7.

Franklin, H. Bruce. "Eternally Safe for Democracy: The Final Solution of American Science Fiction." *Science Fiction, Social Conflict and War.* Ed. Philip John Davies. Manchester, England: Manchester UP, 1990. 151–167.

———. "Robert A. Heinlein: His Time and Place." *Robert A. Heinlein: America as Science Fiction.* New York: Oxford UP, 1980. 3–16.

Fremantle, Susan. "The Power of the Picture Book." *The Power of the Page: Children's Books and Their Readers.* Ed. Pat Pinsent. London: Fulton, 1993. 6–14.

Gose, Elliott. *Mere Creatures: A Study of Modern Fantasy Tales for Children.* Toronto: U of Toronto P, 1988.

Goswami, Amit, with Maggie Goswami. *The Cosmic Dancers: Exploring the Physics of Science Fiction.* New York: Harper, 1983.

Gough, John. "An Interview with John Christopher." *Children's Literature in Education* 15.2 (1984): 93–102.

Griffiths, John. *Three Tomorrows: American, British and Soviet Science Fiction.* London: Macmillan, 1980.

Gunn, James. "The Other Novels." *Isaac Asimov: The Foundations of Science Fiction.* New York: Oxford UP, 1982. 139–184.

———. "Science Fiction and the Mainstream." *Science Fiction, Today and Tomorrow.* Ed. Reginald Bretnor. New York: Harper, 1974. 183–216.

Hall, Peter C. "'The Space Between' in Space: Some Versions of the Bildungsroman in Science Fiction." *Extrapolation* 29 (1988): 153–159.

Hassler, Donald M. *Comic Tones in Science Fiction: The Art of Compromise with Nature.* Westport, CT: Greenwood, 1982.

Heinlein, Robert A. *Grumbles from the Grave.* Ed. Virginia Heinlein. New York: Ballantine, 1990.

Hogan, Patrick G., Jr. "The Philosophical Limitations of Science Fiction." *Many Futures, Many Worlds: Theme and Form in Science Fiction.* Ed. Thomas D. Clareson. Kent, OH: Kent UP, 1977. 260–277.

Hollindale, Peter. *Signs of Childness in Children's Books.* Stroud, England: Thimble, 1997.

Huck, Charlotte, Susan Hepler, and Janet Hickman. *Children's Literature in the Elementary School.* 4th ed. Fort Worth, TX: Holt, 1987.

Hull, Elizabeth Anne. "Asimov: Man Thinking." *Science Fiction for Young Readers.* Ed. C. W. Sullivan, III. Westport, CT: Greenwood, 1993. 47–64.

Hume, Kathryn. *Fantasy and Mimesis.* New York: Methuen, 1984.

Inglis, Fred. *The Promise of Happiness: Value and Meaning in Children's Fiction.* New York: Cambridge UP, 1980.

Jackson, Rosemary. *Fantasy: The Literature of Subversion.* London: Methuen, 1981.

James, Edward. *Science Fiction in the 20th Century.* Oxford: Oxford UP, 1994.

Johnson, Diedre. *Edward Stratemeyer and the Stratemeyer Syndicate.* New York: Twayne, 1993.

Kensinger, Faye R. *Children of the Series and How They Grew.* Bowling Green, OH: Bowling Green State U Popular P, 1987.

Ketterer, David. *New Worlds for Old: The Apocalyptic Imagination, Science Fiction, and American Literature.* Garden City, NY: Anchor, 1974.

Klass, Morton. "The Artificial Alien: Transformations of the Robot in Science Fiction." *Annals of the American Academy of Political and Social Science* 470 (1983): 171–79.

Knight, Damon. *In Search of Wonder: Essays on Modern Science Fiction.* Chicago: Advent, 1967.

Lanes, Selma. "A Series Is a Series Is a Series." *Down the Rabbit Hole: Adventures and Misadventures in the Realm of Children's Literature.* New York: Atheneum, 1971. 128–145.

Larrick, Nancy. "The All-White World of Children's Books." *Saturday Review* 11 Sept. 1965: 63-65+.

Lefanu, Sarah. *Feminism and Science Fiction.* Bloomington, IN: Indiana UP, 1988.

LeGuin, Ursula K. *The Language of the Night.* New York: Harper, 1989.

L'Engle, Madeleine. "Childlike Wonder and the Truths of Science Fiction." *Children's Literature* 10 (1982): 102–110.

Lenz, Millicent. *Nuclear Age Literature for Youth: The Quest for a Life-Affirming Ethic.* Chicago: ALA, 1990.

Lerner, Frederick Andrew. *Modern Science Fiction and the American Literary Community.* Metuchen, NJ: Scarecrow, 1985.

Lewis, C. S. *On Stories and Other Essays on Literature.* Ed. Walter Hooper. San Diego: Harcourt, 1982.

Lukens, Rebecca J. *A Critical Handbook of Children's Literature.* 5th ed. New York: Harper, 1995.

Marx, Leo. *The Machine in the Garden: Technology and the Pastoral Ideal in America.* New York: Oxford UP, 1964.

Mason, Bobbie Ann. *The Girl Sleuth: A Feminist Guide.* Old Westbury, NY: Feminist, 1975.

McCaffrey, Anne. "Hitch Your Dragon to a Star: Romance and Glamour in Science Fiction." *Science Fiction: Today and Tomorrow.* Ed. Reginald Bretnor. New York: Harper, 1974. 278–294.

Mellor, Adrian. "Science Fiction and the Crisis of the Educated Middle Class." *Popular Fiction and Social Change.* Ed. Christopher Pawling. London: Macmillan, 1984. 20–49.

Meyers, Walter E. *Aliens and Linguists: Language Study and Science Fiction.* Athens: U of Georgia P, 1980.

Mogen, David. *Wilderness Visions: Science Fiction Westerns Volume One.* San Bernardino, CA: Borgo, 1982.

Molson, Francis J. "Andre Norton." *American Writers for Children Since 1960: Fiction.* Ed. Glenn E. Estes. Detroit: Gale, 1986. 267–278.

———. "The Boy Inventor in American Series Fiction: 1900–1930." *Journal of Popular Culture* 28.1 (1994): 31–48.

———. "Great Marvel: The First American Hardcover Science Fiction Series." *Extrapolation* 34 (1993): 101–122.

———. "Three Generations of Tom Swift." *Children's Literature Association Quarterly* 10 (1985): 60–63.

———. "The Tom Swift Books." *Science Fiction for Young Readers.* Ed. C. W.

Sullivan, III. Westport, CT: Greenwood, 1993. 3–20.

———. "The Winston Science Fiction Series and the Development of Children's Science Fiction." *Extrapolation* 25   (1984): 34–50.

Molson, Francis J., and Susan G. Miles. "Young Adult Science Fiction." *Anatomy of Wonder 4: A Critical Guide to Science Fiction*. Ed. Neil Barron. New Providence, NJ: Bowker, 1995. 393–452.

Morgan, Chris. *The Shape of Futures Past*. New York: Webb, 1981.

Moskowitz, Sam. "Teen-Agers: Tom Swift and the Syndicate." Strange Horizons: The Spectrum of Science *Fiction*. New York: Scribner's, 1976. 160–181.

Nahin, Paul J. *Time Machines: Time Travel in Physics, Metaphysics, and Science Fiction*. New York: American Institute of Physics, 1993.

Newsinger, John. "Rebellion and Power in the Juvenile Science Fiction of John Christopher." *Foundation* 47 (1989-90): 46–54.

Nicholls, Peter. "Children's SF." *Science Fiction Encyclopedia*. Ed. Peter Nicholls. New York: Doubleday, 1979. 113–114.

———. "Pulp SF." *The Encyclopedia of Science Fiction*. Eds. John Clute and Peter Nicholls. New York: St. Martin's, 1995. 980.

Nodelman, Perry. "The Other: Orientalism, Colonialism, and Children's Literature." *Children's Literature Association Quarterly* 17 (1992): 1, 29–35.

———. *The Pleasures of Children's Literature*. White Plains, NY: Longman, 1992.

Owen, Leslie E. "Children's Science Fiction and Fantasy Grows Up." *Publisher's Weekly* 30 Oct. 1987: 32–37.

Parrinder, Patrick, ed. *Science Fiction: A Critical Guide*. New York: Longman, 1979.

Patterson, Nancy-Lou. "Angel and Psychopomp in Madeleine L'Engle's 'Wind' Trilogy." *Children's Literature in Education* 14.4 (1983): 195–203.

Pierce, Hazel. "'Elementary, My Dear . . . ': Asimov's Science Fiction Mysteries." *Isaac Asimov*. Writers of the Twenty-first Century Series. New York: Taplinger, 1977. 32–58.

Pierce, John J. *Great Themes of Science Fiction: A Study in Imagination and Evolution*. New York: Greenwood, 1987.

Pinsent, Pat. "'Such Agreeable Friends'—Children and Animal Literature." *The Power of the Page: Children's Books and Their Readers*. Ed. Pat Pinsent. London: Fulton, 1993. 34–44.

Pohl, Frederick. "Science Fiction for the Young (at Heart)." *Children's Literature* 10 (1982): 111–112.

Rabkin, Eric S. *The Fantastic in Literature*. Princeton, NJ: Princeton UP, 1976.

———. "Science Fiction Women Before Liberation." *Future Females: A Critical Anthology*. Ed. Marleen S. Barr.   Bowling Green, OH: Bowling Green U Popular P, 1981. 9–25.

Raymo, Chet. "Dr. Seuss and Dr. Einstein: Children's Books and the Scientific Imagination." *Only Connect: Readings on Children's Literature*. Ed. Sheila Egoff, Gordon Stubbs, Ralph Ashley, and Wendy Sutton. 3rd ed. New York: Oxford UP, 1996. 184–191.

Reimer, Kathryn Meyer. "Multiethnic Literature: Holding Fast to Dreams." *Language Arts* 69 (1992): 14–21.

Roberts, Robin. *A New Species: Gender and Science in Science Fiction*. Urbana: U of Illinois P, 1993.

Roberts, Thomas J. "Science Fiction and the Adolescent." *Signposts to Criticism of Children's Literature*. Ed. Robert Bator.   Chicago: ALA, 1983. 288–293.

Rose, Mark. *Alien Encounters: Anatomy of Science Fiction.* Cambridge, MA: Harvard UP, 1981.

Rosenberg, Judith K. Assisted by C. Allen Nichols. *Young People's Books in Series: Fiction and Non-Fiction, 1975–1991.* Englewood, CO: Libraries Unlimited, 1992.

Rosenberg, Judith K., and Kenyon C. Rosenberg. *Young People's Literature in Series: Fiction: An Annotated Bibliography.* Littleton, CO: Libraries Unlimited, 1972.

Sale, Roger. *Fairy Tales and After: From Snow White to E. B. White.* Cambridge, MA: Harvard UP, 1978.

Samuelson, David. *Visions of Tomorrow: Six Journeys from Outer to Inner Space.* New York: Arno, 1975.

Sandels, Robert. "UFOs, Science Fiction and the Postwar Utopia." *Journal of Popular Culture* 20.1 (1986): 141–151.

Sargent, Pamela. Introduction. *Women of Wonder: Science Fiction Stories by Women About Women.* New York: Vintage-Random, 1975. xiii–lxiv.

Schelde, Per. *Androids, Humanoids, and Other Science Fiction Monsters: Science and Soul in Science Fiction Films.* New York: New York UP, 1993.

Schmidt, Gary D. "See How They Grow: Character Development in Children's Series Books." *Children's Literature in Education* 18.1 (1987): 34–44.

———. "'So Here, My Dears, Is a New Oz Story': The Deep Structure of a Series." *Children's Literature Association Quarterly* 14 (1989): 163–165.

Schmidt, Stanley. "The Science in Science Fiction." *Many Futures, Many Worlds.* Ed. Thomas D. Clareson. Kent, OH: Kent State UP, 1977. 14–26.

Scholes, Robert. "Boiling Roses: Thoughts on Science Fantasy." *Intersections: Fantasy and Science Fiction.* Ed. Eric S. Rabkin and George Edgar Slusser. Carbondale: Southern Illinois UP, 1987. 3–18.

———. *Structural Fabulation: An Essay on Fiction of the Future.* Notre Dame, IN: U of Notre Dame P, 1975.

Scholes, Robert, and Eric D. Rabkin. "Vision: Forms and Themes: Imaginary Beings." *Science Fiction: History, Science, Vision.* New York: Oxford UP, 1977. 179–185.

Schwarcz, H. Joseph. "Machine Animism in Modern Children's Literature." *A Critical Approach to Children's Literature.* Proc. of the Thirty-first Annual Conference of the Graduate Library School. 1–3 Aug. 1966. Chicago: U of Chicago P, 1967. 78–99.

Shwartz, Susan M. "Series." *The New Encyclopedia of Science Fiction.* Ed. James Gunn. New York: Viking, 1988. 408–411.

Sims, Rudine. "What Has Happened to the 'All-White' World of Children's Books?" *Phi Delta Kappan* 64 (1983): 650–653.

Sleator, William. "What *Is* It About Science Fiction?" *Only Connect: Readings on Children's Literature.* Ed. Sheila Egoff, Gordon Stubbs, Ralph Ashley, and Wendy Sutton. 3rd ed. New York: Oxford UP, 1996. 206–212.

Smith, Nicholas D., ed. *Philosophers Look at Science Fiction.* Chicago: Nelson-Hall, 1982.

Stahl, J. D. "Rocketing to the Mushroom Planet: The Fifties Space Age in Eleanor Cameron's Science Fiction/Fantasy Novels." Paper presented at the International Conference of the Fantastic in the Arts. Fort Lauderdale, FL. March 1994.

Staicar, Tom, ed. *The Feminine Eye: Science Fiction and the Women Who Write It.* New York: Ungar, 1982.

Stephens, John. *Language and Ideology in Children's Fiction.* New York: Longman, 1992.

Sulerud, Grace, and Sue Garness. "Eleanor Cameron." *American Writers for Children Since 1960: Fiction*. Ed. Glenn E. Estes. Detroit: Gale, 1986.

Sullivan, C. W. III. "Heinlein's Juveniles: Growing Up in Outer Space." *Science Fiction for Young Readers*. Ed. C. W. Sullivan, III. Westport, CT: Greenwood, 1993. 21–35.

———. *Science Fiction for Young Readers*. Westport, CT: Greenwood, 1993.

Suvin, Darko. *Metamorphoses of Science Fiction: On the Poetics and History of a Literary Genre*. New Haven: Yale UP, 1979.

———. *Pour Une Poètique de la Science-Fiction*. Montréal: Les Presses de L'Université du Québec, 1977.

Svilpis, Janis. "Authority, Autonomy, and Adventure in Juvenile Science Fiction." *Children's Literature Association Quarterly* 8 (1983): 22–26.

Todorov, Tzvetan. *The Fantastic: A Structural Approach to a Literary Genre*. Ithaca, NY: Cornell UP, 1975.

Townsend, John Rowe. *Written for Children: An Outline of English Children's Literature*. New York: Lothrop, 1965.

Walker, Nancy A. *Feminist Alternatives: Irony and Fantasy in the Contemporary Novel by Women*. Jackson: UP of Mississippi, 1990.

Warrick, Patricia S. *The Cybernetic Imagination in Science Fiction*. Cambridge, MA: MIT P, 1980.

———. "Images of the Man-Machine." *Many Futures, Many Worlds: Theme and Form in Science Fiction*. Ed. Thomas D. Clareson. Kent, OH: Kent UP, 1977. 182–223.

White, Barbara. *Growing Up Female: Adolescent Girlhood in American Fiction*. Westport, CT: Greenwood, 1985.

Williams, Raymond. "Utopia and Science Fiction." *Science Fiction: A Critical Guide*. Ed. Patrick Parrinder. New York: Longman, 1979. 52–66.

Wolfe, Gary K. "Frontiers in Space." *The Frontier Experience and the American Dream*. Ed. David Mogen, Mark Busby, and Paul Bryant. College Station: Texas A&M UP, 1989. 248–263.

———. *The Known and the Unknown: The Iconography of Science Fiction*. Kent, OH: Kent State UP, 1979.

Woolf, Virginia. "Feminist Criticism and Science Fiction for Children." *Children's Literature Association Quarterly* 7 (1982–1983): 13–16.

Wu, Dingbo. "Understanding Utopian Literature." *Extrapolation* 34 (1993): 230–244.

Zipes, Jack. "Taking Political Stock: New Theoretical and Critical Approaches to Anglo-American Children's Literature in the 1980s." *Only Connect: Readings on Children's Literature*. Ed. Sheila Egoff, Gordon Stubbs, Ralph Ashley, and Wendy Sutton. 3rd ed. New York: Oxford UP, 1996. 365–76.

Index

About the Authors

KAREN SANDS is an assistant professor of English at Buffalo State College where her specialty is children's literature.

MARIETTA FRANK is a Curriculum-Reference Librarian at the University of Pittsburgh at Bradford. She has previously worked as a high school librarian.

ISBN 0-313-30192-1

90000>

EAN

9 780313 301926

HARDCOVER BAR CODE